AT THE
CROSSROADS
BETWEEN PEACE AND WAR

AT THE
CROSSROADS
BETWEEN PEACE AND WAR

The London Naval Conference of 1930

EDITED BY JOHN H. MAURER
AND CHRISTOPHER M. BELL

NAVAL INSTITUTE PRESS
ANNAPOLIS, MARYLAND

This book has been brought to publication with the generous assistance of Marguerite and Gerry Lenfest.

Naval Institute Press
291 Wood Road
Annapolis, MD 21402

Library of Congress Cataloging-in-Publication Data
At the crossroads between peace and war : the London naval conference of 1930 / edited by John Maurer, Christopher M. Bell.
    pages cm
    Summary: "This volume provides fresh perspectives on the international strategic environment between the two world wars. At London in 1930, the United States, Great Britain, and Japan concluded an important arms control agreement to manage the international competition in naval armaments. In particular, the major naval powers reached agreement about how many heavy cruisers they could possess. Hailed at the time as a signal achievement in international cooperation, the success at London proved short-lived. France and Italy refused to participate in the treaty. Even worse followed, as within a few years growing antagonisms among the great powers manifested itself in the complete breakdown of the interwar arms control regime negotiated at London. The resulting naval arms race would set Japan and the United States on a collision course toward Pearl Harbor. "— Provided by publisher.
    ISBN 978-1-61251-326-3 (hardback) — ISBN 978-1-61251-331-7 (ebook) 1. London Naval Treaty (1930) 2. Disarmament—History—20th century. 3. Sea-power—History—20th century. I. Maurer, John H., editor of compilation. II. Bell, Christopher M., editor of compilation. III. Title: London naval conference of 1930.
    JZ5615.A82 2013
    327.1'743—dc23
                        2013038916
♾Print editions meet the requirements of ANSI/NISO z39.48-1992 (Permanence of Paper).
Printed in the United States of America.

22 21 20 19 18 17 16 15 14   9 8 7 6 5 4 3 2 1
First printing

CONTENTS

ILLUSTRATIONS

Figure

Tables

ABBREVIATIONS

ADM	Admiralty records
BuAer	Bureau of Aeronautics
BuC&R	Bureau of Construction and Repair
BuEng	Bureau of Engineering
BuNav	Bureau of Navigation
BuOrd	Bureau of Ordnance
BuY&D	Bureau of Yards and Docks
CAB	Cabinet office records
CID	Committee of Imperial Defence (Britain)
CINCUS	Commander in Chief, U.S. Fleet
CNO	Chief of Naval Operations
COS	Chiefs of Staff Committee (Britain)
DBFP	*Documents on British Foreign Policy*
DDI	*Documenti Diplomatici Italiani*
DL	Diet Library (Japan)
FO	Foreign Office
FRUS	[*Papers Relating to the*] *Foreign Relations of the United States*
GB	General Board
GC&CS	Government Code & Cypher School (Britain)
HHPL	Herbert Hoover Presidential Library
HMSO	[Her/His] Majesty's Stationery Office
IJN	Imperial Japanese Navy
JMFA	Japanese Ministry of Foreign Affairs [Archives]
MSDSC	Maritime Self-Defense Staff College (Japan)
NARA	National Archives and Records Administration
NC	Naval Conference
NGB	*Nihon gaiko bunsho* (Documents on Japanese Foreign Policy)

NGS	Naval General Staff (Japan)
NIDS	National Institute of Defense Studies (Japan)
NWC	Naval War College
OpNav	Office of the Chief of Naval Operations (USA)
PHGB	Proceedings and Hearings of the General Board
PRO	Public Records Office
PTSD	post–traumatic stress disorder
RG	Record Group
RN	Royal Navy
SHM	Service Historique de la Marine
TNA	The National Archives, Kew (Britain)
TSM	*Taiheiyo Senso e no michi*
USN	U.S. Navy

AT THE
CROSSROADS
BETWEEN PEACE AND WAR

Introduction

John H. Maurer and Christopher M. Bell

The London Naval Conference opened on 21 January 1930 in the Royal Gallery of the House of Lords in Westminster. The fog that morning was the worst London had seen all winter. Visibility was so poor that traffic flares had to be lit outside the Parliament buildings, and the car bringing King George V to deliver the opening speech was forced to travel at a walking pace so that it could be guided by policemen carrying lanterns. According to one press account, the fog caused the Royal Gallery to be filled with "a strange honey-coloured light."[1] But there is no indication that the assembled delegates regarded any of this as a bad omen. The king, himself a former naval officer, expressed the hope shared by many that the conference would "lead to immediate alleviation of the heavy burden of armaments now weighing upon the peoples of the world" and help pave the way for further disarmament efforts. His words found a receptive audience. Leaders espousing a liberal world order had come together in London to fashion in solemn treaty obligations their goal of curtailing the international competition in naval armaments and promoting mutual security among the great powers.

The statesmen who assembled in London believed they were avoiding the mistakes of the recent past, the rivalries in armaments that had contributed to the seeming inevitability of war between the great powers. They consciously set out to build on the naval arms agreement concluded in Washington in 1922 by

1

the world's five greatest naval powers—the United States, Great Britain, Japan, France, and Italy. The Washington Treaty had prevented a new naval arms race from erupting after the First World War, but it had not eliminated naval rivalry among the great powers. Competition had soon spilled over into areas not covered by the earlier agreement; and some powers had begun to bristle at the limitations they had willingly accepted. The delegates who gathered in London in early 1930 believed they could create a more comprehensive and durable framework for naval arms limitation. Their efforts were crowned three months later by an arms control agreement, signed by the United States, Britain, and Japan, that was lauded at the time as a major step toward constructing an international architecture for peace, an approach using arms control to reduce spending on weaponry, increase international transparency, and thereby build confidence among world leaders.

The London agreement was notable for curtailing competitive building in cruisers, the largest class of warship not regulated by the Washington Treaty. As a rough guideline, the United States, Britain, and Japan accepted that their relative strengths in this category should conform to the 5:5:3 ratio established for capital ships in Washington. To facilitate an agreement on this contentious issue, all sides agreed to concessions. The United States was allowed a slight advantage over Britain in heavy cruisers (those with displacements of ten thousand tons and eight-inch guns), while Britain was conceded a preponderance in light cruisers, giving it a larger overall tonnage in this class. The United States agreed to delay construction of some of its new heavy cruisers so as to allow Japan temporarily to improve its ratio in this class to 5:5:3.5. The agreement also set tonnage limits for destroyers and submarines, laid out which aging capital ships would be scrapped over the life of the treaty, and extended the "building holiday" on battleships for another five years.

The success achieved at London, however, proved short-lived. Two of the principal powers represented at the conference, France and Italy, were unable to overcome their mutual differences and remained outside the new arms control agreement. Before long, Japan's warlords embarked on a path of aggression in China that mocked the aspirations of liberal statesmen to settle disputes among the great powers without recourse to armed conflict. Within Japan, naval leaders, angered by the constraints placed on their navy by arms control obligations, sought to overturn the "unequal" treaty that they believed Great Britain and the United States had imposed upon them. Japan's admirals were determined never again to sign a treaty that did not permit them to build up a more powerful navy. Meanwhile, the Nazi seizure of power in Germany brought into play in the international arena another predatory state, intent upon building up its armed strength to undertake wars of aggression. The efforts at London did not halt these aggressive leaders and their countries from following paths toward war.

Considerable controversy thus swirls around the London Treaty of 1930 and the attempts to fashion an interwar arms control regime to manage international rivalries in naval armaments. The London Treaty was undoubtedly the high point of interwar naval arms control, but its legacy is inevitably tainted by the subsequent collapse of the liberal international order it was meant to serve. To detractors of arms control, London served to disarm the status quo powers, the liberal democracies of Britain and the United States, making the international scene more dangerous. Arms control encouraged public opinion in Britain and the United States to scale back defense preparations because spending on naval strength was to waste resources on acquiring weapons for unthinkable wars during a period of economic hard times. Instead of curtailing naval armaments, critics of the London Treaty maintain, Britain and the United States needed to enlarge their navies.

The London agreement was a pivotal moment in interwar arms control and, by extension, in the history of the interwar period. The last book-length study of the conference was published in 1962, making a reexamination long overdue. This volume fills an important gap in our understanding of what happened at London and why its achievement proved so fleeting. By reexamining the London Conference, it is possible to see how history turns, how one era ends and a new one begins. London marked the end of the First World War's aftermath, of the attempts by world leaders to construct a new international order based on a liberal worldview of cooperation and mutual security, to reduce the danger of war by controlling arms. What was soon to follow would make a mockery of London—the start of a new chapter on the road to another world war.

This volume provides the first comparative examination of the major powers involved in interwar naval arms control negotiations at London in 1930. One of our goals has been to avoid the standard narrative that focuses almost exclusively on Britain and the United States. Sadao Asada offers a compelling account of how Japan's naval leaders were determined to thwart arms control. This account makes clear that rising nationalist sentiment in Japan gave that country's naval leaders an opening to campaign against existing limitations on their ability to arm. In another important contribution, Paul Halpern has mined French and Italian archives to give fresh perspective on the views of political and naval leaders in both countries about the international strategic environment. The naval rivalry between France and Italy reflected deeper, conflicting international ambitions of both countries' leaders. That they could not reach agreement on naval arms underscored the sense in which the London negotiations were proving to mark the end of arms control rather than serving as a springboard for further efforts to limit armaments rivalries.

This study also incorporates new information that was not available to other historians who have examined interwar international relations and arms control. Some of the most important new documents to reach the archives in recent years are those revealing the full extent of the successes enjoyed by Britain's code breakers before and during the conference. Britain's leaders approached the negotiations with an important advantage in the realm of intelligence, but the impact of signals intelligence on Britain's actions and the conference's outcome has not been properly told before this study. This subject is treated at length by John Ferris, whose contribution to this volume examines the role and importance of intelligence in statecraft and strategy.

This volume reexamines a critical moment in the history of the U.S. Navy during the twentieth century. John Kuehn and Norman Friedman give close attention to American ambitions and decision making in approaching the London Conference. The Hoover administration was determined to bring about a reduction in naval spending and find a solution to the vexing question of how to measure and then control the relative cruiser strengths of Britain, Japan, and the United States. The compromises worked out at London to manage the rivalry in cruiser construction and strength did not prove easy to achieve, and the negotiations might readily have failed to reach agreement.

Christopher Bell shows that the London Conference represented an important turning point for Britain as well. The willingness of Ramsay MacDonald, Britain's first Labour prime minister, to overrule his naval advisers and make major concessions to the United States brought to a close a decade marked by deteriorating Anglo-American relations and set the two powers, however tentatively, on the path that would culminate in their wartime alliance. But at the same time, the sacrifices accepted at London in 1930 struck a major blow to Britain's ability to defend its global interests and accelerated its naval decline.

With regard to understanding the unraveling of the London agreement between the world wars, this volume can also provide insight into the pitfalls and perils of attempting to arrest international rivalries through arms control negotiations. Today, prominent public commentators have invoked the interwar arms control agreements as models and inspiration for establishing a framework for cooperation with the rising power of China. In his recent book *On China,* Henry Kissinger calls on the leaders of China and the United States to develop a multinational framework—a "Pacific Community"—to foster collaboration among the great powers of Asia and reduce the chances of conflict.[2]

China's rising power, however, is fraught with problems that work against a smooth transition of power in Asia. The dramatic growth of China's economy is producing strategic consequences that will prove difficult to manage for even the cleverest of world leaders.[3] For example, as the Chinese economy surges ahead over the coming decade, China's leaders confront increasing strategic vulnerability, with other countries holding the means to disrupt critical sea lines of communication. China's economic growth is and will remain heavily dependent on access to overseas resources. China's industrialization and growing demand for automobiles requires oil imports from the Middle East and Africa. The growing appetite for food imports is another strategic vulnerability facing China. As a consequence, its rulers will likely feel compelled to undertake arms programs and pursue a foreign policy that they believe minimizes these risks. The aspiration of Chinese naval leaders to possess four large aircraft carriers by 2020 is motivated in part by this drive to provide for China's security on the high seas.[4] Further, China's growing economy enables its armed forces to compete more effectively in the maritime and aerospace domains against rivals, including the United States. China's development of more powerful submarine and surface naval forces, antiship ballistic and cruise missiles, and space and cyberwarfare capabilities, as well as efforts to improve combat readiness, are eroding the long-standing lead of the U.S. Navy in the western Pacific. China's arms buildup means that the United States must make a greater effort just to stay in place in the competition. To maintain the current balance of power in the western Pacific will require that the United States put even more effort into countering China. Otherwise, America's ability to fight effectively on the maritime commons will erode. Whether American decision makers remain willing to maintain the lead in the arms competition occurring in Asia is one of the most consequential questions now facing the country. Paul Kennedy has noted that the United States is "frantically trying to figure out what this rise of Asian sea-power means for its own overstretched world position."[5] New naval rivalries in the Pacific will thus pose problems that make imperative an understanding of the interwar competitions in sea power.

Troubling too is the attempt by China's rulers to garner legitimacy and popular support by manipulating Chinese nationalism. The Chinese regime, Nicholas Kristof has observed, by "constantly excoriating the Japanese nationalists of the 1930s, [is] emulating them."[6] Not surprisingly, China's military leaders show themselves as ardent nationalists, eager to develop and deploy the latest generations of weaponry in an attempt to promote their country's foreign policy ambitions, provide for its security, and avenge past wrongs. Professor Huang Jing has presented the provocative view: "The young officers [in China] are taking control of strategy and it is like [the] young officers in Japan in the 1930s. They are thinking what they can do, not what they should do. This is very dangerous. They are on a collision course with a U.S.-dominated system."[7] Kissinger is also concerned by the strident calls of "triumphalist" nationalists within China who call for their country to become stronger militarily and act more assertively in the international arena as its economy grows.[8] The combination of weak political leadership and aggressive military chiefs, as Japan's experience of the 1930s attests, can prove a formula for strategic disaster. American leaders must try to shape the debate among China's rulers, policy advisers, and defense planners that self-restraint in armaments might best serve their country's and the regime's interests. Whether that effort can prove more successful than the attempt by liberal statesmen at London remains the challenge for statecraft in the twenty-first century.

NOTES

1. *Register News-Pictorial*, 23 January 1930, 4.

2. Henry Kissinger, *On China* (New York: Penguin, 2011), 527–30.

3. On the international strategic consequences of economic crises, see James Kurth, "A Tale of Four Crises: The Politics of Great Depressions and Recessions," *Orbis: A Journal of World Affairs* 55, no. 3 (Summer 2011), 500–523.

4. Jeremy Page, "China Flexes Naval Muscle," *Wall Street Journal*, 11 August 2011, 1.

5. Paul Kennedy, "Rise and Fall," *World Today* 66, nos. 8–9 (August–September 2010), 6.

6. Nicholas D. Kristof, "The China Threat?" *New York Times*, 20 December 2003.

7. Ambrose Evans-Pritchard, "China's Young Officers and the 1930s Syndrome," *Telegraph*, September 7, 2010, accessed online at blogs.telegraph .co.uk/finance/ambroseevans-pritchard/100007519/china%E2%80% 99s-young-officers-and-the-1930s-syndrome/.

8. Kissinger, *On China*, 503–7.

CHAPTER 1

A Turning Point in Anglo-American Relations?

The General Board of the Navy
and the London Naval Treaty

John T. Kuehn

*I have always been a great advocate of a real entente between us
[the United States and the United Kingdom] but do not believe in
written alliances. As I think I have told you in the past, Great Britain
makes me pretty hot under the collar sometimes, but I admire the
nationalism that is always manifest in all that they do. If ever we
could get them really at heart to recognise that the US must be treated
as a co-equal and must march in international affairs shoulder
to shoulder with her, it would go a long way to straightening out
questions between us.*

—Rear Admiral Hilary Jones to Rear Admiral W. V. Pratt, February 1926

The U.S. Navy has played a significant role in the foreign policy of the
United States for most of its existence.[1] Its role in preparing for and
influencing the London Naval Conference from 1927 to 1930 was of
great importance and perhaps the acme of direct diplomatic agency by the U.S.
Navy during the period between World Wars I and II.[2] Until recently, some
naval historians regarded that role in a negative light. In this view, stodgy "battleship" admirals saw Great Britain rather than Japan as the enemy and had

stymied British and U.S. cooperation. This chapter does not argue that the General Board approved of the results of the Washington Conference in 1922 or London in 1930—far from it: its members were very vocal in their opposition to both treaties, especially the one in 1930.[3] However, that vocal opposition, after Washington, to Geneva in 1927, and after London, had serendipitous results. By being contrarian and offering the "minority" opinion, as it were, the General Board helped to reconcile the naval policies of the United States and Great Britain (unintentionally at first).[4] Additionally, by being so intimately involved in the arms limitation process, the board created a cadre of diplomat-admirals, well versed in naval arms limitation on both sides of the treaty issue, who provided outstanding expertise at London in 1930—expertise that arguably put the U.S. Navy in a better position for the trials ahead.[5]

In order to provide context for the actions of the General Board at the London Naval Conference of 1930, this chapter will first discuss how the Navy came to have a substantially more important role in American foreign policy. It will then briefly discuss the genesis of the General Board and the role it came to play in naval arms limitation. Additionally, the organizational process of how the board worked will add value as well as a taxonomy for a better understanding of its actions prior to and during the arms conferences. Finally, the narrative of its involvement with the London Conference must begin with the failed Geneva Naval Conference, to provide essential context to the run-up to London in 1930 and its eventual outcome.

The Navy, the General Board, and Foreign Policy

From the 1880s, due to the efforts of men like Stephen B. Luce, A. T. Mahan, and, especially, Theodore Roosevelt, the Navy played an increasingly pivotal, even dominant, role in American foreign policy. Two policies propelled the Navy as an institution into the very heart of the foreign-policy decision processes of the United States—the Monroe Doctrine and the Open Door. The building and acquisition of a modern steel fleet contributed to the formulation of the famous "Roosevelt Corollary" to the venerable Monroe Doctrine. Theodore Roosevelt promised not only to oppose "Old World" attempts at new territorial acquisitions in the Americas but to "assist" nations that needed U.S. help. This assistance was in large part enabled by Roosevelt's use of "his" navy.[6]

However, the U.S. Navy's role in foreign policy, already quite important due to the Monroe Doctrine and maritime trade, expanded profoundly with the acquisition of the Philippine Islands and Guam because of the

Spanish-American War. Here territorial defense requirements and the Open Door intersected and interacted in such a way as to add to the list of the Navy's maritime and diplomatic responsibilities overseas.

What was the Open Door? It is best, perhaps, simply to quote its author, Secretary of State John Hay, to gain a sense of its tenets: "Earnestly desirous to remove any cause of irritation and *to insure at the same time to the commerce of all nations in China* the undoubted benefits which should accrue from a formal recognition by the various powers claiming 'spheres of interest' that they shall *enjoy perfect equality of treatment for their commerce and navigation* within such 'spheres.'"[7]

In other words, the United States declared a policy of open commerce and navigation inside China as that ancient civilization opened up during the last years of the Qing Dynasty. Additionally, the Open Door involved free navigation, not just for trade but also to permit access for Christian missionaries from the United States. President Theodore Roosevelt provides a clear explication of how the acquisition of the Philippines interacted with Hay's enunciation of the policy: "The inevitable march of events gave us the control of the Philippine Islands at a time so opportune that may without irreverence be called providential."[8] Sea-power theorist A. T. Mahan wrote, "We can scarcely fail to see that upon the sea primarily must be found our power to secure our own borders and to sustain our external policy, of which at the present moment there are two principal elements; namely, the Monroe Doctrine and the Open Door."[9] As such, the Open Door and the defense of the Philippines both required support by the fleet of the United States for the foreseeable future.

The General Board of the Navy was arguably the nation's first modern general staff. Its creation was very much a reflection of the reformist spirit of the times, a spirit that would later give birth to the Army War College, the Army General Staff, and the office of Chief of Naval Operations.[10] The General Board was born out of an honest study of the lessons of the Spanish-American War. That conflict had been poorly managed by both the Army and, to a lesser degree, the Navy; these lessons had been learned the hard way.[11] One of the few bright spots in its conduct involved the establishment of the Naval War Board of 1898 by Secretary of the Navy John D. Long. This board included Capt. Alfred Thayer Mahan, Assistant Secretary of the Navy Theodore Roosevelt, and several senior Navy captains. Long freely acknowledged that since he lacked "professional experience and the Navy being without a General Staff, it was necessary that he should have the assistance of such a Board." Based on this recent experience and at the urging of the chief of the Bureau of

Navigation, Admiral H. C. Taylor, Secretary Long issued General Order 544 on 13 March 1900 establishing the General Board of the Navy. Its purpose was "to insure efficient preparation of the fleet in case of war and for the naval defense of the coast."[12]

The board's early years were dominated by its one and only president, the hero of the battle of Manila Bay—Admiral George Dewey. Dewey served in this capacity until his death in January 1917. Its charter was as broad or as narrow as the secretary of the Navy chose to make it, since only he determined the agenda. The position of the board was always precarious, since its creation had been the result not of congressional legislation but of executive fiat. Nonetheless, the longer it existed the more recognized it became as an institutional authority on important strategic issues in the Navy, as well as in the language of legislation. Until 1909 the board was overwhelmingly concerned with fulfilling its role as a strategic and operational planning entity, as envisaged by Admiral Henry Taylor and others.[13]

By 1908–1909, during the design battles over the first U.S. dreadnoughts, the General Board finally became preeminent in fleet design. Up to that point the bickering naval bureaus had dominated the process of warship design. These bureaus warrant explanation. Semiautonomous entities, they largely "ran" those parts of the Navy that built ships, provided resources, and generated administrative policy prior to World War I. They worked for the secretary of the Navy, and coordination between them was informal. Disputes between the bureaus were resolved at the secretarial level. The major bureaus consisted of Navigation (which included personnel management), Ordnance (sometimes called the "gun club"), Construction and Repair (C&R), Engineering, Yards and Docks, and (after World War I) Aeronautics.[14] Throughout the Navy they were known by their abbreviations: BuNav, BuEng, BuOrd, BuC&R, BuY&D, and BuAer. Each was usually headed by an unrestricted-line admiral, often destined for higher command, except BuC&R, which fell under the leadership of the senior Construction Corps officer. The General Board came to serve as a coordinating staff, and even referee, between the office of the secretary, the Chief of Naval Operations, and the bureaus.

A conference convened at the Naval War College in 1908 by President Theodore Roosevelt set out to resolve the bickering between the bureaus. The attendees reached a consensus that line officers should be more intimately involved in the process of warship design and decided that the General Board would fulfill this function. This decision had the force of a presidential order.[15] Navy Regulations later formalized this precedent, reading, by the time of the first London Naval Conference, "When the designs are to be prepared for a new ship, the General Board shall submit to the Secretary of the Navy a recommendation as to the military characteristics to be embodied therein." By this process the General Board became the final arbiter in the design of warships and, by extension, the fleet.[16]

It took time for this to happen, but once this precedent established an expansion of the General Board's authority, its influence in fleet design gradually increased. Some naval historians regard the establishment of the Office of the Chief of Naval Operations (OpNav) by congressional legislation in 1915 and 1916 as the beginning of the end of the influence of the board. Although OpNav replaced the General Board as the principal war-planning entity in the Navy, the board retained its authority over fleet design and building policy. In fact, its role was to connect the two, since it was still required to remain cognizant of the war plans: "The General Board shall be furnished, for information, with the approved war plans, including cooperation with the Army and employment of the elements of naval defense."[17]

For the purposes of this chapter, however, it was the Great War (World War I) that catapulted naval officers, and in particular the members of General Board, into the uppermost levels of foreign policy as "diplomats in blue."[18] The impact of the World War I was indirect, but no less profound, because it was in the aftermath of that conflict that the mechanism of collective-security agreements and institutions—for example, the League of Nations—gave impetus to the idea of naval arms limitation. Statesmen identified the naval arms race between Great Britain and Germany prior to the outbreak of World War I as a contributing factor that had led to the catastrophes and stalemates in the trenches. The new American president, Warren G. Harding, opened the Washington Naval Conference in 1921 by referring explicitly to this factor: "Out of the cataclysm of the World War came new fellowships, new convictions, new aspirations. . . . A world staggering with debt needs its burden lifted. Humanity which has been shocked by wanton destruction would minimize the agencies of that destruction. Contemplating the measureless cost of war and the continuing burden of armament, all thoughtful peoples wish for real limitation of armament and would like war outlawed."[19]

After the president's short speech, Secretary of State Charles Evans Hughes delivered his now-famous proposal that "sank" more warships than any navy had in history, to paraphrase the words of a contemporary observer. It was by this means that that the U.S. Navy, which lost in that conference the most warship tonnage of any power (over 800,000 tons), ironically found its role

in foreign policy enhanced by naval arms limitation.[20] Once the dust had settled, the diplomats turned over the execution of the Washington Naval Treaty's
terms to their naval establishments. In the United States, that task fell exclusively to the General Board of the Navy.[21]

Thus, by two mechanisms—fleet design and naval disarmament stemming
from naval arms limitation—the General Board became the primary agent to
execute and uphold the Washington Treaty system. Its members influenced
Navy policy and programs in a way that was meant to wring every advantage
possible allowed under the treaty. These habits informed its approach to naval
conferences at Geneva in 1927 and London in 1930. Board members crafted
advice, delivered in the 438/438-1 series of General Board Reports (or "serials"), that was meant to shape future treaty negotiations to the advantage of the
United States. They came to perceive themselves as a group of subject-matter
experts on the clauses of the naval treaties.

By the time of the Geneva Conference the organization of the General
Board was relatively fixed. It was composed of an executive committee of twelve
officers, up to seven of them admirals, either coming from sea duty or going
to sea duty. It also included four significant ex officio members—the Chief of
Naval Operations (CNO), the Commandant of the Marine Corps, the president
of the Naval War College (NWC), and the Director of Naval Intelligence. Also
assigned was a secretary (usually a senior Navy commander or a captain), and
other officers could be temporarily attached as needed by the Navy secretary.
The chairman of the General Board was often one of the most senior admirals
on active duty. In 1930, the entire board met regularly on the last Tuesday of
every month and as directed by the secretary, whereas the executive committee
met at ten o'clock every morning, Monday through Friday.[22]

The mechanics of the General Board's processes highlight how its structure
and function influenced its role in naval diplomacy. First, the General Board
was *authoritative*, in the sense that other Navy entities, and often the secretary
of the Navy, considered its advice "the last word" on a particular issue.[23] For
example, the correspondence of the interwar period is full of references to "the
opinion of the Board" or "the judgment of the Board." These opinions and judg-
ments were reference points that the secretary of the Navy, CNO, NWC, and
the bureaus would use in making decisions, initiating programs, and spending money.[24] At the time of the London Treaty the General Board too perceived
itself as an important entity in the formulation of plans, policy, and strategy:
"Although the General Board is not established by [congressional] Statute, it

has long been recognized in legislation by Congress. In the organization of the Navy Department it has a very definite standing as a *personal* advisory board to the Secretary of the Navy. Its membership being composed of officers of long experience and special qualification, its advice is available to the Secretary on broad questions of naval policy and specific questions referred to him from time to time."[25]

The General Board's process was an "open" one—in today's terminology it would be called a "flat hierarchy." There were open lines of communication between the board and other organizations, both internal and external to the Navy. These lines of communication were not limited to governmental entities (see figure 1.1). The board examined a broad array of ideas and testimony, either written or in formal hearings. It could invite experts from anywhere to testify on any topic of interest. These hearings favored a collaborative, and sometimes confrontational, exchange of ideas.[26] The board posed potential courses of action about topics ranging from naval policy (such as arms limitation) to the thickness of armor on a battleship's bridge.

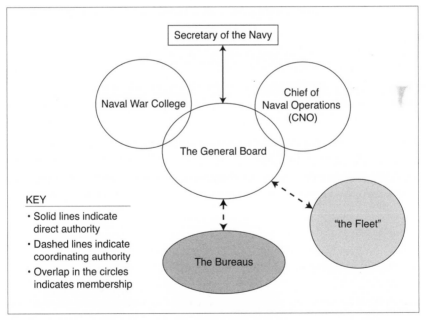

Figure 1.1 Navy Organizational Relationships during the Interwar Period

The historical record suggests that the General Board was good at working multiple issues at the same time. It tended to withhold judgment and instead to subject new or competing ideas to analysis, collaborating with other Navy organizations in the process. It often simply deferred making recommendations until a concept or ship design had been tested by war gaming at the Naval War College and then experimented with by the fleet in the annual fleet exercises. Results of fleet exercises, which were usually built around "battle problems" and the college's war-gaming results, were used by the General Board in its deliberations.[27]

The General Board advised the secretary of the Navy at meetings and by written products. The meetings could be either closed, informal discussions—often restricted to the membership of the board—or formal hearings before the board, as discussed above. In 1929 the board explained the purpose and initiation of its hearings as follows:

> When the General Board has a subject before it for consideration on which the advice or recommendation of materiel bureaus, other officers of the Department, or civilian experts, is desired, a hearing is held at which these various representatives are requested to be present and present such information as they may have for consideration by the Board. These hearings are recorded, bound kept in the General Board offices, and form an excellent set of reference papers for further use. From such hearings and personal knowledge of the members, the General Board formulates its recommendations to the Secretary.[28]

Closed meetings could include the entire membership of the board but more often, prior to 1932, were limited to the executive committee. The purpose of both the closed meetings and the hearings was to provide advice in the form of a written study.[29] For most issues—policy, tactics, arms limitation, and ship design—the board consulted a broad variety of expertise. The board could use the transcribed hearings either to draft a new study or make changes to an existing one. Once the draft had been revised, it was submitted as a numbered serial to the secretary of the Navy. The General Board assigned the serial numbers in chronological fashion, based on when a topic was received by the board. For example, serial 1427 on "The Reduction and Limitation of Armaments" was referred to the board on 31 May 1929. On 8 June the board spent the entire morning discussing this serial after being briefed by Admiral Hilary Jones, member at large, concerning his attendance at the sixth session of the Preparatory Commission (for naval armaments) at the League of Nations in Geneva. On the same day the finalized serial was forwarded to the secretary of the Navy, who directed further action in preparation for the upcoming London Naval Arms Conference in 1930. These numbered serials were retained for reference. Sometimes serials were referred to other Navy organizations (typically the bureaus) for work—that is, in the Navy terminology of the time, "for action."[30]

During the interwar period the mechanics and membership of the General Board changed with the times. The fundamental process remained one whereby the secretary of the Navy largely set the agenda. However, the Navy was a collaborative collection of suborganizations and individuals. The board was at the center of these collaborative processes, especially those implementing the treaties that produced a balanced fleet. As mentioned, after the conclusion of the Washington Conference it fell to the General Board to implement the Washington Naval Treaty (also known as the Five Power Treaty).[31] The General Board began this implementation before the Senate had even ratified the treaty and soon issued the 1922 naval policy that spelled out its long-term shipbuilding goals and policies vis-à-vis the treaty. The members of the General Board, most of whom initially opposed the Washington Naval Treaty, soon came to see it as something they could use to build and modernize a navy "second to none." However, by the time of the Geneva Naval Conference of 1927 the General Board had seen many of its hopes for programs to carry out the construction allowed by the Washington system stymied. It perceived the U.S. fleet as having lost ground against both the British and, especially, Japanese fleets.[32]

Also by the time of the Geneva Conference, the General Board had created a cadre of officers with considerable experience in arms limitation. Admirals Hilary Jones (see note 28) and William Veazie Pratt, both former General Board members who had implemented the Washington articles, were acknowledged arms-limitation experts. The board may in fact have organized itself into sections the better to deal directly with arms limitation. The proceedings of the General Board delineate four numbered "sections" and detail assignments to those sections of various members. Cdr. H. C. Train and Rear Admiral Jehu V. Chase constituted the "Fourth Section." Since Train was regularly detached to Geneva as the assistant to Hugh S. Gibson (the chairman of the American delegation) for most of the period and he was assigned to this section, it stands to reason that this section's duties included naval arms limitation.[33] There were also technical experts in the bureaus, such as Cdr. A. H. Van Keuren from BuC&R and Rear Admiral William Moffett, chief of BuAer. In fact, Moffett and Van Keuren can be considered de facto members of the General Board, given their frequent testimony at hearings.[34] For the Geneva Conference in 1927 the

Navy secretary picked Jones, senior member of the General Board, as the lead naval technical delegate.[35]

Historians identify the failure to impose a comprehensive limit on auxiliary warship tonnages as the most significant shortcoming of the Washington Naval Treaty. Ever since the adoption of that treaty the naval powers had aimed at another conference to address this "unfinished business," because naval competition had moved to these other categories of warships—especially cruisers. The failure to cap cruiser construction had worked in Japan's favor, because of the paucity of naval construction during the Warren Harding and first term of the Calvin Coolidge administrations. Japan was free to build as much as it could to further ameliorate the "inferior" position conferred by the ratio for capital ships—and it did (although Japan too was restrained by its government). Japan's auxiliary warship construction exceeded that of the United States during the same period (1924–29), especially for submarines and cruisers.[36] The U.S. Navy desired to build as many heavy cruisers as possible. This desire stemmed from its need for long-range ships that could operate independently of their bases for extended periods in the opening phases of operations as outlined in War Plan Orange. However, by 1927 lagging naval construction had brought the Navy to a crisis beyond any "cruiser gap" vis-à-vis the British or Japanese.

The General Board attempted to leverage the treaty system by liberally interpreting the various treaties. It attempted to wring every advantage allowable or implied by the treaties—often without consulting the State Department. For example, board members believed improving propulsion systems on battleships did not constitute "reconstruction" as defined in the treaty. This was true not just of those who had initially opposed the Washington settlement but of men like Rear Admiral Pratt, an outspoken supporter. Pratt came to see problems with anemic naval construction authorizations—although he continued to support the treaty system.[37] The chairmen of the executive committee of the board also attempted to achieve advantages within the treaty system, altering or adding language to international proposals that were favorable to the strategic situation of the United States. This would be the case with the flying-deck-cruiser proposal at the London Conference, as we shall see. However, the General Board was often frustrated in its efforts to leverage the treaty system for most of the period, tending to lose rather than gain ground.

General Board serials reflected this pessimism, deepening with each subsequent year after 1922, about the prospects for building a full-strength treaty navy. In a December 1926 serial the board again emphasized the need to build to treaty limits, because that would afford "the only fleet that will provide adequate national defense." However, its assessment of the status of the existing fleet was blunt: "We have not such a fleet at the present time."[38] By the next year, as building continued to be delayed by both parsimony and hopes for further arms reductions, the board's tone became more urgent: "We have fallen behind and continue to fall behind the treaty ratio of 5:5:3 in certain classes of auxiliary combatant craft [cruisers, carriers, and submarines]."[39] Note how the General Board gauged "falling behind" on the basis of extrapolating the capital-ship ratios to auxiliaries, a policy enacted in 1922.[40] Faced with no additional authorizations for new naval construction, the board was forced to trim its fiscal year 1929 building program to what it viewed as absolutely essential. The Navy's priorities incorporated elements of modernization within a program meant to build up to treaty limits. The following list illustrates how the board identified and prioritized the most important programs:

a. Modernize five oil burning battleships in accordance with previous recommendations of the General Board.
b. Lay down eight 10,000-ton modern cruisers.
c. Lay down three fleet submarines.
d. Lay down one aircraft carrier, not to exceed 23,000 tons.
e. Construct aircraft in accordance with five-year building program recommended [by BuAer].
f. Lay down one floating dry dock.[41]

Only the most fuel-efficient battleships were chosen for modernization in the following year. Likewise, large cruisers and submarines were given priority, in order to support the battle fleet and provide long-range reconnaissance.[42]

Often in the interwar period ships were authorized but not built until later. If a new arms-limitation treaty reduced tonnages and sizes, the ships might not be built at all. For example, the language in House Resolution 8687 that authorized naval construction in 1924 clarified the relationship between construction and the treaty system: "That in the event of an international conference for the limitation of naval armaments the president is hereby empowered, in his discretion, to suspend in whole or in part any or all alterations or construction authorized in this Act."[43] Congress, whose membership also included arms-reduction advocates, could also scale back the president's budget submissions during the allocation process. Legislators often saw no sense in building ships that might be scrapped under the terms of a new treaty, as they had been in the Washington treaties. This dynamic became manifest with a particular vengeance after the London Naval Conference.[44]

From Geneva to London

Rear Admiral Hilary Pollard Jones of the General Board was, as noted above, dispatched to Geneva as the senior observer of the United States to the League of Nations Preparatory Commission for Disarmament in 1926. Jones was assigned despite the clear differences over naval construction between the secretary of the Navy, Curtis Wilbur, and the General Board—an indication of the power and influence of the General Board during this period. The League established this commission to discuss the basis for a comprehensive arms-reduction conference tentatively scheduled in 1927 at Geneva. Jones took with him an agenda that Secretary Wilbur had asked him to "reconsider" the previous year. Prior to leaving for Geneva, Jones had reflected the frustration of the board in a response to a query from Rear Admiral Pratt, now the president of the Naval War College: "No one has been able to get any information regarding the reasons why the Secretary declines to sign such a precept, nor have any specific modifications to it been suggested."[45]

Jones' assignment to the leadership of the General Board capped a very successful career in the Navy that had included a tour as commander in chief of the U.S. Fleet. His personality was often (and has been since) the target of invective and has been used as an explanation for the failure of the United States and Great Britain to come to terms at the Geneva Naval Conference in 1927. However, as both the epigraph to this chapter and more recent scholarship make clear, Jones was not the instinctive or reactionary Anglophobe that some have portrayed him to be.[46] His correspondence prior to the Geneva Conference with another of the expert admirals on naval arms limitation, W. V. Pratt, reflects an emerging consensus among the senior Navy leadership on the need for a rapprochement and a good working relationship between the two English-speaking maritime powers. Responding to Jones' letter of 1 February 1926, Pratt wrote: "For so long as she [Britain] maintains equality or preponderance *with us* and preponderance of sea strength against any possible European combination of naval powers, she can remain secure in what is to her vital—the economic factor" [emphasis mine]; Pratt continues in a vein marked far more by self-interest and realpolitik than is true of Jones in emphasizing that Britain "should never make the mistake of 1776 with America again. Hence equality in cruisers and all else."

Jones ably defended U.S. interests at the Preparatory Commission meetings. Forewarned by the U.S. naval attaché in London about British proposals for the conference, Jones emphasized the opposition of his country to any initiatives to abolish the battleship or the submarine.[47] The retention of the battleship has been viewed as evidence of the interwar Navy's obsession with this vessel. If one looks at this issue from the perspective of the General Board at the time, however, one finds instead that the battleship was viewed as the one element of the treaty navy that the United States had managed to maintain at close to parity with Great Britain. More importantly, this ratio gave the United States a 40 percent advantage over the Imperial Japanese Navy in this category of warship. As for the submarine, it was viewed as essential to strategy in the Pacific, based on the courses of action in the Orange plan. Jones had been a party to the extensive board hearings on the topic of fleet submarines in 1924–25 and regarded the submarine as an essential reconnaissance and screening asset for the fleet.[48]

Jones' primary purpose at the 1926 Geneva meetings was to maintain the primacy of the Washington formula in the face of French proposals to limit navies by using a "global tonnage approach." This method simply gave nations maximum tonnage figures, within which they could build as they saw fit; a variation on this theme was to add merchant tonnages to those for warships. Jones found willing allies in the officers assigned to the Japanese and the British naval delegations for maintaining the Washington formula as the correct basis for future conferences—tonnages and ratios by class. Jones judged seeking a universal consensus in these meetings to be a "hopeless task." However, Jones and the administration held out hope for a successful effort in 1927 outside of the aegis of the League. The State Department called for a three-power conference to meet the next year at Geneva "independent of the League," in part due to Jones' recommendations. Jones visited his British Admiralty counterparts in November 1926. Jones and the British ended up talking past each other on the issue of cruiser tonnages and ratios. This was due to a British reluctance to reveal their overall cruiser requirements, which were substantially higher than the United States was willing to accept.[49]

The cruiser issue was critical. The British wanted to build large numbers of cruisers to secure the sea lines of communication of their empire. They wanted a cruiser ceiling that was double (600,000 tons) what the General Board had recommended. The General Board knew it would never get Congress or the president to approve a building program to reach 600,000 tons of cruisers; in fact, the board had calculated that 300,000 tons was probably the maximum that could be authorized for cruisers, built and building. Jones continued his shuttle diplomacy, meeting with British naval representatives again in March 1927 to ascertain if they were more flexible on the cruiser issue than they had been the previous November. The British led him to believe they were.[50] Some historians have identified Jones', and by extension the Navy's, intransigence on the cruiser issue as obstinacy and Anglophobia. The fact of the matter is that the Japanese were the board's, and Jones', real concern. If a much higher cruiser tonnage cap were adopted to accommodate the British, the Japanese could build to 60 percent of that total figure. The problem was that the Republican administration in Washington had no intention of building up to 400,000 tons, never mind 600,000 tons. That meant that the Japanese might actually exceed the United States in cruiser tonnage. One historian in particular claims it was Jones' Anglophobia that drove this position, when in point of fact it hinged entirely on War Plan Orange—a plan aimed not at Great Britain but at Japan! However, it is the subsequent declassification and complete accessibility of War Plan Orange that makes it now clear that the only overt budgetary enemy was Japan; at the time, war planning was highly classified.[51] It was no accident that Jones' primary aide at the 1927 Geneva Conference was none other than Rear Admiral Frank Schofield, fresh from a tour as the chief of the OpNav War Plans Division, which had produced the latest update of War Plan Orange.[52]

The real question, often obscured by the focus on Jones, is why the British seemed so intent on limiting the U.S. Navy's acquisition of ten-thousand-ton 8-inch-gun cruisers. They had no Japan-like naval threat in the wings as the most likely adversary. Versailles limited (or more truthfully, eliminated) the German navy, and the Washington system limited the French and Italians. So the question remains, who was really the more phobic naval institution—the U.S. Navy or the Royal Navy? Might Jones, as historian William Braisted suggests, been merely have responding to a British animosity—an animosity that would have made no sense on his part, given his regard for the British Empire as one of "two main pillars of civilization," alongside the United States?[53]

Article XIX of the Washington Treaty exacerbated the American position, because it established a status quo on U.S. naval bases in the western Pacific. These bases were barely adequate to maintain the small Asiatic Fleet.[54] This "nonfortification" clause caused the General Board to desire to build cruisers of the treaty limit of ten thousand tons, in order to possess as large an operational radius of action as possible, in the absence of bases. The British, in contrast, had less need of these largest cruisers, given their mature and extensive system of imperial bases. The Americans could not afford to build to match British tonnages.[55] The difference between the United States and British positions was profound—the gap separating the extremes of the two positions was 300,000 tons. Jones and his civilian counterpart, Ambassador Hugh S. Gibson, however, proceeded to the Geneva Naval Conference in June 1927 with no idea that the difference was so great.[56]

The hope of the U.S. delegation was that a treaty agreement would restrict the other powers' cruiser construction programs. At the same time, Jones and the General Board regretted the negotiating position in which their country's anemic construction program had placed them vis-à-vis Japan and Great Britain. At the time of the Geneva Conference the United States had begun construction on only two of the eight cruisers first authorized in 1924.[57] For their parts, Great Britain had laid down thirteen new cruisers and Japan eight. Clearly, U.S. construction was lagging in this category, as the General Board had repeatedly emphasized. The U.S. plan was to propose a cruiser limitation of 300,000 tons for the United States and Great Britain and to restrict the Japanese to 60 percent or less of this total (180,000 to 150,000 tons). However, the context for the Geneva Conference was completely different from that existing at Washington in 1921–22. At the earlier conference, the United States had negotiated from a position of strength, with capital ships built and building. However, at Geneva it was in a position of relative inferiority in the numbers of cruisers, both commissioned and under construction. It was thus less likely that either Great Britain or Japan would agree to any substantial limits without significant concessions from the U.S. delegation.[58]

A complete breakdown of the conference occurred over the cruiser disagreement between the U.S. and British delegations. Worse, the Japanese delegation, ably led by Admiral Saito Makoto, was already engaged behind the scenes in negotiations with the British over the "inferior" 60 percent cruiser ratio. The vice navy minister, Osumi Mineo, remained "intransigent" and committed Japan to a 70 percent cruiser ratio for Japan, vetoing all compromises proposed by Saito. The Geneva Conference might still have faltered on the Japanese position vis-à-vis cruiser tonnages even if the British and Americans had worked out their disagreement.[59]

The breakdown of the naval arms-limitation process at Geneva prompted the Coolidge administration to take decisive action. Taking advantage of the impression of bad faith on the part the British, and perhaps reflecting lingering Anglophobia on his own part, Coolidge proposed, and the House passed, a second "cruiser bill" shortly after the end of the conference. The Senate rejected this bill, due to fierce lobbying by powerful peace groups. However, a modified "cruiser bill" was submitted in 1928. This new bill authorized the construction of fifteen additional cruisers and a small aircraft carrier. Even so, the Senate delayed approving it until after the 1928 fall elections.[60] This legislation, often identified as an act of anger directed at Great Britain, was the first substantial demonstration in over four years that the United States might build to match its rhetoric about treaty ratios. As such, ironically, it constituted a positive step—albeit a stormy one—on the path toward British and American rapprochement. The Americans had real concerns and intended to act on them; they would not be bullied into a position of inferiority vis-à-vis what they perceived as their real threat—Japan. Like a stormy fight between committed marriage partners, the dispute promised in the aftermath more, rather than less, stability in the relationship.

Despite the setback at Geneva, the governments of Japan, the United States, and Great Britain remained interested in naval limitation as a means to cut spending. Admiral Jones was dispatched to Geneva again—this time for the third meeting of the Preparatory Commission on the Reduction and Limitation of Armaments in early 1928. This forum evolved into an organizational agency through which British and American positions on naval limitation slowly improved. A February 1928 letter to the secretary of the Navy from Jones clarified the progress being made in discussions with the British about how to establish ship classes and types for the next naval-limitation conference, now scheduled in London for 1930. On the issue of setting ratios for naval "effectives" and trained reserves, "the British Empire and the United States" stood together in mandating that personnel limitation would be implemented only if concurrent tonnage ratios on ships were also agreed to. The two powers also made common cause on the issue of reserve stock and material, the British in the lead, while "the American delegation [headed by Jones] viewed with the sympathy the British attitude." These sorts of agreements on the peripheral issues boded well for a continuing thaw in the relationship between the American and British naval delegations, and they occurred before the Quaker Herbert Hoover's election.

By this time Admiral Jones had left the board and been moved to the retired list, but he certainly does not seem to have retired. The CNO, Admiral C. F. Hughes, acting in his capacity as an ex-officio member of the board, endorsed Jones' letter as the basis for further General Board discussion. This letter also mentioned for the first time a French proposal to separate cruisers and destroyers into separate classes for the purposes of tonnage limitations.[61] The General Board proceedings (minutes) for this period are full of references to Jones, as well as to members of the board detached to support him in his ongoing discussions.[62]

Later that year (1928) the board denounced a separate, draft Anglo-French proposal that established limits on the 8-inch-gun/ten-thousand-ton cruisers but left smaller, 6-inch gun cruisers and below unrestricted. This seeming reversal of course by the British might be explained as a move by British diplomats without reference to their naval representatives, since the idea had come out of the British Foreign Office. The board opined that using this proposal as the basis for further limitation would make U.S. participation "fruitless."[63] However, the Anglo-French proposal may have served as the motivation for a new means, nicknamed the "yardstick," of measuring cruiser equivalencies. The yardstick was a formula developed in the United States—initially by Jones, according to one account—to calculate "equivalent" cruiser tonnages. It used "tonnage, age, and gun power" as factors.[64] The sixth meeting of the Preparatory Commission met in April–May 1929 at Geneva, again with Jones as the primary U.S. naval representative to Hugh S. Gibson. Commander Train of the General Board was detached to serve as Gibson's technical adviser. Jones and Train both returned that June, with Jones briefing the entire General Board on the meeting on 4 June 1929. It was at this conference that Jones acceded to, and perhaps refined, the idea of the yardstick.[65]

Shortly after the meeting, while Jones was briefing the General Board, Secretary of State Henry Stimson notified the U.S. ambassador to Great Britain, Charles G. Dawes, that he had been contacted by the British ambassador about the positive outcome of the meeting in Geneva. The British were proposing a head-to-head meeting between the new prime minister, Ramsay MacDonald, and President Hoover in the fall. Perhaps Stimson was alluding to the General Board when he wrote, "While it was of course impossible that [Hoover and MacDonald] could settle all the details of the naval disarmament matter they might announce that they had reached an agreement in principle leaving the details *to be worked out by others*."[66] The "others" had already started working the details and would do so right up until the moment the prime minister arrived in October.

The change in the willingness of Jones and members of the General Board (including the CNO) to reach a modus vivendi with Great Britain was given much more momentum by Hoover, a one-time delegate to the original Washington Conference and advocate of worldwide disarmament.[67] Hoover wanted to bring the British back into negotiations, while accommodating the General Board's desire to build no fewer than twenty-three 8-inch cruisers. This makes sense only if one attributes to the Americans, and the General Board specifically, a desire to build with Japan in mind as the adversary, not Great Britain. This intent clearly comes out in a communication of Stimson to the new secretary of the Navy, Charles F. Adams, in July 1929, after the utility of the yardstick—really a conversion formula—was in hot debate between the two departments and the General Board. Stimson stated unequivocally, "At the moment I am interested only in the results vis-à-vis Great Britain." However, Stimson had alarmed the General Board in the same letter by proposing to include destroyers in yardstick calculations as well. Its members cited in reply an earlier 1921 opinion about the impracticability of any attempt "to commute combatant value of one class of ships into combatant value of another." They reminded both secretaries that the Anglo-French proposal in the Third Preparatory Commission meetings was the basis for naval limitations everyone had agreed to—laying down that destroyers and cruisers would be limited separately and in no way linked for the upcoming London Conference.[68] The sense one gets is of the U.S. naval and diplomatic polity trying to come to consensus on the cruiser issue in a way acceptable to only the British.

To this end, Hoover presided over a marathon meeting of the entire General Board, Secretary Stimson, and Secretary Adams, as well as the Chief of Naval Operations and the undersecretary of the Navy, in the White House on 11 September 1929. Notably absent was anyone from the War Department. The meeting lasted until past midnight, as the president and the board attempted to draft a telegram to Prime Minister MacDonald that proposed a yardstick acceptable as a basis for negotiation. The meeting was convened again the following day and lasted until past 8:00 p.m. before the final wording laying out the U.S. position on cruisers was approved by the president. In it the United States proposed to limit itself to twenty-one 8-inch-gun (heavy) cruisers, ten older *Omaha*-class light cruisers, and five new 6-inch-gun (light) cruisers.[69] These new light cruisers would eventually include an experimental new type with a substantial complement of aircraft, a design that came to be known as the "flying-deck cruiser." The results were captured in a subsequent presidential memorandum to the General Board on 24 September 1929. The memorandum included five versions of the yardstick formula: the General Board's, Admiral Jones', and three proposals by Hoover. The memorandum also included a series of questions and answers as to why the General Board had modified certain yardstick components in Jones' formula, especially as regards "gun factor." It seems clear that Jones and Hoover were more closely aligned than Hoover and the General Board!

The preferred yardstick formula (this is the Jones Yardstick) looked like this; it gives a sense of the intricacies involved and of Hoover's obsession with the details:

$$E = D \, x \, A - D \, x \, (1 - G)$$

Original tonnage $= D$
Age factor $= A$ (60 percent for Jones version)
Gun factor $= G$ (6-inch versus 8-inch)
Equivalent tonnage $= E$

Essentially, a tonnage correction is made for ships scrapped at obsolescence (which could allow more, rather than less, to be built, ton for ton), and the result would be modified by the gun factor. As Hoover stated at the end of his memorandum to the board, "The purpose of the above calculation is to determine the maximum and minimum to be placed upon this example . . . and it is a good opportunity for further illumination of the mathematical background adopted in the determination of gun factors."[70]

A variation on this formula was eventually adopted for use at the London Conference in 1930. It limited both classes of cruisers (8- and 6-inch guns) separately but linked them by the yardstick using $E = D$ x A x G.[71] This yardstick led to rapprochement on the cruiser issue between the United States and Great Britain, which in turn laid the ground for the success of the London Naval Conference of 1930. It was an elegant way for the British and Americans to have their cake and eat it too. The British could have more absolute cruiser tonnage but of the smaller, light-cruiser type, while the United States would have less overall tonnage but more of the heavy-cruiser type. Both navies would have the optimal cruiser inventories for what they respectively perceived as their most critical strategic needs: in the British case, patrolling the sea-lanes of the empire; in the U.S. case, screening the fleet for the decisive battle outlined in War Plan Orange.

When Prime Minister MacDonald arrived that October in the United States, President Hoover went to great lengths to ensure that the British and American positions would be closer than they had been at Geneva. The series of meetings with MacDonald and their diplomatic advisers from 5 to 11 October 1929 finalized the combined front of the two great maritime powers. In an initial policy memorandum for the president, Stimson again highlighted the importance of the General Board in the ongoing process as regarded rapprochement over the issue of naval bases, heretofore an item of concern in the board's calculations of sea power:

> The President presented our proposition to divide the world into two hemispheres in the western one of which the British will not maintain naval or

military stations which are a menace to us and in the eastern one of which we shall not maintain such bases which are a menace to them. . . . They were willing that the armament should extend only the ability to stand off raids of privateers and to do ordinary police work against internal troubles. Finally, it was decided *that the best way was to have our General Board advise us as to the truth of the British statement* that their bases are thus innocuous and then to have them agree not to increase them so that they would not become a menace to us.[72]

The memorandum went on to emphasize that any joint statement would reassure the Japanese that article XIX (the nonfortification clause) of the Washington Treaty remained germane, as did the Four-Power, or Pacific, Treaty.[73] Later in the papers generated during the meeting, Stimson emphasized that the goal was to reduce armaments and seek a "moral influence and not a military one"—in other words, not to establish a bilateral grand naval alliance that divided the maritime world between Great Britain and the United States.[74] This tortured conciliatory language was aimed at Japan.

Most interesting in the material generated by the meetings was an entire section, composed of two annexes (VI and VII), dedicated to a detailed articulation of equivalent cruisers strengths based on the work Hoover had done with the General Board the previous month. Most of annex VI was written by Hoover, who zeroed in on the key issue of heavy cruisers, using various permutations of the yardstick. He used a combination of the General Board's yardstick (for age) with Jones' yardstick (for the gun factor). These calculations led to a possible impasse over the number of ten-thousand-ton heavy cruisers—the United States wanted twenty-one, but the British wanted to limit them (mostly for reasons of economy) to eighteen.[75] Using the yardstick to bring the numbers closer together, these annexes show that both parties understood prior to the London Conference that the United States would have to come down to eighteen heavy cruisers but that the tonnage lost could be transferred to light cruisers. Hoover's closing comment emphasized that, based on the yardstick correction, "we are two ships in excess." The final cruiser numbers that would be agreed upon at the London Conference were to be, for reasons discussed below, very similar to the British revised proposal that October—eighteen heavy cruisers and 119,500 tons of light cruisers of varying ages. At the upcoming conference the United States would gain over 20,000 tons extra for its light-cruiser tonnage in compensation for the reduction of the three heavy cruisers. Robert Craigie's proposal the previous October during MacDonald's visit had outlined much of what would become the American-British compromise.[76]

Prior to MacDonald's departure the General Board delivered its opinion on the "menace" posed by British bases. The memorandum signed by the president stated, "With the further view to reducing fear and the friction that comes from fear, we have obtained the opinion of our General Board of the navy, that the existing military and naval stations of Great Britain in the Western Hemisphere are not in a condition to be a menace to the U.S." The initial input of the president for the joint statement of the two political heads of state emphasized the hard work of "the past three months [resulting] in such an approximation of views as has warranted the calling of a conference of the naval powers in the belief that at such a conference all views can be reconciled. (Between ourselves we have agreed upon parity, category by category[,] as a great instrument for removing competition between us.)"[77] The language of the British was similarly positive: "The exchange of views on naval reduction has brought the two nations so close to agreement *that the obstacles in the previous conferences . . .* seem now substantially removed."[78] There is no mention of the yardstick in these formal papers, but it is in the fine print, so to speak. The date for the London Conference was set for 21 January 1930, and the invitations to the other powers were sent out.[79]

Despite Admiral Jones' good work to date, Hoover hedged his bets by including other personnel in the delegation in order to ensure that compromise would occur. Jones' presence on the delegation was balanced by the inclusion of Admiral William V. Pratt, former president of the Naval War College and still nominally the commander in chief of the U.S. Fleet (CINCUS). Pratt, a known supporter of the treaty system, had the confidence of Secretary Stimson, the overall head of the delegation. Stimson had consulted with Theodore Roosevelt Jr. (assistant secretary of the Navy at the time of the Washington Naval Conference). Roosevelt had worked closely with Pratt at Washington and recommended him as the senior technical adviser. Pratt then handpicked a veritable "dream team" of innovators and leaders to assist him, including:

Rear Admiral William Moffett, chief of the Bureau of Aeronautics
Rear Admiral J. R. P. Pringle, president of the Naval War College and regular attendee at Preparatory Commission meetings from 1928
Rear Admiral Harry Yarnell, former chief of the Bureau of Engineering
Rear Admiral Arthur J. Hepburn, chief of the Bureau of Engineering and a former and future General Board member
Capt. A. H. Van Keuren of the Bureau of Construction and Repair, frequent expert visitor to the General Board

Capt. W. W. Smyth, from the Bureau of Ordnance
Cdr. H. C. Train, from the General Board
Lt. Cdr. "Jimmy" Campbell (Pratt's flag aide).[80]

Pratt would effectively become the key senior Navy adviser for the conference. Jones' role in the conference became muted, although he was not without
influence. The British representative, Craigie, recognized Jones' influence in the
U.S. Senate, which might be an obstacle to ratification, noting that Stimson still
listened closely to Jones.[81] However, Pratt, a man who could more readily compromise, departed from Jones on the issue of the American delegation's tentative willingness to accept less than twenty-one 8-inch heavy cruisers. Pratt put
in writing his disagreement with Jones' memo, arguing for a return to the base-
line proposal. In this manner Pratt went on record as siding with the civilian
diplomats. Health problems eventually prompted Jones to return to the United
States before the conclusion of the conference.[82] Despite his break with Pratt
over the cruiser issue, Jones' later opposition to the London Naval Treaty arose
from its compromises adopted regarding 14-inch guns for battleship replacements, the extension of the capital-ship building "holiday," and its accommoda-
tions in naval ratios vis-à-vis the Japanese—not from Anglophobia.[83]

In contrast to the Geneva Conference, the London Conference almost
foundered on the increasingly hard-line attitude of the Japanese over the inferiority it would impose with respect to the American fleet—especially the
proposed ratio for treaty cruisers.[84] They now had a much larger number of
auxiliaries already built than the 10:6 ratio proposed by the Americans. The
Japanese delegation regarded 70 percent as the absolute minimum for any
ratio, because they already had an 80 percent equivalence to the United States
in cruisers—and these were mostly heavy cruisers. When it appeared that
the conference might break up with a Japanese withdrawal, Stimson notified
Washington that he was fully prepared to proceed, as he had denied being earlier in October, with a "two-power" agreement with Great Britain.[85]

At the eleventh hour, a compromise was brokered by Senator David Reed
of the American delegation with Japan's Ambassador Matsudaira Tsuneo.
Under this compromise the Japanese were given the 70 percent ratio for all
auxiliaries except heavy cruisers (which would be 60 percent) and parity in
submarines (although not for the higher tonnages they requested). In order to
make this bitter pill easier to swallow for the Japanese, the Americans promised not to build three of their own heavy cruisers until at least 1936, the year
the London Treaty was to expire, along with the original Washington Naval

Treaty.[86] Perhaps as important in the long run, Great Britain, Japan, and the United States agreed to extend the capital-ship building holiday to 1936.[87] This last element had been opposed from the start by the General Board but accorded well with President Hoover's commitment to both fiscal restraint and disarmament.[88] The General Board now had to delay its plans to begin building replacements for the Navy's battleships until after 1936. This in turn kept the focus of innovation on those classes that could be built—including carriers, submarines, cruisers, and other auxiliaries.

The Role of the Flying-Deck Cruiser at London

One important result of the Reed-Matsudaira compromise was that the relative importance of light cruisers increased, because under the treaty they could actually be laid down prior to 1936 and still displace as much as ten thousand tons. Not so well known were some interesting codicils in the language of the treaty about light cruisers. The focus on cruisers generated by the treaty system also offered the Navy a means to address another problem—its dearth of naval aviation for Pacific operations.[89]

At the suggestion of Admiral Moffett, the Navy came to see the smaller classes of cruisers in a new light. The still-anemic pace of carrier construction in the United States due to costs had led Moffett to suggest that perhaps cruisers were another way to get more aviation into the fleet. Moffett, in reference to light cruiser design, testified two months prior to the London Conference to the board, "I would say briefly that Aeronautics thinks that we should carry as many planes on cruisers as can be done without interfering with the proper mission of the ship." Moffett recommended that these light cruisers carry at least six aircraft—launched by catapult.[90] The idea of putting as many airplanes as possible on cruisers was not new; a 1925 OpNav War Plans Division study had recommended installing flying decks on all U.S. light cruisers.[91] The Navy's plan "to build aircraft carriers at such a rate that the United States shall not fall behind treaty ratios" had been put on hold by the expectations generated by the treaty system.[92] However, because of the London Conference there was an opportunity to redress this paucity of naval aviation in the fleet with cruisers. A treaty allowance opened the door for long-range, ten-thousand-ton *light* cruisers equipped with as many aircraft as possible—the flying-deck cruiser.

Admiral Moffett had grown frantic on the issue of carrier introduction by the late 1920s. He had asked the Navy secretary to recommend that five carriers of the smaller size be built and had gotten only one. The secretary duly forwarded Moffett's correspondence to the General Board. Moffett was coming to believe that spreading aviation around on smaller decks would allow the Navy more operational flexibility in using aircraft carriers. Not only would they support the battle fleet, but they could provide air cover for the increasingly important fleet train, ferry aircraft, and act as an element of the scouting fleet. The General Board concurred with most of this reasoning, although it was loath to abandon the big carriers until more evidence was available, from experience gained in the fleet with the new smaller carrier *(Ranger)* authorized in the Butler "cruiser bill."[93] With only the *Saratoga, Lexington,* and the old, slow *Langley,* there were hardly enough carriers to support the battle line. Even with every ton built, Admiral Pratt at the Naval War College was convinced, there would not be enough carriers to do everything that needed to be done. According to a 1927 annual fleet report, "In a Pacific War, Navy control of the air cannot be attained by any arrangement of tonnage of aircraft carriers within the allotment of 135,000 tons, whether all were of 10,000 tons, or all of 27,000 tons displacement, and that in order to secure this, quantity production will have to be resorted to."[94]

Admirals Mark Bristol (as commander in chief of the Asiatic Fleet) and Moffett had emphasized the urgent situation of the Asiatic Fleet and its bearing on strategy, and they were supported in their views by Pratt: "One of the outstanding lessons of the overseas problem played each year is that to advance into a hostile zone the fleet must carry with it an air force that will ensure, *beyond a doubt,* command of the air. This means not only superiority to enemy fleet aircraft but also to his fleet and shore based aircraft combined."[95] A few months after Moffett's memorandum to the secretary, Admiral Schofield of the War Plans Division added his voice to the clamor for more carriers. In a memorandum addressing the aircraft building program Schofield bluntly stated, "I consider the greatest need of naval aviation today is more carriers."[96]

Moffett's memorandum showed that he was not alone in identifying the critical need for naval aviation as an operational means to enable the strategy of the Orange plan by ameliorating the impact of the prohibition against basing aviation ashore in the western Pacific. Buried in Moffett's memorandum was the following recommendation: "Within 10,000 tons displacement it is practicable to build an aircraft carrying cruiser which can operate upward of 40 planes of the intermediate or smaller types. Such a complement of planes can be used alternately on gunnery observation, tactical scouting, fighting [air defense], smoke laying or bombing missions with bombs carrying at least 400 pounds of explosive."[97] Here was the outline for a new type of naval vessel—a hybrid cruiser/aircraft carrier. Moffett was clearly worried that the Japanese might take this path, given their ambitious cruiser construction programs.

Moffett's solution was a new vessel with the ten-thousand-ton displacement of a cruiser and ability to operate substantial numbers of aircraft. After the extreme disappointments and delays of the late 1920s, the board held hearings on light cruiser design in November 1929, on the eve of the London Naval Conference. Admiral Moffett was asked for his views on how many planes the new light cruisers recently authorized in the Butler cruiser bill should have. BuAer responded that the "minimum number should be six." Interestingly, after an extended discussion of how these planes were to be positioned aboard the ship, the transcript noted, "at this point a discussion took place not for the record." Moffett, who was to be a member of the London Conference delegation, may have shared his flying-deck-cruiser ideas with the board. The board certainly had access to these views via Moffett's secret correspondence of the previous year in which he had first broached the idea. The nature of the topic— and the plan to propose a new class of ship at London—may have been viewed as too sensitive to commit to the hearing transcript.[98]

At the same time, Moffett lobbied the General Board to recommend formally that the London delegation propose "transferring these carriers [*Lexington* and *Saratoga*] to the experimental class" of carriers allowed by the Five Power Treaty. In this way the United States could replace these two carriers with four "16,500-ton carriers," which had "several advantages over" the larger carriers. Moffett's purpose here was to try to retain the large ships while building even more of the smaller ones. The General Board forwarded Moffett's advice and endorsed it by recommending that should the naval conference in London advocate a reduction in overall carrier tonnage "below 135,000, the General Board is of the opinion that the United States should insist that the SARATOGA and LEXINGTON be placed in the experimental class as a necessary provision for agreement." However, its bottom line was that treaty allowances for carrier tonnage should not be decreased under any circumstances, since "the United States must conduct any naval war at greater distance from home than would be the case of other Powers signatory to the Washington Treaty."[99]

The needs of U.S. fleet aviation could be augmented by cruisers with up to twelve aircraft on board. In later hearings before the General Board, the numbers would go as high as forty aircraft. Additionally, Fleet Problem IX in 1929 had emphasized a need for more aviation vessels. Limited to two large aircraft carriers, the fleet could lose most of its aviation support if either of these ships were sunk or damaged. All the eggs were in two baskets. Flying-deck cruisers would spread the risk across the fleet and ensure that its aviation was not so vulnerable through the sinking of the precious carriers.[100] The risk of losing one of the two big carriers, as had happened in the Fleet Problem IX, and thus losing a significant percentage of the aviation available to protect and assist the battle line would be ameliorated by the addition of such ships.[101]

It was against this background that the Admiral Moffett inserted his idea for a flying-deck cruiser into the language of the 1930 London Naval Treaty. Such a ship would serve multiple purposes. First, it would get naval aviation into the fleet, by employing a different class of ship—ships that could carry more than just two or three planes but not as many as the larger carriers. Such ships promised operational flexibility, because aviation would be distributed more evenly throughout the fleet. Moffett used his advisory role at the London Conference to proceed with his idea for flying-deck cruisers. He jotted a note to himself making reference to the key design engineer, A. H. Van Keuren from the Bureau of Construction and Repair, who was also at the conference: "Aircraft will settle next war. Don't care how many surface vessels we build. The more the other nations build, the less money they will have for aircraft. Friday Mar 21st proposed to Captain Van Keuren he get up a design for a 6-inch gun cruiser that would have a landing deck for aircraft."[102]

Using the opportunity presented, Moffett proposed language to include in the London Treaty creating a new "loophole" using two separate articles. Article 3 of the London Treaty prevented the counting of "landing-on or flying-off platforms" against a nation's overall carrier tonnage, "provided such vessel was not designed or adapted exclusively as an aircraft carrier." Also, article 16 of part III of the treaty stipulated, "Not more than twenty-five percent of the allowed total tonnage in the cruiser category may be fitted with a landing-on platform or deck for aircraft."[103]

This loophole may have in fact been the key to the willingness of the U.S. naval delegates, especially Admirals Hepburn, Pringle, and Yarnell, but Pratt above all, to accept the lower heavy-cruiser number (eighteen) proposed by the British. This was because they believed the flying-deck cruiser (which could be counted as a light cruiser) was probably superior to heavy cruisers in what they called "combat power." Certainly Moffett believed as much, as the quotation above makes clear. Pratt and many other naval officers, if they were not yet convinced that the design had more "combat power," came to believe that it did after the ratification of the London Treaty.[104] At the same time, the British were unconvinced of (or maybe oblivious to) the potential of the concept.[105] They and the Japanese allowed the Americans to insert the language allowing conversion of heavy-cruiser to light-cruiser tonnage in article 18 and also to insert the language in article 16 that allowed the Americans to convert that tonnage to the flying-deck type.[106] The irony here is too rich to ignore—article 18 led to eighteen heavy cruisers!

The Navy's—and Moffett's—purpose in creating the treaty language for the flying-deck cruiser has been misunderstood to some degree. Some historians have listed the flying-deck cruiser, along with Moffett's advocacy of lighter-than-air dirigibles, as simply another "wrong" idea. However, others have been less critical but still use the case as an example of the General Board serving admirably as "umpire," preventing the Navy from making an "unfortunate" construction decision. Still others regard the concept as "before its time" and argue that the flying-deck cruiser might have measurably improved the performance of the Navy during the first year of World War II.[107]

What is clear is that the situation as perceived by Navy leaders in 1930 was urgent. The Navy had only just begun to experiment with the big carriers *Saratoga* and *Lexington*. The General Board was still undecided as to the relative utility of large carriers versus small carriers. Meanwhile, the one thing everyone in the Navy did agree on was that there were not enough aviation ships in the fleet—be they carriers, tenders, or flying-deck cruisers. Moffett's purpose was congruent with the consensus in the Navy: whatever means could be used should be used to get aviation ships. Any attempt to do so must account for the constraints of the naval treaties, support by the administration, and support in Congress. Although because of the London Treaty Moffett could no longer purposefully build small carriers, he could build flying-deck ships as long as they looked like, and were armed as, 6-inch cruisers. In order to get to the fleet, the more numerous, smaller, flying-decked ships would have to be half carrier and half cruiser. Moffett's view carried certain risks. First and foremost was the risk that building flying-deck ships might mean that other aviation ships would not get built. Clearly, Moffett wanted aircraft carriers as well. Also, the concept, however promising, would remain unproven until one of these ships could be built and tested with the fleet.[108] Admiral Pratt, addressing the General Board after the London Conference, warned, "We have to be very careful. This ship is a cruiser first according to the treaty. Otherwise you will have Japan and every other country on your neck."[109]

Because the light cruiser was smaller and cheaper per unit, it was hoped that more of them could be built than aircraft carriers. Having more cruisers meant that they could be assigned to provide, or dispute, command of the air in the remote areas of the Pacific and provide air cover for assets for which larger carriers were considered inappropriate (such as the fleet train or portions of the scouting forces). As a cruiser, the ship could also perform all the functions—screening, reconnaissance, and commerce raiding—at which cruisers excelled. And it could do these missions, and new ones like convoy protection and anti-submarine warfare, in ways that aviation would only enhance, because of its operational reach. Instead of defending or screening a convoy or patrol area within visual range, the cruiser could extend its search area over hundreds of square miles.[110] Finally, it would be a "treaty" ship, one that naval officers could point to in the language of a naval-limitation treaty in order to justify construction. It stood a good chance of being constructed by stingy administrations and Congress, because it was relatively inexpensive. As it turned out, Congress authorized the construction of the flying-deck cruiser before the Navy was ready to build it.[111] It was only by the "slimmest of circumstances" that the United States did not build the prototypes for the flying-deck class codified and allowed for by the London Naval Treaty. The great irony is that this concept—never built—*convinced* the U.S. naval delegation to some degree to accept the cruiser compromises at London.[112]

The Japanese, however, did lay down scouting cruisers with increased floatplane complements beginning in 1934—the *Tone* class.[113] This they did as a direct result of the London Naval Treaty's flying-deck language. However, the *Tone*s were eventually armed with 8-inch rather than 6-inch guns.

Conclusion

The London Conference and the diplomats who negotiated there have been widely condemned for failure to put in place political agreements commensurate in importance to what had been achieved at Washington. Many observers identify the London Treaty as the key turning point on Japan's path to aggressive militarism in the 1930s.[114] In the United States the treaty was roundly criticized, and the ratification process was not nearly as smooth as it had been for the Washington Naval Treaty. The treaty was publicly opposed by the General Board and many in the Navy.[115] Many in the Navy blamed Admiral Pratt, and when Pratt became CNO, his predecessor, Admiral C. F. Hughes, reputedly refused to shake hands with him at the change of command. However, some historians identify a new spirit of cooperation between the United States and Great Britain as having emerged from the London Conference.[116] Certainly the pre-London level of effort toward accord between the two nations on the part of the Hoover administration, as well as the installation of the anglophile and treaty-friendly Pratt as CNO thereafter, did much to pave the way for increased U.S.-British amity.

This chapter looked primarily at the role of the General Board, including the actions of Admiral Hilary Jones, prior to the London Arms Limitation Conference of 1930. It also recounted how the General Board colluded to a degree with Admiral William Moffett to create a potential "loophole" in the London Treaty to solve pressing operational problems with naval aviation. This loophole may have in fact been a key factor that persuaded the American naval delegates to accept the lower heavy-cruiser number (eighteen) proposed by the British.

Admiral Jones was in fact, if not in name, a supernumerary member of the General Board (and, one might add, the State Department) after November 1927. He was what today might be termed "the go-to guy" when it came to the ongoing arms-limitation process in Geneva, through the agency of the various preparatory commissions that met throughout the 1920s. The same might also be said of Moffett, who almost never missed an opportunity to testify before or write his opinions to the General Board. Just as Jones was the man for general naval arms-limitation issues as they affected sea power writ large, Moffett was the point man for all things involving naval aviation.

This examination suggests the following observations regarding both the significance of the General Board's influence and a possible revisionist argument about the efficacy of the London Conference and the 1930 Naval Arms Limitation Treaty signed there. First, the board's influence was significant and beneficial. Far from retreating into Anglophobia or a Stimsonesque "dim religious world" or peering narrowly through a porthole, Jones and the General Board offered considered and sober advice to both the Coolidge and Hoover administrations about arms limitation in general and naval limitation in particular.[117] In the process the president and the secretaries of the Navy and State partnered with the General Board in crafting the technical solution (the "yardstick") that allowed a British-U.S. rapprochement on the key issue that separated them and stood in the way of a closer relationship—treaty cruisers.

Finally, historians who have generally found the 1930 London agreement to be a failure on the grounds of its lack of commensurate collective political agreements have missed the critical accomplishment of a de facto united British-American political-military front. This relationship was codified at London in 1930.[118] To a degree, the foundation for the grand alliance of World War II can be found in the fine print of the correspondence leading up to, and the language of, the London Naval Treaty.

The following exchange between Admiral Sir Roger J. B. Keyes and a confidant of Franklin Delano Roosevelt over lunch in March 1934 captures the new spirit in all its complexity:

> [Admiral Keyes said] "I agree that you are not a prospective enemy, but (and he smiled) you are a prospective bully." We all laughed and the Admiral continued, "You know you did object to some of our naval policies at the beginning of the last war and greater naval strength gives weight to such objections"—"to answer your question I think we should approve of your building what you like so long as we may do the same." . . . The net impression which I gained from this conversation was one of great friendliness toward the U.S.A., which this letter has not fully expressed.[119]

Shortly thereafter, following naval conversations in June and July with British officials in London, the General Board reported to the secretary of the Navy that "the British officials were most cordial and friendly and on every occasion evidenced their desire for cooperation with the United States, both in matters affecting the 1935 Conference [on naval armaments in London] and, so far as might be practicable, in general political affairs, such as a common understanding with reference to the Orient."[120] It is true that the actions of Japan in 1931 and 1932 in Manchuria and Shanghai clarified the common interests of the Great Britain and the United States in East Asia; however, these events merely reinforced an already improving relationship.

Finally, the beneficial presence of William Veazie Pratt reflected to a degree the wise statesmanship of his Japanese predecessor and analogue at the Washington Naval Conference—Admiral Kato Tomosaburo—for his role within the U.S. Navy in the success of the London Conference.[121] Pratt too represents a more liberal and innovative tradition fostered at times by the General Board; like Jones and Moffett, Pratt can be considered a de facto member of the board.

Perhaps we need to look at London from a different perspective—looking forward instead of back. From this perspective, understanding about the fundamental progress in British-American relations comes into clearer focus. A turning point had occurred, opaque perhaps to us but not to the generation watching the storm clouds gathering again over Europe and Asia.

NOTES

1. For the epigraph, Hilary Jones, cited in Michel Simpson, ed., *Anglo-American Naval Relations, 1919–1930* (Burlington, Ver.: Navy Records Society, 2010), 70. Hilary Jones was the senior member of the General Board of the Navy at this time, and William V. Pratt was the president of the Naval War College, a position that included ex-officio membership on the General Board, a secondary duty that Pratt took seriously. Pratt had served two previous tours on the General Board as a regular member. See Gerald E. Wheeler, *Admiral William Veazie Pratt, U.S. Navy: A Sailor's Life* (Washington, D.C.: Navy History Division, 1974), 240–44.

2. The present chapter is based on the author's material used for chapters 2–4 and 6 in *Agents of Innovation: The General Board and the Design of the Fleet That Defeated the Japanese Navy* (Annapolis, Md.: Naval Institute Press, 2008) and from " Naval Arms Limitation: 1922–1937," *Journal of Military History* 74, no. 4 (October 2010), 1129–36.

3. The most objective essay that makes this point is William F. Trimble, "Admiral Hilary P. Jones and the 1927 Geneva Naval Conference," *Military Affairs* 43, no. 1 (February 1979), 1–4; see also Thomas H. Buckley, "The Icarus Factor: The American Pursuit of Myth in Naval Arms Control, 1921–36," in *The Washington Conference, 1921–22: Naval Rivalry, East Asian Stability and the Road to Pearl Harbor,* ed. Erik Goldstein and John Maurer (London: Frank Cass, 1994), 124–46.

4. B. J. C. McKercher, "From Enmity to Cooperation: The Second Baldwin Government and the Improvement of Anglo-American Relations, November 1928–June 1929," *Albion: A Quarterly Journal Concerned with British Studies* 24, no. 1 (Spring 1992), 67. McKercher makes an argument similar to the one in this chapter, except from a British political perspective.

5. The originator of this position is William R. Braisted; see especially "On the General Board of the Navy, Admiral Hilary P. Jones, and Naval Arms Limitation, 1921–1931," in *The Dwight D. Eisenhower Lectures in War and Peace, No. 5* (Manhattan: Kansas State University, Department of History, 1993); and "The Evolution of the United States Navy's Strategic Assessments in the Pacific, 1919–1931," in *Washington Conference, 1921–22,* ed. Goldstein and Maurer.

6. For the key argument about the Navy's increasing importance in foreign policy see William Reynolds Braisted, *The United States Navy in the Pacific, 1897–1909* (New York: Greenwood, 1969, first published 1958), vii–ix, 244–45. For references to the Navy's role in the Monroe Doctrine and Roosevelt Corollary see Henry J. Hendrix, *Theodore Roosevelt's Naval Diplomacy* (Annapolis, Md.: Naval Institute Press, 2009), 31, 52–53; see also Edmund Morris, *Theodore Rex* (New York: Random House, 2001), 201–202.

7. John Hay to Andrew D. White, 6 September 1899, cited in *Papers Relating to the Foreign Relations of the United States, 1899* [hereafter *FRUS*], 129–30, www.vlib.us/amdocs/texts/opendoor.html (accessed 03/06/2011) [emphasis mine].

8. Morris, *Theodore Rex*, 229.

9. A. T. Mahan, *Naval Strategy*, reprinted as Fleet Marine Force Reference Publication 12–32 (Washington, D.C.: Government Printing Office, 1991), 110.

10. See Kuehn, "U.S. Navy General Board and Naval Arms Limitation"; Philip L. Semsch, "Elihu Root and the General Staff," *Military Affairs* 27, no. 1 (Spring 1963), 16–27; see also Ronald H. Spector, *Professors at War: The Naval War College and the Development of the Naval Profession* (Newport, R.I.: Naval War College Press, 1977), passim.

11. Williamson Murray and Alan Millett, "Innovation: Past and Future," in *Military Innovation in the Interwar Period* (Cambridge, U.K.: Cambridge University Press, 1996), 313–14.

12. Jarvis Butler, "The General Board of the Navy," U.S. Naval Institute *Proceedings* 56, no. 8 (August 1930), 701. See also the extremely valuable discussion of Admiral Taylor's role in Henry P. Beers, "The Development of the Office of the Chief of Naval Operations," *Military Affairs* 10, no. 1 (Spring 1946), 40–68.

13. Kuehn, *Agents of Innovation*, chap. 2, passim.

14. The Bureau of Ordnance was nicknamed the "gun club" due to its advocacy of all calibers of guns for ships, as well as of other ordnance, such as torpedoes. It also made recommendations for armor for the various classes of ships and tended to be the home of the fiercest partisans of the battleship.

15. Norman Friedman, "The South Carolina Sister: American's First Dreadnought," *Naval History* (February 2010), 16–23.

16. Kuehn, *Agents of Innovation, chap.* 3, passim; Butler, "General Board of the Navy," 703.

17. Ibid. For the view that OpNav replaced the General Board as a general staff see Beers, "Development of the Office of the Chief of Naval Operations."

18. The author derives this usage from Williams Reynolds Braisted, *Diplomats in Blue: U.S. Naval Officer in China, 1922–1933* (Gainesville: University of Florida Press, 2009); see also pages ix–x for the editor's comments about the Open Door policy.

19. Senate Document no. 77, "Address of the President of the United States at the Opening of the Conference on the Limitation of Armament at Washington, November 21, 1921" (Washington, D.C.: Government Printing Office, 1921), 6–7. Indirect evidence existed prior to the war's end in point four of Woodrow Wilson's famous "Fourteen Points" speech to Congress, available at www.firstworldwar.com/source/fourteenpoints.htm (accessed 3/17/2011).

20. Cited in Herbert P. Le Pore, *The Politics and Failure of Naval Disarmament, 1919–1939: The Phantom Peace* (Lewiston, N.Y.: Edward Mellen, 2003), 75.

21. For a full discussion of the General Board's executive role in the execution of the Washington Naval Treaty see the author's *Agents of Innovation*, 33–39.

22. Herbert Hoover Presidential Library [hereafter HHPL], General Board memorandum dated 14 December 1929, 2. Hoover had asked the board to give a short history of itself, via the assistant secretary of the Navy, and the secretary, Cdr. Robert L. Ghormley, drafted a short history on its behalf.

23. National Archives and Records Administration [hereafter NARA] Record Group [hereafter RG] 80, GB 449, 27 January 1931 CNO memorandum, "Naval Air Operating Policy." Pratt uses the term "authoritative" in referring to the promulgated policy, which had been written by the General Board. The U.S. Army uses the word "authoritative" to refer to the role that military doctrine plays in conducting operations. See U.S. Army Dept., *Operations,* FM 3-0 (Washington, D.C.: U.S. Government Printing Office, 2001), 1–14.

24. General Board [hereafter GB] 449 War Department, 21 October 1919; GB 420-2 Secretary of the Navy, 7 September 1928; Curtis D. Wilbur, "To Authorize Major Alterations to Certain Vessels" (HR 8353), 27 March 1924; GB 438 Secretary of the Navy, 18 January 1927; Correspondence of the CNO, 11 July 1936; GB 420-2, CNO 9 September 1941. These are all representative examples of correspondence that refer to the authoritative nature of the General Board's advice.

25. HHPL, Ghormley memorandum, 14 December 1929, 2 [emphasis mine].

26. See also NARA RG 80, Proceedings and Hearings of the General Board [hereafter PHGB], "Developments in Naval Aviation," 3 April 1919, for a somewhat confrontational hearing before the board by Gen. "Billy" Mitchell.

27. For how this process worked see Albert A. Nofi, *To Train the Fleet for War: The U.S. Navy Fleet Problems* (Newport, R.I.: Naval War College Press, 2010), chap. 3, passim, and 55. Nofi also discusses how General Board members served occasionally as umpires during the annual fleet problems.

28. HHPL, Ghormley memo, 4.

29. The General Board produced minutes (which the archives term "proceedings") for every single meeting, but these were usually no more than one page and did not include transcripts of discussions. For example, the minutes for 3 March 1922 listed the membership in attendance, recording the reading and approval of the minutes of the previous meeting, and simply stated that "the Committee discussed Naval Policy" and gave the names of the transcribers for the hearing held on that topic.

30. PHGB, roll 1, Index of General Board Serials and archivist comments. Information for serial 1427 comes from roll 7, Proceedings, including the

index of serials on pages i–v. Between the Geneva (1927) and London (1930) naval conferences Admiral Hilary Jones served as the primary U.S. naval delegate to all arms limitation meetings of the Preparatory Commission in Geneva, often traveling to London as well for talks with the Royal Navy.

31. The five major naval powers referred to are the United States, Great Britain, Japan, France, and Italy. See Kuehn, "U.S. Navy General Board and Naval Arms Limitation," 1129–36.

32. Ibid., 1129–47. See also *Washington Conference, 1921–22,* ed. Goldstein and Maurer. For the details of the treaty see Kuehn, *Agents of Innovation,* app. 1.

33. NARA, RG 80, PHGB, roll 7, pp. 81, 209. Chase had just come from a major fleet command and later testified before Congress against the London Treaty after taking over command of the fleet from Admiral Pratt (who became Chief of Naval Operations). Chase became chairman of the General Board in 1932.

34. See Kuehn, *Agents of Innovation,* especially chapters 5–7, for examples of the ubiquity of presence at hearings by these two officers.

35. See Trimble, "Admiral Hilary P. Jones and the 1927 Geneva Naval Conference," and Braisted, "On the General Board of the Navy, Admiral Hilary P. Jones, and Naval Arms Limitation, 1921–1931," both passim for more on Jones at Geneva.

36. See Buckley, "Icarus Factor," and Emily Goldman, *Sunken Treaties: Naval Arms Control Between the Wars* (University Park: Pennsylvania State University Press, 1994), 31. For Japanese cruiser construction programs see Dave Evans and Mark Peattie, *Kaigun* (Annapolis, Md.: Naval Institute Press, 1997), chap. 7, passim, especially 224.

37. W. V. Pratt, "Some Considerations Affecting Naval Polity," U.S. Naval Institute *Proceedings* (November 1922), 1845–62. See also Wheeler, *Admiral William Veazie Pratt,* 185–86. Pratt also wrote articles supporting the treaty in *The North American Review* (1922) and *Current History* (1923).

38. NARA RG 80 GB 420-2 ser. no. 1338, 11 December 1926.

39. NARA RG 80 GB 420-2 ser. no. 1345, 5 April 1927. Admiral Jones signed this serial.

40. See Kuehn, *Agents of Innovation,* app. 2 (1922 Naval Policy, Naval Building Policy section).

41. NARA RG 80 GB 420-2, ser. 1345. Reference (e) was serial 1315 of the previous year.

42. NARA RG 80 GB 420-2, ser. 1345. See also Norman Friedman, *U.S. Aircraft Carriers: An Illustrated Design History* (Annapolis, Md.: Naval Institute Press, 1983), 67–71.

43. NARA RG 80 GB 420-2, HR 8687, 26 May 1924, attached to serial 1271.

44. See Kuehn, "U.S. Navy General Board and Naval Arms Limitation" 1154–56, for a discussion of the cancellation of approved naval construction by President Hoover after the London Conference.

45. NARA RG 80 GB 438-1, 23 January 1926. Letter from the General Board to Rear Admiral Pratt, president of the Naval War College. The "precept" was the board's recommended guidance on the subject.

46. For the Anglophobe position see Trimble, "Admiral Hilary P. Jones and the 1927 Geneva Naval Conference," 1–3. Trimble in this article wholeheartedly agrees with Stephen Roskill that Jones was "the most difficult character" for the British to deal with. See also Braisted, "On the General Board of the Navy, Admiral Hilary P. Jones and Naval Arms Limitation, 1921–1931" for a more balanced portrayal. Interestingly, Trimble cites the same letter this author cites in the epigraph.

47. NARA RG 80 GB 438-1, 2 March 1926, London Naval Attaché's report, 4, 8.

48. Jeffrey K. Juergens, "The Impact of the General Board of the Navy on Interwar Submarine Design" (unpublished master's thesis, Fort Leavenworth, Kans., U.S. Army Command and General Staff College, 2009), 53–54.

49. NARA RG 80 GB 438-1, 2 March 1926 London Naval Attaché's report, 8. Trimble, "Admiral Hilary P. Jones and the 1927 Geneva Naval Conference," 2; Braisted, "On the General Board of the Navy, Admiral Hilary P. Jones and Naval Arms Limitation, 1921–1931."

50. Trimble, "Admiral Hilary P. Jones and the 1927 Geneva Naval Conference," 2–3.

51. See ibid. For the role of War Plan Orange see Edward S. Miller, *War Plan Orange* (Annapolis, Md.: Naval Institute Press, 1991), and William R. Braisted, "The Evolution of the United States Navy's Strategic Assessments in the Pacific, 1919–31," 110–18, in *Washington Conference, 1921–22,* ed. Goldstein and Maurer.

52. "Frank H. Schofield: Rear Admiral, United States Navy," *Arlington National Cemetery,* www.arlingtoncemetery.net/fhschofield.htm (accessed 3 May 2011).

53. For the British and American attitudes see Braisted, "On the General Board of the Navy, Admiral Hilary P. Jones, and Naval Arms Limitation, 1921–1931," passim.

54. See Kuehn, *Agents of Innovation,* chap. 6, and the discussion regarding aviation tenders for the Asiatic Fleet.

55. See George W. Baer, *One Hundred Years of Sea Power: The U.S. Navy, 1890–1990* (Stanford, Calif.: Stanford University Press, 1994), 109; Thomas Buckley "The Washington Naval Limitation System: 1921–1939," in *Encyclopedia of Arms Control and Disarmament,* vol. 2, ed. Richard Dean Burns (New York:

Charles Scribner's Sons, 1993), 645; and Robert W. Love, Jr., *History of the U.S. Navy*, vol. 1, *1775–1941* (Harrisburg, Pa.: Stackpole Books, 1992), 554–55. All cite a fight without bases as the reason for the Navy's commitment to the ten-thousand-ton cruiser.

56. Trimble, "Admiral Hilary P. Jones and the 1927 Geneva Naval Conference," 2.

57. HR 8686, 26 May 1924 (copy attached to GB 420-2, ser. no. 1271).

58. Braisted, "On the General Board of the Navy, Admiral Hilary P. Jones and Naval Arms Limitation, 1921–1931," passim. See also the discussion in Kuehn, "U.S. Navy General Board and Naval Arms Limitation," 1147–50.

59. Sadao Asada, *From Mahan to Pearl Harbor: The Imperial Japanese Navy and the United States* (Annapolis, Md.: Naval Institute Press, 2006), 112–19.

60. McKercher, "From Enmity to Cooperation," 75. See also Samuel Eliot Morison, *The Two-Ocean War: A Short History of the United States Navy in the Second World War* (Boston: Little, Brown, 1963), 7. The original bill had called for five aircraft carriers and twenty-five new cruisers to be constructed in the next nine years. This bill is also known as the Butler Bill, after its congressional sponsor.

61. NARA RG 80 438-1, papers used for ser. 1371 including 20 February 1928 from Hilary Jones to Secretary of the Navy Curtis Wilbur and 28 February 1928 from Wilbur to Jones. The fact that this letter was in the GB 438-1 series means that the board was cognizant of it, having filed it after using it to write the 1371 serial. PHGB, roll 1, membership by year of the General Board, reveals that Jones retired 14 November 1927 but spent considerable time meeting with the board throughout 1928 and 1929.

62. PHGB, roll 7, see especially volume 20. Members detached included the president of the Naval War College, Rear Admiral Pringle, and Cdr. H. C. Train.

63. NARA RG 80 GB 438-1 ser. no. 1390, 21 September 1928. The General Board rejected this pact "even as a basis for discussion."

64. Braisted, "On the General Board of the Navy, Admiral Hilary P. Jones and Naval Arms Limitation, 1921–1931," passim.

65. NARA RG 80, PHGB, volume 21 of the proceedings (1929); see also Braisted, "On the General Board of the Navy, Admiral Hilary P. Jones and Naval Arms Limitation, 1921–1931."

66. *FRUS*, 1929, 3:1, Stimson to Dawes [emphasis mine].

67. For an equivalent "new attitude" by the British see McKercher, "From Enmity to Cooperation," 65–68, 87–88. McKercher argues for more continuity in the thawing of the relationship, not a sharp departure with the arrival of Ramsay MacDonald.

68. Letter attached to GB 438-1 ser. 1437, 9 July 1929, and GB ser. 1437 approved 13 July 1929.

69. NARA RG 80 GB 438-1 ser. no. 1444-A, 11 September 1929 memorandum. This memorandum was attached to the serial and shows the lengths to which the new president went in order to accommodate both the British and the General Board.

70. Letter attached to GB 438-1 ser. 1449 dated 24 September 1929 via Capt. A. Buchanan from Herbert Hoover to the Navy Department (and subsequently delivered to the General Board).

71. This final formula is referenced in GB 438-1 ser. 1430 of 1 August 1930.

72. *FRUS*, 1929, 3:6–7 [emphasis mine].

73. The Four-Power Pact was an ostensible alliance between Japan, the United States, Great Britain, and France in the Pacific and was meant to replace the old Anglo-Japanese Naval Alliance; see Kuehn, *Agents of Innovation*, 3, 206.

74. *FRUS*, 1929, 3:3, Stimson's Statement on Comment in the Press, 11 October 1929.

75. See Christopher Bell's chapter on British fiscal calculations for the London Conference, as well as his article "Winston Churchill and the Ten Year Rule," *Journal of Military History* 74, no. 4 (October 2010), 1097–128.

76. *FRUS*, 1929, 3:25–31; see also Goldman, *Sunken Treaties*, app. 2, article 16, for the final cruiser tonnages after the Reed-Matsudaira compromise. Robert Craigies was head of the Foreign Office's American section, and he proposed three solutions, one of which was to "transfer American 8" tonnage to 6" tonnage."

77. *FRUS*, 1929, 3:9.

78. *FRUS*, 1929, 3:34, from the joint statement also signed by Hoover [emphasis mine].

79. See the chapter by Sadao Asada for the preconference negotiations after the Hoover-MacDonald October meetings. Today we would call such a meeting a summit.

80. Wheeler, *Admiral William Veazie Pratt*, 297–314. All these admirals publicly supported the treaty after the fact. Hepburn is most famous as head of the famous Hepburn Board that addressed naval preparedness in the late 1930s and was responsible for much-needed base improvements prior to World War II. He chaired the General Board from August 1942 to the end of that war; see NARA PHGB, roll 1, membership of the General Board.

81. Simpson, *Anglo-American Naval Relations*, 138–38, from minutes of the meeting of the British delegation, 9 February 1930.

82. Ibid. See also Braisted, "On the General Board of the Navy, Admiral Hilary P. Jones and Naval Arms Limitation, 1921–1931", 138–39.

83. Jones reviews these positions in a very critical paper on naval policy that he gave to the Navy League and provided to the board in 1933 on the occasion of the arrival of a new president and, he hoped, a new policy for naval limitation and naval construction. GB 438, memorandum of Jones to Navy League, dated May 1933.

84. See the chapter by Sadao Asada for a complete discussion of the intricacies of the Japanese cruiser ratio position.

85. *FRUS*, 1930, 1:171. See the chapter by Sadao Asada in this anthology for more on this discussion.

86. Asada, both in this collection and in *From Mahan to Pearl Harbor*, 178–79. See also James B. Crowley, *Japan's Quest for Autonomy: National Security and Foreign Policy, 1930–1938* (Princeton, N.J.: Princeton University Press, 1966), 66–71, for a retelling of the political crisis that occurred in Japan as a result of the London Naval Treaty.

87. Italy and France were allowed 70,000 tons of new capital-ship construction.

88. Herbert Hoover Presidential Library and Museum, box 34, Cabinet Papers, 22 November 1930 memorandum to the secretary of the Navy. Hoover would go even farther by delaying construction on all ships to generate goodwill for the 1932 Geneva general disarmament conference. He closed many Navy bases and yards and for a time put the fleet on an operating schedule reduced by 33 percent. See also NARA RG 80 Correspondence of the Secretary of the Navy, 7 September 1930, "Reduction in expenditures in forces afloat."

89. NARA RG 80 GB 420-2, 7 September 1928, 1–13. This document was a lengthy memorandum by Admiral Moffett forwarded to the General Board via the CNO recounting the poor state of aircraft carrier construction vis-à-vis the Japanese.

90. PHGB, 27 November 1929, 398.

91. PHGB, 11 March 1925, 98–104. This Op-12C War Plans Division study was attached to testimony given by Capt. M. G. McCook before the General Board.

92. See Kuehn, *Agents of Innovation*, app. 2, *U.S. Naval Policy, 1922*, "Building and Maintenance Policy."

93. BuAer 31 July 1928 to Secretary of the Navy, attached to GB ser. no. 1345. Moffett wrote this extremely important 13-page memorandum on the occasion of the development of the 1929 aircraft building policy.

94. BuAer 31 July 1928. Moffett included CINCUS' annual report for 1927 [A9-1/OF1(4)] ending 30 June 1927 in his memorandum as well as Pratt's endorsement.

95. Cited in BuAer 21 July 1928 [emphasis original].

96. Op-12-CD, 8 October 1928, memorandum from War Plans Division to CNO and BuAer. This correspondence was attached to serial 1376, the building program for 1930.

97. BuAer 21 July 1928, 8.

98. PHGB, 27 November 1929, "Light Cruisers NOS. 37 to 41 Authorized by the Act of 13 February 1929—General Characteristics." Preconference negotiations for London had been under way for some time, and November 1929 was the "eleventh hour." The conference convened barely two months later, on 21 January 1930. See Stephen Roskill, *Naval Policy between the Wars,* vol. 2 (Annapolis, Md.: Naval Institute Press, 1976), 51–57.

99. GB 438-1 ser. no. 1464, 3 January 1930; BuAer 23 November 1929 to secretary of the Navy, forwarded 3 December 1929 to the General Board.

100. Kuehn, *Agents of Innovation,* chap. 6: NARA RG 80 GB 420-2, BuAer 28 May 1930. Moffett emphasizes all these points and recommends construction of all flying-deck cruisers allowable to meet the shortage of aviation in the fleet. From article 3 and article 16, paragraph 5 of the London Naval Treaty; Alan D. Zimm, "The U.S.N.'s Flight Deck Cruiser," *Warship International* no. 3 (1979), 220–21.

101. Zimm, "U.S.N.'s Flight Deck Cruiser," 220; Norman Friedman, Thomas C. Hone, and Mark Mandeles, *American and British Aircraft Carrier Development, 1919–1941* (Annapolis, Md.: Naval Institute Press, 1999), 48–49. Fleet Problem IX was the debut of the *Lexington* and *Saratoga.* It included Pratt and King as commanders of the forces and highlighted the offensive potential of the carriers, but it also highlighted their vulnerability. See also Nofi, *To Train the Fleet,* 109–17.

102. Zimm, "U.S.N.'s Flight Deck Cruiser," 221, excerpt from Moffett's diary.

103. Zimm (at ibid.) discusses Moffett's alleged subterfuge in proposing the flying-deck cruiser at London.

104. See Kuehn, *Agents of Innovation,* 107–23, for the hearings after London associated with the flying-deck design. There was significant dissent on the General Board in opposition to the flying-deck concept, but it did not come from any of the naval delegates to the London Conference, and Admirals Bristol and later Harris Laning (of the Naval War College) strongly favored the final design as having more combat power than a standard 8-inch-gun heavy cruiser.

105. For British carrier and naval aviation development between the wars see Hone, Friedman, and Mandeles, *American and British Aircraft Carrier Development;* see also Geoffrey Till's chapter on the British Fleet Air Arm in *Military Innovation in the Interwar Period,* eds. Williamson Murray and Alan Millett (Cambridge, U.K.: Cambridge University Press, 1996).

106. See Goldman, *Sunken Treaties,* app. 2, 314–15, for these articles. Article 16 allowed 25 percent to be "fitted with a landing on platform or deck for aircraft," and article 18 allowed the conversion of 15,166 tons of heavy cruiser tonnage to light-cruiser tonnage.

107. Roskill, *Naval Policy between the Wars,* 2:81–82; Barry Watts and Williamson Murray, "Military Innovation in Peacetime," *Military Innovation in the Interwar Period,* 394. For a more moderate view see Hone, Friedman, and Mandeles, *American and British Aircraft Carrier Development,* 191; for the most favorable view of the flying-deck cruiser see Zimm, "U.S.N.'s Flight Deck Cruiser," 243–45. Zimm posits that the concept was not given a proper chance to be tested and was canceled "without a trial."

108. See Simpson, *Anglo-American Naval Relations,* 144–45, undated 1930 memorandum by Rear Admiral Moffett. Moffett states any aircraft carrier tonnage less than the Washington limit of 135,000 tons would be a "calamity."

109. PHGB, 4 December 1930, "Military Characteristics of Cruisers with Landing-on Decks." Moffett, in the same memorandum emphasizes the importance of experimenting with all sizes of carriers.

110. At this time, and for some time to come, torpedo aircraft, because of the relatively low power of their engines, were considered too heavy for the necessarily small flight decks being proposed for the flying-deck cruiser—around 325 to 350 feet. See Zimm, "U.S.N.'s Flight Deck Cruiser," 230–36.

111. PHGB, 15 February 1934, "Flying Deck Cruiser." The amount cited by 1934 was $19–20 million. See also Kuehn, *Agents of Innovation,* chap. 6, passim.

112. Zimm, "U.S.N.'s Flight Deck Cruiser," 216. See also Kuehn, *Agents of Innovation,* chap. 6.

113. Peattie and Evans, *Kaigun,* 244. These ships used floatplanes and catapults and played a critical role at Midway in 1942. They were probably a response the U.S. flying-deck program.

114. Buckley, "Washington Naval Limitation System," 646–47. Asada, *From Mahan to Pearl Harbor,* 183–84.

115. Wheeler, *Admiral William Veazie Pratt,* 110–23. Wheeler provides one of the better post-London accounts of the discord within the Navy and the General Board over the London Treaty, but the opposition, while vocal and even principled (including that of Bristol, chairman of the General Board), never had a chance of preventing ratification, given the strong support of the influential and charismatic Pratt.

116. Baer, *One Hundred Years of Sea Power,* 116–17. Roskill, *Naval Policy between the Wars,* 2:65. Wheeler, in his biography of Pratt, says nothing of this snub, although his description of the change of command gives the impression of a very formal and impersonal ceremony.

117. For the Stimson reference see Philip A. Crowl, "Alfred Thayer Mahan: The Naval Historian," in *Makers of Modern Strategy,* ed. Peter Paret (Princeton, N.J.: Princeton University Press, 1985), 444; for the porthole reference see Trimble, "Admiral Hilary P. Jones and the 1927 Geneva Naval Conference," 1. Stimson made his famous comment about the Navy in 1947, not 1930, after serving as secretary of war during World War II.

118. For example see Goldman, *Sunken Treaties.*

119. Franny Colby to President Franklin Roosevelt, 25 March 1934, found in material with GB 438–1 ser. 1640E of 12 March 1934.

120. GB 438-1, letter of July 30, 1934, "Participation in Naval Conversations at London, June 18–July 10, 1934," from the Chairman of the General Board to the Secretary of the Navy.

121. See the Asada chapter in this volume for more discussion of the role and wisdom of Kato Tomosaburo.

CHAPTER 2

Great Britain and the London Naval Conference

Christopher M. Bell

In the aftermath of the First World War, Britain's decision-making elite recognized that the tremendous industrial and financial strength of the United States would enable it to surpass Britain as the world's dominant maritime power if it ever chose to: Britain simply did not possess the resources to prevail in an all-out naval race with such a powerful rival. Lloyd George's coalition government temporarily averted this threat in 1921 by conceding parity to the United States in capital ships at the Washington Naval Conference. This agreement diminished Britain's prestige, but it did not involve the sacrifice of any vital interests.[1] Britain retained sufficient naval power during the 1920s to defend its empire against any naval threat that was likely to emerge, and it maintained a maritime advantage over the United States by virtue of its superiority in auxiliary warships, merchant shipping, naval bases, and fueling stations. Stanley Baldwin's second Conservative government entered the Geneva three-power naval conference in 1927 hoping for little more than new qualitative restrictions on warships to help ease its financial burdens. When the United States demanded parity in all classes of warship, the government let the conference break up without an agreement rather than make concessions that might undermine British security.[2] Anglo-American relations deteriorated alarmingly following the conference, and they hit a low point the following year when news leaked out that Britain and France had reached a poorly conceived compromise agreement on naval limitations. In late 1928, the outgoing U.S. president, Calvin Coolidge, announced his support for a large program of new cruiser construction.

Faced with a crisis in Anglo-American relations and the emergence of an overt challenge to British maritime supremacy, Baldwin's government could not afford to ignore the problem of naval arms control during its final months in power. Two schools of thought emerged within Whitehall as to the best means to avert an expensive and acrimonious naval competition with the United States. The first, represented by the Admiralty and the chancellor of the exchequer, Winston Churchill, held that no urgent action was required. The United States, in their view, did not share Britain's need for a great navy: it was a largely self-contained continental power that did not depend on the sea for either survival or prosperity. Consequently, American enthusiasm for expensive naval programs would subside, as long as Britain did nothing to sustain American ill will. The best course, therefore, was to pursue a moderate building program and avoid further discussion of naval arms control, which would only reopen old wounds and increase tensions.[3] A second school of thought emerged from the Foreign Office. The foreign secretary, Austen Chamberlain, and his advisers were considerably more alarmed about the state of Anglo-American relations and concluded that positive steps had to be taken to improve them.[4] The hard line adopted by the Admiralty and the cabinet in 1927 on the question of cruiser parity seemed to rule out a dramatic breakthrough in this area. The British government therefore decided to investigate the contentious issue of maritime belligerent rights. Britain's blockade of the Central Powers and interference with American trade during the First World War had caused considerable bitterness in the United States, but the British had blocked President Woodrow Wilson's efforts during the Paris Peace Conference to establish "freedom of the seas" for neutral shipping in wartime. The Foreign Office hoped that a settlement of this issue would improve Anglo-American relations, pave the way for a resolution of the contentious cruiser issue, undermine the "big navy" lobby in the United States, and fend off any overt American challenge to Britain's naval supremacy.

Winning support for this course proved to be difficult. At Chamberlain's urging, the cabinet established a subcommittee of the Committee of Imperial Defence (CID) to consider the question of belligerent rights.[5] From the outset of its deliberations in January 1928, opinion was sharply divided.[6] Foreign Office officials were inclined to think that because Britain could not hope to impose any future blockade in the face of American opposition, some concessions to the United States were unavoidable and desirable. The Admiralty and

Sir Maurice Hankey, the influential cabinet secretary, believed that it was a mistake to offer to the United States any concessions that would limit Britain's ability in wartime to apprehend and search neutral ships and condemn contraband cargoes before a nationally constituted prize court. This insistence on "high" belligerent rights stemmed from a conviction that economic pressure exercised through maritime blockade had historically been one of the most powerful weapons in Britain's arsenal; that it had been a decisive factor in securing Germany's defeat in the First World War; and that it would continue to be a valuable offensive weapon in future conflicts, especially against Japan.[7]

The committee's final report, issued in March 1929, concluded that it was in Britain's best interests to maintain belligerent rights as high as possible. However, a majority of members supported the Foreign Office view that these rights should be made the subject of compulsory arbitration when Britain concluded a new arbitration pact with the United States. The committee's first report, issued the previous month, outlined the strong objections of several members, including the First Lord of the Admiralty. In their opinion, this course would inevitably lead to the erosion of Britain's traditional belligerent rights and was unlikely to bring either a significant improvement in Anglo-American relations or a moderation of the American naval program. Any cabinet debate on these questions was bound to be divisive, and with a general election approaching the government preferred to let the matter drift. Foreign Office officials were impatient, however. The difficulty was finding a path forward. The strength of the Admiralty's opposition to the new arbitration treaty or any weakening of belligerent rights meant that these issues were unlikely to be resolved quickly. Moreover, the new U.S. president, Herbert Hoover, seemed to be more interested in naval limitation than in belligerent rights or arbitration. Consequently, Robert Craigie, the head of the American section at the Foreign Office, proposed in late March 1929 that a fresh attempt should be made to address the problem of naval arms control.[8]

Chamberlain obtained the consent of the cabinet on 11 April to send Craigie to the disarmament conference in Geneva in order to sound out American opinion on naval limitations and prepare the groundwork for an agreement by impressing on "the Americans that we were anxious to work with them and that we meant business."[9] This proposal immediately ran up against opposition from the Admiralty, which warned the Foreign Office against raising American expectations, as it could see "no possible basis of an agreement at the present moment."[10] With the United States seemingly unwilling to put forward proposals of its own, there appeared to be little hope of progress in the short term.[11]

The Foreign Office was caught, according to Robert Lindsay, the permanent undersecretary, "between the Devil of America, who sits back and says 'you may make further proposals if you like' (the very worst sort of diplomacy) and the Deep Sea of the Admiralty, who say 'lets sink rather than say a word.'"[12]

The situation was transformed on 22 April 1929 when the American delegate to the Preparatory Commission in Geneva, Hugh Gibson, announced that his government was prepared to develop a formula that made allowances for age, displacement, and armament of warships in calculating relative strength in any class of vessel.[13] Such a formula, Gibson informed the British delegates privately, was designed to facilitate a naval agreement with Britain by making a settlement of the cruiser issue possible.[14] The Coolidge (i.e., Geneva) Conference had broken down in 1927 because the Royal Navy and its supporters in cabinet had been unwilling to make concessions on Britain's cruiser requirements.[15] The Admiralty insisted that seventy of these vessels were the minimum necessary to safeguard Britain's far-flung interests in wartime; that the smaller cruisers the British favored should not be limited by treaty; but that the larger Washington Treaty cruisers preferred by the United States should be regulated. While willing in principle to concede parity in this class to the United States, the British insisted that it must be at a level that suited their own requirements, not the Americans'. Gibson's proposed formula—soon referred to as the "yardstick"—promised to break the deadlock by allowing the United States to equate its relatively small fleet of predominantly large, 8-inch-gun cruisers with the much larger fleet of smaller 6-inch-gun cruisers that the British wanted. This would enable both sides to emerge from an agreement with the cruiser force it needed, while allowing them to claim that overall parity existed, even though there would be a difference in numbers of ships and overall tonnage.

Foreign Office officials were enthusiastic about these new overtures from President Hoover. "If we play our cards properly," Craigie commented, "there is now a chance of placing Anglo-American relations on a better footing than they have been at any time in the past—a chance, in fact, of initiating that wholehearted cooperation with the United States which would have such a beneficent effect not only on the position of the British Empire but on world affairs generally."[16] The Conservative government immediately welcomed the American initiative but did not wish to begin detailed discussions until after the British general election at the end of May.[17] Chamberlain nevertheless asked the First Lord of the Admiralty, Sir William Bridgeman, to have the Admiralty begin calculating a suitable yardstick so that no time would be lost "when we come back."[18] In the event, the election brought Ramsay MacDonald back to power with a Labour minority government. MacDonald, a harsh critic of the Baldwin government's foreign policy and a passionate proponent of disarmament, shared the Foreign Office's enthusiasm about the prospects of resolving naval issues and improving Anglo-American relations.[19] He assumed the premiership in early June 1929 and—while he chose not to act as his own foreign secretary, as he had during his previous administration—he made clear his intention to retain personal control over the settlement of Anglo-American differences.

The Foreign Office briefed the new prime minister on the history of deliberations over naval limitations, belligerent rights, and the arbitration treaty soon after he took office.[20] MacDonald's first meeting with the new U.S. ambassador, Charles Dawes, on 16 July left both men optimistic that the political will existed to reach an accommodation on naval matters. Dawes readily agreed to leave the question of belligerent rights and arbitration "in abeyance" in order to concentrate on the reduction of naval armaments, and, most importantly from the British perspective, he reaffirmed his government's commitment to the application of a yardstick to resolve the cruiser issue.[21] Subsequent conversations with the Americans reinforced MacDonald's confidence that there were no serious obstacles to a settlement of naval issues. Both sides agreed that negotiations should remain in the hands of political leaders rather than technical experts, that the Washington Treaty ratios in battleships and aircraft carriers should not be disturbed, and that parity could be established in both destroyers and submarines on the basis of tonnage alone.[22] On the cruiser question, the British trusted to the American yardstick to overcome any difficulties.

Gibson had claimed at Geneva that a formula had already been worked out by the Americans and was resting "in the President's safe at Washington." Details were not forthcoming, however. Gibson informed Craigie on 26 June that the formula had been sent back to "the Navy Department for certain repairs and modifications," and the British were unable to obtain specifics.[23] Nevertheless, discussions with both Gibson and Dawes had been so cordial that there did not appear to be any reason in London to worry. The Admiralty initially assumed that Britain might not expect to effect *any* reductions in cruisers, as the yardstick would be designed to establish parity on the basis of vessels already built, building, and authorized by both sides.[24] The Foreign Office was more cautious but still tended to think that Britain and the United States would determine their cruiser requirements based on a calculation of their own needs and then devise a formula that would produce the desired result.[25] This view was encouraged by Gibson during discussions with Craigie when he suggested that the two countries might simply set their respective minimum requirements and that the resulting figures "could be taken as constituting parity between the two countries and that the 'yardstick' could be made to fit in with the result thus achieved."[26]

MacDonald was eager to secure an invitation to visit the United States, which depended on first removing the obstacles to a naval agreement. He pressed on the Americans the "wisdom of striking whilst the iron is hot and the public are expectant." All that was needed to "make our agreement complete," he wrote to Dawes on 17 July, were the details of the yardstick.[27] The American reply, handed to the prime minister on 22 July, was a bitter disappointment. Dawes warned that the United States wanted large reductions in cruisers and proposed to decrease its projected strength by as many as twenty-two vessels. The current gap between British and U.S. cruiser strength—estimated at 102,800 tons—was too great to be "bridged by any yardstick," and the gap was only likely to increase if the United States cut its authorized construction program.[28] This was MacDonald's first intimation that the Americans expected a commitment from Britain to substantial reductions in its cruiser force before they would proceed with preparations for a conference.

Neither the prime minister nor the Foreign Office wished to see negotiations break down over the same issue that had wrecked the Geneva Conference two years earlier. Craigie had no doubt that the Admiralty's demand for seventy cruisers would have to be abandoned before progress could be made. He had noted several weeks earlier that the Royal Navy only had fifty-three cruisers afloat at the time, making it "thoroughly bad tactics" to enter into negotiations looking for an initial figure of seventy. In his opinion, sixty would be a more reasonable figure to start with.[29] The Admiralty independently reached the same conclusion. On 3 July, MacDonald invited the First Lord of the Admiralty, A. V. Alexander, to outline possible concessions on the cruiser issue.[30] Two days later, the First Sea Lord, Admiral Sir Charles Madden, stated that he was prepared to drop to sixty cruisers—fifteen large and forty-five small. This figure, he remarked, would result in rough equality in fighting strength and, with the application of the yardstick, approximate parity in tonnage. He doubted this would be acceptable to the United States, however, and insisted that Britain could not go any lower unless substantial reductions were also obtained from Japan, Italy, and France.[31]

MacDonald warned the First Lord that he hoped to reduce Britain's cruiser requirements from sixty to fifty and asked him to begin sounding out Admiralty opinion on this possibility.[32] In the meantime, he proposed the higher figure to the Americans on 29 July, suggesting that parity could be achieved on this basis if the United States accepted eighteen large cruisers and ten small ones. Anticipating the American reaction, he reassured Dawes the following day that he would work to obtain lower figures once the other major naval powers were brought into an agreement.[33] He wrote to the ambassador again on 1 August to justify Britain's need for large numbers of cruisers, emphasizing the country's extensive global commitments and the need to take other powers besides the United States into its calculations. If Britain had only the United States to consider, "my task would be easy," he explained, "because you and I could just agree not to continue to build against each other and off would go the cruisers on both sides." He regretted that "your device of a 'yardstick' . . . has disappeared from recent dispatches. I still trust to it," he concluded, "and wish we had it so that we could work on 'effective' and not absolute tonnage."[34]

The American response was received with dismay. Henry Stimson, the U.S. secretary of state, charged that Britain's position on small cruisers had not altered since the Geneva Conference. He reaffirmed that the current gap in cruiser strength was too wide to be bridged by a yardstick and warned that the United States would not accept any agreement that would require new construction to achieve parity.[35] This communication was regarded as a virtual renunciation of the yardstick concept and a return to the U.S. position of 1927. Craigie complained that its tone was "as disappointing as its substance" and recommended that no new proposals be put forward until the Americans have "a more satisfactory communication to make."[36] MacDonald too was unhappy with the American position. "The U.S. is really not behaving well," he complained in his diary:

> They want parity & wish to set the standard of building to suit themselves. The[y] assume us to be a possible enemy & quarrel with me when I assume other powers to [be] mine. It is a rather egotistically one sided arrangement with the U.S. the boss all the time. Hoover has big difficulties only too plainly & wants me by forgetting my own responsibilities to save his virtue & his face. Parity joined with reductions with the U.S. settling both to its own requirements presents a hard proposition.[37]

MacDonald feared that the disappearance of the yardstick would make agreement impossible, but he remained determined to find a solution.[38] In the absence of some new American initiative, there seemed to be no option but to scale back British cruiser requirements.

Naval leaders by now realized that a reduction to fifty cruisers was unavoidable and set out to strike the best deal they could. The Admiralty was concerned about the composition of its cruiser force after 1936, the date when a naval treaty would expire. If new ships were not built during the first half of the 1930s, Britain would be left with an alarming number of older cruisers. If a steady program of new construction took place, Britain would only maintain its current strength as older vessels were scrapped, but the fighting strength of the cruiser fleet would be significantly enhanced by the addition of more modern and efficient ships. New construction was therefore more important to the Admiralty at this time than a nominal commitment to a strength of sixty or seventy cruisers that would not be achieved for the foreseeable future. As Capt. Roger Bellairs, the navy's Director of Plans, explained to Lord Beatty, "the figure 50 now represents the only figure practicable under a reasonable building programme of 3 cruisers a year."[39] The Labour Party's return to power in 1929 had put the question of future construction in doubt. The Conservatives had cut three cruisers from the 1927 and 1928 construction programs, and MacDonald's government suspended work on two more authorized cruisers from the 1928 program in July 1929.[40] Naval leaders feared that Labour would also cancel the 1929 program, authorized by the Conservatives before leaving office, when it came up for reconsideration later in the year. The Admiralty therefore expressed its willingness to reduce its requirements to fifty in return for a steady annual program of new cruisers for the duration of the treaty.[41]

Craigie calculated that if the Americans were willing to accept ten small and twenty large cruisers, the reduced British figure would narrow the gap between U.S. and British tonnage to 90,000. He was concerned, however, that such a large British reduction would encourage the Americans to think that additional pressure would bring even greater concessions.[42] MacDonald nevertheless outlined this new offer to Dawes on 8 August. He began by emphasizing again that the United States was not considered a possible enemy: Britain's minimum cruiser requirements stemmed from the threat posed by other powers and the very large areas that the Royal Navy had to cover in peacetime. "The cruiser category for me is therefore only partly a fighting category," he remarked, "and is to a considerable extent a police category." He then offered to scrap more ships each year than previously planned but to implement a new construction scheme that would leave Britain with no more than fifty cruisers in 1936. To make this prospect more attractive, the prime minister held out the possibility that Britain might develop a smaller type of cruiser for police purposes. "I hope I have made it clear that I shall go to the utmost possible length to meet Mr. Hoover," he concluded. "But there are things I cannot do. I cannot take the necessary police off the seas, and I cannot make an agreement with America alone which leaves me at the mercy of Powers with which I have no agreement or a very imperfect one. I believe that our somewhat different requirements can be met, but give and take and a yardstick are required."[43]

The American response, though encouraging, dealt another blow to British hopes for the development of a favorable yardstick. Because the American public thought primarily in terms of displacement, the U.S. government stated, it could accept a yardstick only as a means to cover a relatively small gap in overall tonnage. Nevertheless, Washington was prepared to continue discussions on the understanding that the British cruiser tonnage in 1936 would not exceed 330,000. This meant that the replacement ships MacDonald proposed would have to be of a new type of "police cruiser," with an individual displacement of about four thousand tons. The United States, in turn, would continue to plan for a fleet with twenty-three large cruisers, totaling 300,500 tons. The remaining gap in tonnage was sufficiently narrow that the Americans would be willing to cover it with a yardstick.[44]

These proposals received a mixed response in London. The Foreign Office was disappointed by the virtual disappearance of the yardstick, a development that Lindsay, the permanent under secretary, attributed to campaigning by "the big navy party and by the wealthy armament firms." He hoped, however, that some further reductions by the United States and the acceptance of a new class of cruiser by Britain might provide the basis for an agreement.[45] The Admiralty was less optimistic. Officials there concluded that negotiations were now being dominated on the American side by the Navy's uniformed leadership and lamented that Gibson's Geneva proposals had "completely disappeared." They dismissed the idea of building small "police cruisers" and insisted that the United States could not be allowed such a large superiority in heavy cruisers.[46] MacDonald was probably encouraged by a report from Esmé Howard, the British ambassador in Washington, that Stimson and Hoover would accept an agreement with Britain even if it did not result in a reduction of American cruiser tonnage.[47] But he was clearly disappointed by the direction negotiations had taken. "I am more depressed than I have been since we began our conversations," he wrote to Dawes on 22 August.

> You will remember that we started on the yardstick which was the proposal which brought back hope after Geneva. You were to give me the formula and we both agreed that it should be examined by subordinate experts. That has all gone. In your speech at the Pilgrims, you said so truly that the statesmen

should handle this matter and that as there was the desire for an agreement, and as a naval conflict between the countries was unthinkable, the technicians should not thwart the statesmen. That has gone, and we are back into exactly the same atmosphere and facing exactly the same presentation of the problem as we were at Geneva. We are now drifting away from the only road which offers a solution of a problem which does not consist of reality at all, but of words and appearances.[48]

In a more formal message the following day, MacDonald expressed his disappointment with the proposed yardstick and held out little hope of further British concessions. The figures he had presented in his previous message "go right to the bone," he insisted, "and must be taken as the minimum to which the Government at present can commit itself." He also took a firm stance on the U.S. proposal to build twenty-three large cruisers as against Britain's fifteen. Like the Americans, he pointed to the effects of public opinion. If his government accepted an inferiority of eight large cruisers and labeled it "parity," the British public, he claimed, "would turn and rend us. An agreed parity must commend itself to our people as well as to those of the United States."[49] The reply from Dawes on 29 August demonstrated that the gap between the two sides had in fact narrowed appreciably. The Americans expressed willingness to go to a conference if British cruiser tonnage was kept to 330,000 tons, although they pressed for details of the proposed replacement program, which MacDonald had yet to supply. They also attempted to bolster the United States' claim to twenty-three large cruisers by disputing Britain's classification of its four *Hawkins*-class cruisers, armed with 7.5-inch guns, as light cruisers.[50]

The British remained firm on the question of large cruisers. To simplify the situation, MacDonald proposed to scrap the anomalous *Hawkins* class prematurely. He also explained to Dawes the difficulties created by Japan. If the United States possessed twenty-three 8-inch-gun cruisers, the Japanese, applying the 5:5:3 ratio, would be entitled to sixteen, one more than Britain. However, if the United States reduced its number to eighteen, Japan would be restricted to thirteen, which Britain was willing to accept. The most serious problem for MacDonald, however, was the Admiralty's flat rejection of the four-thousand-ton cruiser. MacDonald informed the Americans on 30 August that the fourteen replacement cruisers would each displace 6,500 tons, thereby increasing Britain's overall tonnage in this class to 339,000.[51] The response from Washington was discouraging. Stimson maintained that MacDonald's new proposals involved "revolutionary changes" and would have to be examined carefully by the Navy Department before a response could be made. The difficulties, he concluded, "seem to us greater today than they have been for a long time past."[52]

While the Americans considered their response, MacDonald and the Foreign Office attempted to ensure that a setback in naval negotiations would not upset the tentative plans that had developed for a prime-ministerial visit to the United States in October. In the event, there was no need to worry. MacDonald was informed on 12 September that American naval leaders had agreed to the British replacement program, although it continued to hold out for twenty-one heavy cruisers and now proposed a total displacement of 315,000 tons in this class for the U.S. Navy.[53] In a separate telegram, President Hoover expressed his confidence that the remaining differences between the two countries would be settled and extended a formal invitation for MacDonald to visit the United States.[54] With a tentative deal now in place, MacDonald moved to reassure the Conservatives that no vital interests were being sacrificed. Thomas Jones wrote to Baldwin on behalf of the prime minister on 14 September reassuring him that the "Admiralty are behind the P.M. without reserve, and that if there is any opposition, the Admiralty support will be publicly announced." Jones also appealed to Baldwin to use his influence to restrain Winston Churchill. MacDonald was concerned, he wrote, "that at the last moment the agreement with Hoover may be imperiled, if not wrecked, by some speech by, or interview with, Winston," who was touring the United States at the time.[55]

Preparations now began for a five-power naval conference. Hoover indicated that he did not wish to enter into further negotiations over cruisers with MacDonald during his visit, but he did appeal to the prime minister to reconsider Britain's tonnage requirements and replacement program. The prospects for peace were so great, the president remarked, that he still hoped for an agreement that would reduce rather than increase naval armaments.[56] MacDonald's mind was moving in a similar direction. He was already uneasy about the deal he had made the previous month with the Admiralty, and two days before Hoover's message arrived the prime minister had written to Alexander expressing concern about the British program. "Generally," he wrote, "my suspicion is that the Admiralty is getting from us not only fifty ships, which of course is quite a good reduction, but is increasing the fighting efficiency of the Navy so that, from that point of view, it is more formidable than it would be if we had more ships with a total efficiency for war purposes of a decidedly lower level than our fleet will be in 1936." He therefore invited the First Lord to turn his thoughts to this matter "and see to it that your experts are not controlling

you more than you imagine." He particularly disliked the replacement program of fourteen new 6,500-ton cruisers, and Alexander was told that he "must
insist upon a proportion of these being of the smaller tonnage."[57] MacDonald
later told Craigie that he would ask the Admiralty to make half of the planned
replacement cruisers smaller ships, not exceeding 4,500 tons. The resulting
reduction of overall tonnage by 14,000 would be sufficient, he hoped, to induce
the Americans to drop some of their proposed heavy cruisers.[58]

Craigie was sympathetic to this idea but advised MacDonald to wait until
the Americans offered concessions before raising the idea with them, noting
that "they have been too prone in recent weeks to take anything offered from
our side and to do nothing in return."[59] The prime minister apparently agreed.
He informed Alexander around this time that he would adhere to the agreed
replacement program during his visit to the United States but warned that
he had not discussed the figures with the chancellor of the exchequer, Philip
Snowden, and was doubtful that the new cruisers would survive the scrutiny
of the cabinet's Fighting Services Committee.[60] But MacDonald had no desire
to force a showdown with the Admiralty, which continued to reject American
claims to twenty-one heavy cruisers, and he continued his efforts to modify
the American position on heavy cruisers. In a lengthy letter to Dawes on 23
September, the prime minister restated the British case. "This parity business
is of Satan himself," he commented sympathetically. "I am sure it has struck
the President as it has me as being an attempt to clothe unreality in the garb of
mathematical reality. Opinion in the United States demands it and the Senate
will accept nothing which does not look like it. On my side I am not interested in it at all. I give it to you with both hands heaped and running down."
But Britain, unlike the United States, could not afford to ignore the fleets of the
other major naval powers. "There are shadowy entities behind me," MacDonald
stated. "A spirit photograph would show you unaccompanied, but round me
would be the ghosts of the other nations." Neither one, he concluded, "can get
away from the fact that the standard [of parity] must be fixed by British needs."[61]

The cruiser question came up for discussion during MacDonald's visit to
Washington in October 1929. The prime minister believed that Hoover was
willing to accept eighteen large cruisers for the United States and would use
his personal influence to bring this about but that he hoped in return to obtain
a modification of Britain's replacement program and a reduction in tonnage.
MacDonald's account of his meeting notes that he and the president agreed to
"continue to examine ways and means by which the remaining gap [between
British and American cruiser strength] might be bridged."[62] The American

account of these discussions, however, reveals that MacDonald put forward a tentative plan to reduce Britain's tonnage to 325,280 by forgoing two replacement cruisers and reducing five more to 4,500 tons displacement.[63] Craigie suggested to the Americans that the Admiralty might be willing to accept a larger number of the smaller 6-inch-gun cruisers if other powers—"with the possible exception of the United States"—agreed to limit half their cruiser strengths to vessels of 4,500–5,000 tons.[64]

An examination of other classes of auxiliary warships during the visit did not reveal any serious obstacles to an agreement. MacDonald indicated his willingness to reduce Britain's destroyer tonnage to 150,000, while Hoover agreed to a reduction of submarine tonnage to 50,000. When discussion turned to battleships, MacDonald adhered to the Admiralty's brief. Naval planners assumed that Britain would have to embark on a battleship building program in 1931, when the Washington Treaty expired. This would involve enormous expense, but naval leaders were adamant that there was no alternative but to replace Britain's aging battle fleet, as this formed the cornerstone of British naval power. To bring down the cost of the replacement program, the Admiralty hoped to use the naval conference to obtain large qualitative reductions in battleships. The Plans Division therefore proposed a reduction in displacement for capital ships from 35,000 to 25,000 tons and in gun caliber from 16-inch to 13-inch guns, as well as an increase in the life of ships from twenty to twenty-six years.[65] Hoover indicated that he would prefer to continue the building holiday in battleships for the duration of the treaty, but discussions between Craigie and the State Department suggested that the Americans might be willing to accept the British proposals provided the United States was allowed to build a new battleship of 35,000 tons to offset Britain's existing superiority in this class. MacDonald was optimistic about a compromise and concluded that there would be no serious disagreements with the United States over battleships.[66]

A more difficult subject proved to be maritime belligerent rights. Although this issue had not been the subject of previous discussions, Hoover suggested that good relations between the two countries could "never be fully established until the problems associated with the capture of property at sea in time of war had been squarely faced." The president was enthusiastic about making ships carrying food or medical supplies immune from capture, and he hinted that an agreement along these lines might make further discussion of the belligerent rights issue unnecessary. MacDonald warned that this was a contentious subject and that while he was happy to investigate it further, any formal discussion should wait until after the naval conference. He was willing, however, to issue a joint statement with the president noting that the two statesmen had agreed to "examine this question fully and frankly" and making reference to the president's food-ship proposal.[67] This immediately produced a storm of protest from London, where Hankey mobilized support from the Chiefs of Staff Committee (COS), the Foreign Office, and the chancellor of the exchequer.[68] Telegrams were dispatched to warn the prime minister against making any public statement that, in Snowden's opinion, would signify the government's "tacit acquiescence" in the president's proposal and "load the dice against us at [a] later discussion."[69] The COS similarly rejected any statement that might commit Britain "prematurely to a course of action in a grave matter of Imperial defence," while the Foreign Office reminded the prime minister that any agreement along these lines might conflict with Britain's commitments to the League of Nations.[70] The force of these objections induced MacDonald to persuade Hoover and Stimson to remove any reference to belligerent rights from the final communiqué.[71]

MacDonald's return to London in mid-October signaled the beginning of discussions to settle Britain's policy for the upcoming naval conference. The Treasury, which had been excluded from earlier high-level discussions with the United States, was now determined to reassert some measure of control over naval expenditure. Its first opportunity came when the cabinet sent the navy's new construction program for 1929, which included the first of the replacement cruisers, to the Fighting Services Committee for review.[72] Treasury officials argued that the two cruisers included in the 1929 estimates should not be treated as the final installment of the program laid down by the Conservative government in 1925 but rather as the first installment of an entirely new program, one that had not yet been formally approved by the current government or submitted to Parliament.[73] They accepted that the figures of fifty cruisers and 339,000 tons agreed with the Americans might be incorporated into a treaty but insisted that they should be regarded "as *maxima*, within which we and America may build if we choose, but not necessarily, and that we should aim at reducing our actual strength substantially below those figures in time."

Treasury officials were also concerned that if the Admiralty's views on British requirements in other classes of warship—capital ships in particular—gained general acceptance, as appeared to be happening, naval estimates would inevitably rise. P. J. Grigg, the chancellor's principal private secretary, warned Snowden in mid-December that Hankey believed "it was perfectly clear that we were tied hand, foot and finger to the standards of naval strengths set up by the Admiralty and put forward by the Prime Minister in his conversations with Dawes and Hoover."[74] Grigg believed that MacDonald would prefer not to have this issue raised at all but suggested that it would be necessary to take the Treasury's case to the cabinet if there was to be any chance of breaking "out of the vicious circle into which we appear to have been trapped by the Admirals and the Americans." The chancellor evidently preferred not to confront the prime minister at this stage, and a detailed Treasury memorandum outlining the financial repercussions of the Admiralty's figures was circulated only to the Fighting Services Committee.[75] This document, dated 16 December, warned "that if the parity agreement is interpreted as the Admiralty seems to be interpreting it, and if other Governments follow suit, there is no hope that limitation will lead to reduction." On the contrary, if the navy's proposals for auxiliary warships were accepted, its annual budget would increase by around £2 million. And, if Britain also began to build capital ships and aircraft carriers, estimates would increase by considerably more than that. The Treasury recommended instead a "drastic revision" of the Admiralty proposals. By permanently trimming the size of the fleet and slashing future construction programs, it hoped to achieve a reduction of "at least £10 million a year below the present amount."

These recommendations provoked a strong counterattack from the Admiralty. Madden complained bitterly that the Treasury was proposing to cast aside the previous "four months endeavour" and force a complete reevaluation of British policy only weeks before the opening of the conference. The cuts proposed by the chancellor, he charged, were completely arbitrary; the Treasury "desired reduction for the sake of reduction, quite regardless of the effect on security." Alexander also offered a strong defense of the Admiralty's position, noting the substantial cuts already made to the navy's programs, including the suspension of work on the Singapore naval base. He noted as well the deleterious effects of the Treasury's proposals on the well-being of the naval shipbuilding industry. But the "real issue," he concluded, is "whether this country is now prepared to take a definitely inferior position in the world. . . . I would remind my colleagues that our land and air forces are very much below those of many nations having smaller commitments and that the main arm of defence of the British Commonwealth of Nations is the Navy."[76]

The Fighting Services Committee was reluctant to interfere with the prime minister's preparations for the naval conference and postponed consideration of the Admiralty's long-term building plans. It was willing, however, to take up the less contentious problem of the 1929 construction program, and in late December the decision was made to build only one of the two cruisers that had previously been authorized.[77] This assault on the navy estimates was a tremendous disappointment to the Admiralty, and the Sea Lords asked Alexander to deliver their formal protest to the cabinet.[78] With the cruiser replacement program looking like it might disintegrate, Admiralty officials no longer felt bound to support the reduction of Britain's cruiser requirements to fifty. On 5 January, Alexander circulated a memorandum to the Fighting Services Committee by Admiral of the Fleet Lord Jellicoe, who was in London as one of New Zealand's delegates to the conference, strongly condemning the government's cruiser proposals for the conference.[79] There was virtually no chance of overturning this decision at this late stage, but the Sea Lords probably hoped to gain leverage in their fight against the Treasury by reminding the prime minister that their support for his proposals should not be taken for granted.

The Admiralty also faced growing opposition to its position on battleships. This had not been a contentious issue during the preliminary Anglo-American discussions, and as late as October 1929 MacDonald had seemed content to accept naval advice on this question. The Admiralty's first intimation of difficulty came when the prime minister told the French ambassador in November 1929 that "based upon their size, their guns and their vulnerability, His Majesty's Government were coming more and more to the conclusion that capital ships were not worth the money they cost to construct."[80] Bellairs commented optimistically that MacDonald presumably intended to "refer to 'the present type' of capital ships and did not mean to suggest that we could do without 'some type' of capital ship, possibly smaller and less expensive than the present type."[81] Admiral William Fisher, the deputy chief of the Naval Staff, was less sanguine. The record of the conversation "is quite clear," he remarked, "and if it correctly represents the Prime Minister's views—as we must assume that it does—I think no time should be lost in giving him the Admiralty views."[82] The Admiralty also had to worry about a renewed attack by the Treasury, which was bound to resist the enormous cost entailed in the Admiralty's plans to resume battleship construction.

Having already committed itself to qualitative reductions of capital ships as a means to economize, the Admiralty now accepted the necessity of reducing the size of its proposed building program. "The laying down of more than *one* capital ship in any year is no longer practical politics," Fisher observed in December.[83] Earlier plans had envisaged the rapid rebuilding of Britain's aging battle fleet with the construction of two battleships in both 1931 and 1932, then alternating between one and two battleships in subsequent years. This was now altered to one battleship annually, starting in 1933. Madden presented the Admiralty's proposals to an ad hoc cabinet committee charged with coordinating Britain's preparations for the forthcoming naval conference. He rejected the idea, favored by the United States, of extending the building holiday until 1936, as this would leave Britain with a preponderance of overage ships and lead to the loss of specialized industrial capacity and skilled workers on which the navy depended.[84] These proposals were incorporated into the first draft of the instructions for British delegates to the conference.[85] When they were discussed by the conference committee again on 9 January 1930, the only dissenter was Arthur Henderson, the foreign secretary, who suggested Britain might cease construction of capital ships altogether or propose even more drastic qualitative reductions, perhaps going as low as ten thousand tons displacement.[86] The latter suggestion, inspired by recent articles in *The Times* by Admiral Herbert Richmond, was immediately dismissed by Madden, who maintained that an effective modern battleship with a displacement less than 23,000 tons was not possible.[87] MacDonald then spoke out *against* the idea of a naval holiday, arguing that it would entail the retention of some British battleships until they were "hopelessly obsolete" and lead to a building rush when the treaty expired in 1936. He also defended the Admiralty's proposals for both qualitative and quantitative reductions in the replacement program, which promised to reduce construction costs by £30 million over the course of fifteen years. The committee duly approved the draft proposals and sent them to the cabinet for consideration at its meeting on 16 January, less than a week before the start of the conference.[88]

Treasury officials, who had not yet seen the navy's proposals for capital-ship construction, were alarmed when they received the draft document the following day. G. C. Upcott, the deputy controller of establishments, calculated that even if lower qualitative limits were established, the Admiralty's proposals would drive the navy estimates to £63 million by 1935, a huge increase over the £52 million proposed for 1930.[89] It was now clear that the Treasury case would have to be taken to the cabinet. The chancellor of the exchequer dispatched a strong rebuke on 12 January from The Hague, where he was attending an international conference on reparations. Snowden expressed his dismay that the draft proposals would result in larger navies and a substantial increase in the size of Britain's naval estimates. He was especially upset by the Admiralty's plans to resume battleship construction. Britain, in his view, should at the very least aim to reduce the number of capital ships in commission from twenty to fourteen. However, he personally "would have much preferred to go further and put forward a proposal for the abolition of the capital ship, which is a useless ornament." MacDonald's recent visit to the United States had "aroused great expectations of naval reductions," Snowden concluded, "and when the public realise that our own proposals to the Conference involve millions a year of increase in Naval Estimates, the reaction will be terrific. . . . I do feel that everything—the future of disarmament and our good faith—is at stake in the line we take at this Conference."[90]

The prime minister now began to express doubts of his own about Britain's position on battleships. Meeting with Japanese delegates the following day, he claimed that many younger British naval officers believed that aircraft and submarines would make capital ships obsolete and that it would be futile to spend more money on them.[91] When the cabinet took this matter up on 14 January, MacDonald supported Snowden's view that Britain should make a stronger effort to secure a reduction in armaments and that the battleship offered the best prospects for achieving this goal.[92] The cabinet agreed. "The Battleship," it decided, "is essentially and solely a ship of war, and as political security is strengthened, it must stand to disappear and the composition and operations of fleets be altered accordingly." Britain would therefore go into the conference advocating a postponement of construction in this class. Only if this did not prove possible would it press for qualitative reductions.

Alexander was asked to inform his naval colleagues of these changes in policy and to "indicate that they were based on political grounds, and that the most careful consideration had been given to the views of the Admiralty throughout."[93] MacDonald announced this new policy to journalists the following day.[94] This was another clear setback for the navy. "The Admiralty," according to Hugh Dalton, "were furious, not without reason. Here was a completely new policy, a clear reversal."[95] Naval leaders had no faith in the idea of global disarmament, but they recognized that Britain only stood to lose from unrestricted naval competition between the great powers and thus took a pragmatic view of the arms control process. If an agreement could be secured that enhanced Britain's maritime security, the Admiralty was willing to pursue it. The naval staff had therefore been prepared to cooperate with MacDonald during his negotiations with the United States in order to help secure a favourable deal. The prime minister, in turn, had shown considerable deference to the Admiralty's views in most technical matters. But while MacDonald was eager to maintain the support of naval leaders, he also had to worry about unity within his government. When these goals directly clashed in December and January, the Admiralty found itself seemingly abandoned by the prime minister and virtually isolated in cabinet. The Labour government's preference for a battleship construction holiday and its doubtful commitment to the cruiser replacement program threatened to turn the naval conference into an unwinnable proposition for the Admiralty.

MacDonald and the Foreign Office, in contrast, had every reason to be satisfied in January 1930. They regarded the conference primarily as a means to secure an improvement in Anglo-American relations, and this goal was substantially accomplished before the proceedings formally opened. MacDonald believed Britain must play an important leadership role in the path toward global disarmament and regarded cooperation with the United States as an essential precondition for progress. But even though he was willing to take some risks to advance this cause, he was under no illusion that the process would not be long and difficult. He was therefore less concerned about securing reductions in armaments at this time than he was with achieving an international agreement that would begin to eliminate the political obstacles to peace and disarmament. MacDonald outlined his thoughts to the Americans in September 1929:

> Now what am I trying to do? First and foremost, I am trying to stop the daily swell [in armaments] so that we may fix levels which cannot be exceeded and then create a confidence which will permit those levels to be steadily lowered. I want to substitute the security of peace for that of military preparation. But if in the lowering we act impatiently there will be a break back. That psychological fact fixes my present limits. Stabilisation downwards is the only road by which Europe will move to disarmament.[96]

To further this agenda, MacDonald needed to ensure that the London Conference produced an agreement, although not necessarily one including all five participants. He assumed from the outset that France and Italy might not adhere to a final agreement, but going into the conference he was prepared to accept a treaty by Britain, the United States, and Japan as a success.[97]

To facilitate an agreement, MacDonald attempted to resolve the remaining differences with the United States before the conference opened. The first item on his list was belligerent rights. Hankey had written privately to the prime minister in October to warn him in strong terms that this subject was bound to be contentious, both at home and abroad, and should be avoided if at all possible.[98] Nevertheless, MacDonald raised the issue in the cabinet in early November, shortly after returning from his American visit. The final report of the belligerent rights subcommittee—a report that had taken over a year to produce—was immediately denounced by Lord Parmoor, Lord President of the Council, who complained that the entire document was "based on assumptions which the Labour Party and the Labour Government have publicly rejected, and that its conclusions are such as my colleagues could not well accept, at least until the whole subject has been thoroughly considered afresh."[99] The cabinet agreed to refer the subject to an entirely new subcommittee for reconsideration. MacDonald, having now seen at first hand the strong feelings aroused by the subject, was clearly eager to prevent this issue from interfering with the work of the naval conference. On 19 November he informed Hoover that a new committee had been set up to consider freedom of the seas and the president's food-ships proposals, but he warned that progress was likely to be slow. "If a storm is not to break out to swamp us before we have got the people to apply reason to our work we must put the issues carefully before the country. As I put it at New York our people have a deep sentimental regard for their historical position on the sea and however much conditions of to-day demand a re-examination of the position, the simple fact of re-examination is apt to unsettle and stampede them."[100]

MacDonald was undoubtedly relieved to learn that the president was not determined to press the matter.[101] Once the cabinet accepted the Americans' position on capital ships, the only potential obstacle to a three-power treaty was the final settlement of the cruiser issue.[102] MacDonald and the Foreign Office were unwilling to concede twenty-one heavy cruisers to the United States, and they went into the conference prepared to decrease the displacement of some of Britain's replacement cruisers if necessary to secure a reduction from the Americans. However, it remained unlikely that the Admiralty would support this proposal. At the conference committee meeting of 9 January, Craigie revealed his plan to reduce British cruiser tonnage by accepting a larger number of ships below six thousand tons in exchange for an agreement limiting other powers (still excluding the United States) to the same proportion of the smaller ships. However, he now proposed that the figure be set at 35 rather than 50 percent, as he had suggested to the Americans in October. Madden objected that this might mean building cruisers below four thousand tons in order to retain fifty ships of this class, but Craigie suggested that Britain might get around this problem by securing more tonnage than actually required in destroyers and transferring the excess into cruisers. When the First Sea Lord rejected this suggestion as well, MacDonald proposed to defer further discussion of the issue until he could confer with the U.S. delegation.[103]

Japan's cruiser demands presented another challenge. The Japanese ambassador, Matsudaira Tsuneo, informed MacDonald in September 1929 that if Britain and the United States agreed to different numbers of heavy cruisers,

Japan would demand that its allowance be based on the higher of the two figures.[104] The British were dismayed to learn two months later that Japan, while accepting the perpetuation of the Washington Treaty's 5:5:3 ratio in capital ships, wanted to improve its ratio to 70 percent in other classes of warship. The Admiralty believed that Japan should be held to 60 percent, and MacDonald agreed that this new demand was an "impossible proposition."[105] It not only would give Japan a numerical advantage over Britain in heavy cruisers but also threaten to disturb the progress toward a settlement with the Americans. MacDonald tried to persuade Matsudaira that Japan should be content with its current figure of twelve heavy cruisers and that an American-British-Japanese ratio of 18:15:12 represented a reasonable "equilibrium."[106] When the Japanese delegation arrived in London, MacDonald hinted that if an agreement could not be reached, Britain would revert to its original demand for seventy cruisers and increase its number of heavy cruisers to eighteen.[107] With the United States also opposed to a 70 percent ratio for Japan, MacDonald, hoping to establish a united front, invited Stimson to join him in private conversations on the cruiser question prior to the opening of the conference.[108] The two statesmen agreed on 18 January to resist Japan's demands and concluded that Japan might be induced to modify its position in return for an agreement to reduce battleship strength.[109]

MacDonald's firm opposition to the U.S. demand for twenty-one heavy cruisers after the conference opened was rewarded with an offer from the American delegation in early February to reduce this figure to eighteen.[110] However, the Americans also proposed to add to their program new 6-inch cruisers with individual displacements of up to ten thousand tons, which would increase their overall cruiser tonnage from 300,000 to 327,000. The Admiralty was disappointed with this offer, which would have left the United States with a significant advantage in 8-inch-gun cruisers while diminishing Britain's earlier lead in 6-inch-gun cruisers. Madden pointed out that this proposal would establish a ratio of 1:1.35 for the relative value attached to 8- and 6-inch-gun cruisers. The Admiralty calculated that a more reasonable yardstick was 1:2.36, a figure that would allow 293,000 tons of cruisers for the United States. The Admiralty wished to hold the Americans to 300,000 tons, but the British delegation decided to accept 315,000 tons, which would produce a slightly more favorable ratio of 1:1.72.[111] But when the two sides met on 11 February, Stimson insisted that the Americans "had really reached bedrock." He explained that he had been able to win the support of Admiral Hilary Jones, one of the hard-liners in his delegation, to his proposals only by agreeing to offset the reduction of three heavy cruisers with new 6-inch-gun ships. But he assured the British that there was little likelihood that the United States would actually build ten-thousand-ton cruisers with the smaller gun.[112]

The Admiralty remained wary about establishing a de facto yardstick of 1:1.36.[113] Madden met privately with Admiral William Pratt of the U.S. Navy the following week to determine whether there was any chance of the Americans' following up an earlier proposal for numerical parity with the British on the basis of fifteen 8-inch cruisers and 339,000 tons overall displacement.[114] Craigie also met separately with Stimson to outline British concerns about his latest proposals. He explained that the British public had resented the hard line taken by the Americans over the settlement of war debts and maintained that the United States could afford to be generous on the question of naval parity.[115] Another hard bargain, he warned, would only stimulate anti-American sentiment after an agreement was concluded. Stimson, whom Craigie described as being irritated at times during their conversation, seemed to feel that the British did not fully appreciate the concessions he had already made and offered no reason to expect any significant modifications of the American proposals.[116] A meeting between members of the two delegations on 27 February was more productive. Stimson agreed to drop the U.S. cruiser tonnage from 327,000 to 323,500 tons, and the British dropped their objections to 6-inch-gun cruisers with ten-thousand-ton displacements.[117] When this offer was considered the following day, the Admiralty was ready to reach a settlement. Alexander claimed that the revised American tonnage could not be taken as constituting parity but that it was nevertheless acceptable as a "statement" of the American program. The British delegation agreed to a cruiser settlement with the United States on these terms.[118]

The American decision to accept eighteen heavy cruisers did not produce any corresponding concessions from the Japanese delegation, which continued to demand a 70 percent ratio in cruisers and other auxiliary craft. The British regarded 60 percent as a reasonable ratio and were opposed to Japan having more than twelve heavy cruisers, which would put its strength at 74 percent of Britain's in this type of ship. They were aware, however, that this would be a difficult proposition to sell. Telegrams between the Japanese delegation and authorities in Tokyo, which the British successfully decoded throughout the conference, revealed that the Japanese were determined to obtain a 70 percent ratio.[119] Moreover, it was clear from this source that the Japanese navy was content to see the conference fail rather than make unacceptable concessions. MacDonald allowed the American delegation to take the lead in negotiations with the Japanese, and a compromise proposal emerged from discussions between U.S. senator David Reed and Ambassador Matsudaira in late February.

The United States now proposed to delay the construction of the final three heavy cruisers in its program so that Japan would achieve a 70 percent ratio in heavy cruisers for the duration of the treaty. The two delegates also outlined figures for small cruisers, destroyers, and submarines that would bring Japan close to its goal of 70 percent of U.S. tonnage in auxiliary ships and place it at nearly 68 percent of British tonnage. This represented a major concession, but the British were willing to accept such an arrangement if it would break the deadlock with Japan.[120]

MacDonald urged the Japanese ambassador on 4 March to take the "very fair offer that had been made" and warned that this was the most favorable deal Britain could accept.[121] Decoded Japanese telegrams revealed that Japan's civilian delegates were willing to accept the compromise but that its naval delegates were not. When the Japanese had still not endorsed the deal a week later, MacDonald was forced to contemplate the possibility that Japan could not be brought into the treaty. Stimson reported on 13 March that he and MacDonald had agreed that if necessary they would "prepare a two-power treaty establishing parity with Great Britain and America in auxiliary categories of fleets by which competitive building in them would be ended."[122] Hope was restored later the same day when the leaders of the Japanese delegation announced that they would recommend the compromise proposal to Tokyo. But it was still far from certain that the Japanese government would respond favorably. Intelligence continued to show that Japan's naval leaders were anxious to block the agreement, even at the risk of breaking up the conference.[123]

On 15 March, Henderson warned Sir John Tilley, the British ambassador to Japan, that the naval members of the Japanese delegation were still opposed to the deal and that the Japanese admiralty would probably put up strong resistance as well.[124] There was little the British could do except try to strengthen the resolve of civilian leaders in Tokyo who favored an agreement. Henderson wrote to Tilley again four days later to inform him of the "most determined effort" on the part of Japanese naval authorities to reject the deal. Nothing, he instructed, "should be left undone to prevent such a disaster occurring." To this end, he recommended a meeting with the Japanese prime minister and minister for foreign affairs in order to impress upon them that rejection of the cruiser compromise would likely lead to a two-power treaty between Britain and the United States and would preclude any agreement on battleship reductions. "So far as Japan is concerned," he concluded, "the era of naval competition will recommence."[125] Tilley conveyed these views to the Japanese foreign minister on 21 March, but this did not produce any immediate results. The Japanese government conveyed its acceptance to the British and American delegations in London only on 2 April.[126]

The obstacles to a five-power treaty proved more formidable. MacDonald acknowledged that the size and composition of the French and Italian navies would ultimately affect Britain's own naval requirements, but he showed little interest in this problem prior to the conference. The most serious obstacle to bringing the two European powers into an agreement was the question of relative naval strength. The Washington Treaty had given Italy parity with France in capital ships. Italy was determined to obtain the same ratio in all classes of warships; France was equally determined to resist. The British were also alarmed to learn that the French intended to use the conference to raise broader questions relating to security. René Massigli, chief of the League of Nations Service at the French Ministry of Foreign Affairs, explained to Craigie in December that Paris hoped to conclude a treaty of mutual guarantee and nonaggression among the Mediterranean powers, modeled on the four-power Pacific Treaty of 1922. Craigie immediately tried to dissuade the French diplomat from this course, warning that British public opinion would be averse to such an agreement. He also hinted that French cooperation at the naval conference would eliminate British opposition to France's position on land disarmament at the Preparatory Commission in Geneva, but the French were not so easily deflected from their goal. The ambassador delivered a formal memorandum on 20 December confirming the French government's interest in new security arrangements in the Mediterranean.[127]

The Foreign Office initially hoped that the French might be satisfied with a general treaty for mutual consultation by the signatories of the Kellogg-Briand Pact, which had been rumored in the American press, but enquiries in Washington soon revealed that Stimson would not enter into any discussions that would create obligations in a region of no direct interest to the United States.[128] The British therefore delivered a lengthy memorandum to the French on 10 January outlining their objections to the French proposal. They acknowledged that the machinery for enforcing the various international agreements already in place was imperfect but maintained that existing treaties and the covenant of the League of Nations already provided facilities for joint consultations and should offer sufficient security to justify reductions in naval armaments.[129] Henderson also warned the French foreign minister, Aristide Briand, that Britain had promised Spain that security arrangements in the Mediterranean would not be discussed at the naval conference. Briand reassured the foreign secretary prior to the conference that though this subject would not appear on the agenda, he hoped private conversations between delegations on political questions would help facilitate an agreement.[130]

Before the question of a Mediterranean security arrangements was raised at the conference, the French released the details of their projected naval program.[131] The British were shocked by the extent of the French demands, which included ten 8-inch-gun cruisers and 99,629 tons of submarines.[132] "France becomes the peace problem of Europe," MacDonald complained when he saw the French figures.[133] His irritation increased when discussions between the two delegations made it clear that the French proposals would be reduced only in return for a Mediterranean pact that would enhance French security. "The French mentality is exactly what it was before the war," he recorded in his diary. "It allows no value for political security. It thinks in guns & bayonets." The British delegation tried unsuccessfully to persuade the French that they did not need additional guarantees beyond those already embodied in the League of Nations, the Kellogg-Briand Pact, and the Locarno Agreement.[134] When the French adhered to their demands, Craigie bluntly informed Massigli that "there was a growing feeling amongst all delegations that it was little use offering France fresh guarantees since she simply pocketed them without apparently experiencing any increase in her sense of security."[135] The French were undeterred, however, and passed the British a draft Mediterranean pact on 26 February.[136]

Henderson was sympathetic to French concerns. He had been one of the architects of the unsuccessful 1924 Geneva Protocol, designed to enhance the League of Nations' ability to impose sanctions on an aggressor, and he was willing in 1930 to consider a security agreement that would alleviate French concerns and help obtain naval reductions.[137] MacDonald, however, had never been enthusiastic about formal security guarantees. He was conscious of the moral obligations that Sir Edward Grey had incurred to France prior to the First World War and feared that any concessions to the French would only give them "a free hand in determining European policy with Great Britain as bound follower or pawn subordinate in the game." He was thus determined not to take on any new commitments to France.[138] "That," he wrote, "will mean alliances & war, & I shall prevent it so long as I am in office."[139] MacDonald therefore overruled his foreign secretary and, on 9 March, stated publicly that Britain would "not agree to base any treaty which may result from this Conference on entangling military alliances."[140]

MacDonald's frustration with the French increased further when he began to receive information in mid-March that they were attempting to persuade

Japan not to conclude a three-power agreement. The British delegation continued to resist French pressure for a Mediterranean pact, and by 22 March negotiations were clearly on the verge of breaking down. Stimson attempted to break the deadlock two days later by suggesting that if Britain and other powers could agree to a consultative pact with France, the United States would consider joining at a later date.[141] The British reopened discussions the following day, hoping the French would be satisfied with assurances that Britain would honor its existing commitments under article 16 of the League covenant. The French were concerned that Britain would not consider itself bound to support military sanctions recommended by the League Council, even though sanctions could be passed only with British support. On 27 March Henderson assured Briand that Britain was prepared to affirm its obligations under article 16.[142] Working out a formula that both sides could agree on was more difficult than expected, however. The French wanted Britain to commit itself to action in the event of a violation of the Pact of Paris. The British would not agree, as this seemed to constitute a "considerable extension" of their existing commitments under the League of Nations.[143] The British delegation prepared a more innocuous draft, but even this proved too strong for the cabinet, which insisted on stipulating that any British action in support of the League would have to receive parliamentary support.[144] This was unacceptable to the French, however, who correctly noted that the British declaration merely "affirmed the present position."[145]

British efforts to resolve the deadlock between France and Italy on the question of parity were also unsuccessful. The Italian delegates refused to specify their country's naval requirements, maintaining that they would be willing to accept virtually any figures, "no matter how low," as long as they provided parity with France.[146] The French were unwilling either to concede parity or to abandon their existing naval superiority over Italy. Craigie made several attempts to persuade the Italians to adopt a more flexible position. "Nothing would ever be achieved," he warned one Italian delegate, "by Italy's simply standing on a formula, and making no constructive contribution to the settlement of our difficulties." But to the dismay of the British delegation, that is precisely what the Italians did. On 19 February Craigie suggested that Italy might adopt the Anglo-American approach and develop a yardstick that would allow France a margin of naval superiority while enabling Italy to claim parity had been achieved.[147] A month later he raised a new idea: that Italy declare a naval program for the duration of the treaty that would effectively maintain the status quo relative to France but would not involve relinquishing Italy's ultimate claim to parity. MacDonald urged this course on Dino Grandi, the Italian foreign minister, on 24 March, but it was clear that the Italian delegation had been allowed no room for flexibility.[148]

As negotiations dragged on and the prospects of a five-power treaty receded, MacDonald became increasingly frustrated with the Italian position. Grandi, he complained at the end of March, "is at a standstill and without resources. Under the absolute control of a chief whom he fears, he can do nothing."[149] The rigidity of the Italian delegation prompted Henderson to contact Sir George Graham, the British ambassador in Rome, to determine whether he might be able to persuade Benito Mussolini to allow a more accommodating position, but Graham warned that this approach was unlikely to succeed and might be counterproductive.[150] Shortly afterward, decrypted Italian telegrams revealed that Mussolini had instructed Grandi to "refrain from any further conciliatory proposals of any kind."[151] MacDonald persevered nonetheless, but further discussions with Grandi during the first week of April only confirmed that the parity problem could not be resolved. The British, French, and Italian delegations, meeting for the last time on 10 April, admitted failure. For MacDonald, the only consolation was a pledge from the European powers to give their blessing to a three-power Anglo-American-Japanese treaty and to continue their negotiations following the conclusion of the conference.[152]

The London Naval Conference was a success for Britain insofar as it improved Anglo-American relations and virtually eliminated naval rivalry as a source of friction with the United States. But the more ambitious goals of Ramsay MacDonald and the Foreign Office were not achieved: the conference failed either to reduce international tensions or stimulate global disarmament. In this respect, the timing of the agreement could not have been much worse. The Great Depression and the emergence of expansionist regimes in Japan and Germany soon demolished the postwar progress toward peace and stability that had inspired MacDonald to take risks with British security. Disarmament was one of the first casualties of the deteriorating global situation. France and Italy never succeeded in resolving their differences over naval limitation, and the League of Nations' long-awaited Disarmament Conference in Geneva broke up without any agreement in 1934. Ironically, one of MacDonald's final duties as prime minister in 1935 was to initiate British rearmament.

The impact of the London Conference on Britain's security is more difficult to judge. Correlli Barnett sees this agreement, together with the Washington Treaty before it, as the major cause of Britain's decline as a great maritime power.[153] Paul Kennedy and Stephen Roskill also consider the treaty to be a failure.[154] This view has been challenged by revisionist scholars, who argue that Britain's unrivaled network of naval bases and massive merchant fleet ensured Britain's position as the world's dominant naval power even after the nation reduced its naval strength and accepted parity with the United States.[155] A more persuasive case has been made by another revisionist, John Ferris, that the London Conference, unlike the Washington Conference, dealt a crippling blow to Britain's maritime power. In his view, the London agreement represents the critical turning point in Britain's naval fortunes.[156] The restrictions imposed on Britain by the Washington Treaty and the reluctance of the governments of the 1920s to build auxiliary warships had already devastated the naval arms industry in Britain before the London Conference opened. The continuation of the capital-ship holiday after 1931 resulted in the further decline of Britain's industrial capacity for warship construction.[157] The treaty also ensured that Britain's naval strength diminished in both absolute and relative terms. The nation's aging capital ships were scrapped rather than replaced during the years 1931–36, and when naval rearmament began in 1937 British shipyards were fully occupied with the replacement of obsolescent ships and could not immediately make up lost ground. Naval construction in Europe by Germany and Italy during the mid-1930s created new threats close to home and eroded Britain's ability to defend its interests in the Far East against Japan. Nevertheless, as Ferris concedes, it is far from certain that Britain's position would have been much better without the treaty, as the nation's financial difficulties during the early 1930s might have been sufficient to preclude large shipbuilding programs.

Charles Madden has been criticized by his naval contemporaries and by historians for not taking a stronger stand against the Labour government over the reduction of Britain's cruiser strength, as Beatty, his predecessor, had with the Conservatives over the negotiations at Geneva in 1927.[158] However, as revisionists have begun to note, this view fails to make allowance for the Admiralty's much weaker position in 1929–30 and does not acknowledge its success in securing a commitment to new cruiser construction.[159] The lion's share of the blame for the negative aspects of the treaty has usually fallen on Ramsay MacDonald and his Labour cabinet colleagues. But charges that these men were overly "eager to give away British power" in order to achieve naive goals and appease the United States have not held up to close scrutiny.[160] Recent studies recognize that MacDonald's idealism was tempered by a pragmatic and cautious approach to matters of security.

Scholars have also been quick to credit MacDonald for the dramatic improvement in Anglo-American relations in 1929–30. Brian McKercher, however, has argued that Britain and the United States were already moving toward a resolution of their differences during the final months of the Conservative government and that MacDonald had to do little more than follow the "blueprint" already laid out by Austen Chamberlain and the Foreign Office in the reports of the belligerent-rights subcommittee.[161] There is some truth in this argument. The Baldwin government genuinely desired to improve Anglo-American relations, responded favorably to conciliatory gestures from the Hoover administration during its final weeks in office, and recognized the opportunities presented by the American proposals for a yardstick. But the belligerent rights committee did not provide a "blueprint" for MacDonald.[162] The committee's prescriptions were built around the assumption that a settlement of the belligerent-rights question or the conclusion of a new arbitration treaty were necessary before progress could be made toward resolving the cruiser controversy. Once the possibility arose of addressing naval limitations first, Chamberlain and the Foreign Office were quick to reverse their priorities. The "blueprint" was thus tacitly abandoned by its authors before MacDonald came to power.

McKercher also underestimates the difficulties that faced any British government in reaching a settlement of the cruiser issue. The shift in the American position signaled by the yardstick proposal proved to be illusory. The United States did not move very far from its position at the Coolidge Conference in 1927, and a Conservative government would have run up against the same obstacles that had led to the breakdown of the previous negotiations. MacDonald's personal role in overcoming these obstacles should not be underestimated. He was willing to go to greater lengths than were other British statesmen of this period, because of the especially high value he placed on close Anglo-American relations, his genuine faith in disarmament, and his willingness to overrule his professional advisers. Moreover, he was better positioned than they to force a naval agreement on the Admiralty, because he had the backing of not only the Foreign Office and the Treasury but also his own political party. Beatty had found powerful supporters in the Conservative cabinet in 1927, but Madden was politically isolated in the months prior to the conference. The Admiralty, realizing how fragile its support was and knowing the extreme views held by many members of the Labour Party, chose to work with the prime minister rather than oppose him. MacDonald, in turn, skillfully avoided an open breach with his naval leaders by siding with them against demands from within the cabinet and the Treasury for even more drastic concessions. The bureaucratic and political deals he struck in Whitehall prior to the conference were as important as his diplomatic negotiations with other powers in shaping the London Naval Treaty and settling Anglo-American differences.

NOTES

1. See John R. Ferris, "The Symbol and Substance of Seapower: Britain, the United States and the One-Power Standard, 1919–1921," *Anglo-American Relations in the 1920s*, ed. B. J. C. McKercher (Edmonton: University of Alberta Press, 1990). See, too, Erik Goldstein and John H. Maurer, eds., *The Washington Conference, 1921–22: Naval Rivalry, East Asian Stability and the Road to Pearl Harbor* (London: Frank Cass, 1994).

2. On British disarmament policy between the wars, see in particular Dick Richardson, *The Evolution of British Disarmament Policy in the 1920s* (New York: St. Martin's, 1989); Carolyn Kitching, *Britain and the Problem of International Disarmament 1919–34* (London: Routledge, 1999), and *Britain and the Geneva Disarmament Conference* (Basingstoke, U.K.: Palgrave, 2003). A multinational perspective on the arms control process is offered in Richard W. Fanning, *Peace and Disarmament: Naval Rivalry and Arms Control 1922–1933* (Lexington: University Press of Kentucky, 1995); Christopher Hall, *Britain, America and Arms Control, 1921–37* (New York: St Martin's, 1987); Raymond G. O'Connor, *Perilous Equilibrium: The United States and the London Naval Conference* (Lawrence: University of Kansas Press, 1962).

3. For example, Churchill cabinet memorandum, 20 July 1927, T 161/295/S34442/2; Churchill cabinet memorandum, 19 November 1928, CP 358(28), CAB 24/199, The National Archives, Kew [hereafter TNA]. Bridgeman to Baldwin, 29 August 1928, in *The Modernisation of Conservative Politics: The Diaries and Letters of William Bridgeman, 1904–1935*, ed. Philip Williamson (London: Historian's Press, 1988), 217–18; B. J. C. McKercher, *The Second Baldwin Government and the United States, 1924–1929* (Cambridge, U.K.: Cambridge University Press, 1984), 183–84.

4. McKercher, *Second Baldwin Government*; McKercher, "Belligerent Rights in 1927–1929: Foreign Policy versus Naval Policy in the Second Baldwin Government," *Historical Journal* 29 (1986), 963–74.

5. Cabinet conclusions 59 (27) 7, 23 November 1927, CAB 23/55, TNA.

6. On the Belligerent Rights subcommittee, see McKercher, *Second Baldwin Government*, and "Belligerent Rights"; Stephen Roskill, *Hankey: Man of Secrets* (London: Collins, 1972), II:451–59.

7. See Christopher M. Bell, *The Royal Navy, Seapower and Strategy between the Wars* (Stanford, Calif.: Stanford University Press, 2000).

8. Craigie minute, 26 March 1929, Foreign Office (FO) 371/13520/A2245/30/45, TNA.

9. Cabinet Conclusions 16 (29) 1, 11 April 1929, CAB 23/60, TNA.

10. Craigie minute, 12 April 1929, FO 371/13520/2740/30/45, TNA.

11. Howard to Chamberlain, 13 April 1929, *Documents on British Foreign Policy 1919–1939*, ed. W. N. Medlicott, Douglas Dakin, and M. E. Lambert (London: Her Majesty's Stationery Office [hereafter HMSO], 1975), series IA [hereafter cited as *DBFP IA*], VI:711; Patteson to Chamberlain, 17 April 1929, *DBFP IA*, VI:713.

12. Lindsay minute, 15 April 1929, FO 371/13520/2740/30/45, TNA.

13. Gibson address before the Preparatory Commission, 22 April 1929, *Papers Relating to the Foreign Relations of the United States 1929* [hereafter cited as *FRUS 1929*] (Washington: U.S. Government Printing Office, 1944), I:92.

14. Cushendon to Chamberlain, 22 April 1929, *DBFP IA*, VI:726–27; also Cushendon to Chamberlain, 23 April 1929, ibid., VI:730–31.

15. On British policy and the Geneva naval conference, see Stephen Roskill, *Naval Policy between the Wars* (London: Collins, 1968), vol. 1, chap. 14; Richardson, *Evolution of British Disarmament Policy*, chap. 9; McKercher, *Second Baldwin Government*, chap. 3; Kitching, *Britain and the Problem of International Disarmament*, pp. 97–109; Tadashi Kuramatsu, "Viscount Cecil, Winston Churchill and the Geneva Naval Conference of 1927: *si vis pacem para pacem* versus *si vis pacem para bellum*," in *Personalities, War and Diplomacy: Essays in International History*, ed. T. G. Otte and Constantine A. Pagedas (London: Frank Cass, 1997); Carolyn Kitching, "Sunk before We Started? Anglo-American Rivalry at the Coolidge Naval Conference, 1927," in *Arms and Disarmament in Diplomacy*, ed. Keith A. Hamilton and Edward Johnson (London: Vallentine Mitchell, 2008), 91–111. Christopher M. Bell, *Churchill and Sea Power* (Oxford University Press, 2012), 112-20.

16. Craigie minute, 30 May 19, *DBFP IA*, VI:758.

17. Chamberlain to Howard, 1 May 1929, *DBFP IA*, VI:746–47.

18. Chamberlain to Bridgeman, 10 May 1929, FO 800/263, TNA.

19. David Marquand, *Ramsay MacDonald* (London: Jonathan Cape, 1977), 466–74.

20. Foreign Office memoranda, "Anglo-American Relations: Memorandum Respecting the Naval Disarmament Question," "Anglo-American Relations: Question of the Conclusion of an Anglo-American Arbitration Treaty," and "Anglo-American Relations: Question of an Agreement with the United States in Regard to Maritime Belligerent Rights," all dated 10 June 1929, Ramsay MacDonald papers, PRO 30/69/267, TNA. See also *Documents on British*

Foreign Policy, ed. E. L. Woodward and Rohan Butler (London: HMSO, 1946), second series [hereafter cited as *DBFP II*], I:3–7.

21. MacDonald memorandum, "Report of conversation between the Prime Minister and General Dawes at Logie House, Forres, Sunday 16th June 1929," 17 June 1929, FO 371/13520, TNA; Henderson to Howard, 24 June 1929, *DBFP II*, I:8–10; Dawes to Stimson, 17 June 1929, *FRUS 1929*, I:117–18.

22. Dawes to MacDonald, 12 July 1929, and MacDonald to Dawes, 17 July 1929, *DBFP II*, I:22–25.

23. Craigie memorandum, 27 June 1929, *DBFP II*, I:14.

24. CP 180 (29): Admiralty memorandum, "Naval Limitation and Armament," 25 June 1929, CAB 24/204, TNA.

25. For example, R. H. Campbell minutes of 27 June and 12 July 1929, FO 371/13521, TNA; Chamberlain to Bridgeman, 10 May 1929, FO 800/263, TNA.

26. Craigie memorandum, 27 June 1929, *DBFP II*, I:15.

27. MacDonald to Dawes, 17 July 1929, *DBFP II*, I:24–25.

28. Dawes to MacDonald, 22 July 1929, *DBFP II*, I:26–27.

29. Craigie minute, 7 July 1929, FO 371/13521/4323/30/45, TNA.

30. Vansittart to Alexander, 3 July 1929, PRO 30/69/267/4, TNA.

31. "Notes by the First Sea Lord," 5 July 1929, PRO 30/69/267, TNA.

32. MacDonald to Alexander, 30 July 1929, FO 371/13522/5059/G, TNA.

33. Memorandum by MacDonald, 29 July 1929; MacDonald to Dawes, 30 July 1929, *DBFP II*, I:33–34.

34. MacDonald to Dawes, 1 August 1929, PRO 30/69/267, TNA.

35. Dawes to MacDonald, 1 August 1929; Stimson to Dawes, 2 August 1929, PRO 30/69/267, TNA.

36. Craigie minute, 3 August 1929, PRO 30/69/267, TNA.

37. MacDonald diary, 6 August 1930, PRO 30/69/1753, TNA.

38. MacDonald minute, 6 August 1929, PRO 30/69/267, TNA.

39. Bellairs to Beatty, 13 December 1929, cited in Phillips Payson O'Brien, *British and American Naval Power* (Westport, Conn.: Praeger, 1998), 209; also Bellair's memorandum of 1 August 1929, *Anglo-American Naval Relations, 1919–1939*, ed. Michael Simpson (Farnham, U.K.: Ashgate for the Naval Records Society, 2010), 112–13. Admiral Sir George Chetwode, the Naval Secretary to the First Lord, later described to Roger Keyes a conversation with Madden in which the latter called the figure of seventy cruisers "a myth, didn't and could never exist." Keyes to Beatty, 1 December 1930, *Keyes Papers* (London: George Allen & Unwin for the Naval Records Society, 1980), II:284.

40. FS [Fighting Services Committee] (29) 7: "First Report Dealing with the Naval Construction Programme," 6 July 1929, CAB 27/407, TNA.

41. Plans division memoranda 0355/29 and 03356/29, 1 August 1929, PRO 30/69/267; cabinet conclusions, 33(29), 13 September 1929, CAB 23/61, TNA. Most historians, following Roskill's inaccurate account of these events, have not recognized that a deal was struck between the Admiralty and MacDonald and have consequently exaggerated the Navy's opposition to this reduction. This problem is corrected in Orest Babij, "The Second Labour Government and British Maritime Security, 1929–1931," *Diplomacy and Statecraft* 6, no. 3 (November 1995), 645–71. See also Keith Neilson, "'Unbroken Thread': Japan, Maritime Power and British Imperial Defence, 1920–32," in *British Naval Strategy East of Suez 1900–2000,* ed. Greg Kennedy (London: Frank Cass, 2005), 79.

42. Craigie minute, 3 August 1929, PRO 30/69/267, TNA; undated Craigie minute, FO 371/13522/5300/G, TNA.

43. MacDonald to Dawes, 8 August 1929, *DBFP II*, I:36–38.

44. Dawes to MacDonald, n.d., *DBFP II*, I:40–45.

45. Lindsay memorandum, 19 August 1929, PRO 30/69/267, TNA.

46. Alexander to MacDonald, 20 and 21 August 1929, PRO 30/69/267, TNA.

47. Howard to Henderson, 21 August 1929, *DBFP II*, I:46–47.

48. MacDonald to Dawes, 22 August 1929, *FRUS 1930*, I:200.

49. MacDonald to Dawes, [23 August 1929], *DBFP II*, I:47–51.

50. Dawes to MacDonald, 29 August 1929, *DBFP II*, I:53–59.

51. MacDonald to Dawes, 2 letters of 30 August 1929, *DBFP II*, I:59–63.

52. Dawes to MacDonald, 4 September 1929, *DBFP II*, I:68–69.

53. Dawes to MacDonald, 12 September 1929, *DBFP II*, I:74–75.

54. Ibid., I:75.

55. Jones to Baldwin, 14 September 1929, in *Whitehall Diary,* ed. Keith Middlemass (London: Oxford University Press, 1969), II:210–11.

56. Hoover to Stimson, 17 September 1929, *DBFP II*, I:87–90.

57. MacDonald to Alexander, 17 September 1929, A. V. Alexander papers, Churchill College Archives Centre, Cambridge, AVAR 5/2/5.

58. Craigie memorandum, 20 September 1929, PRO 30/69/267, TNA.

59. Ibid.

60. MacDonald to Alexander, n.d., AVAR 5/2/4a.

61. MacDonald to Dawes, 23 September 1929, *DBFP II*, I:94–97.

62. CP 312 (29), "Memorandum respecting the Conversations between the Prime Minister and President Hoover at Washington (October 4 to 10, 1929)," CAB 24/207, TNA; a slightly abridged version is printed in *DBFP II*, I:106–22.

63. Henry Stimson "Memorandum of Papers Drawn Up during Prime Minister MacDonald's Visit," 9 October 1929, annex VI, Hoover memorandum, 6 October 1929, *FRUS 1929*, III:25.

64. Craigie memorandum, "Cruiser Problem," 6 October 1929, *FRUS 1929*, III:27–29.

65. Plans Division memorandum, "Proposals for Naval Limitation," 27 September 1929, ADM 116/3372, TNA.

66. CP 312 (29): "Memorandum respecting the Conversations between the Prime Minister and President Hoover at Washington (October 4 to 10, 1929)," CAB 24/207, TNA.

67. Ibid.

68. Roskill, *Hankey*, II:491–94.

69. Snowden to MacDonald, 9 October 1929, CP; *DBFP II*, I:124.

70. Henderson to Howard, two telegrams of 8 October 1929, *DBFP II*, I:119–21; Roskill, *Hankey*, II:493.

71. CP 312 (29): "Memorandum respecting the Conversations between the Prime Minister and President Hoover at Washington (October 4 to 10, 1929), CAB 24/207, TNA.

72. Cabinet conclusions 34 (29) 4, 25 September 1929," CAB 23/61, TNA.

73. FS (29)20: Report by Treasury and Admiralty representatives on the Fighting Services Committee, 13 December 1929, CAB 27/407, TNA.

74. Grigg to Snowden, 13 December 1929, T 172/1693, TNA.

75. FS (29)18: Treasury memorandum, "Financial Aspects of the Naval Conference," 16 December 1929, CAB 27/407, TNA. Acting on Snowden's instructions, Grigg passed a copy of this document to MacDonald on (or slightly before) 13 December. However, he left the chancellor room to retreat by "making it clear" to the prime minister that the memorandum had not yet been seen by Snowden and could not necessarily be taken as representing his views. Grigg to Snowden, 13 December 1929, T 172/1693, TNA.

76. FS (29)19, Alexander memorandum, "Financial Aspects of the Naval Conference," 20 December 1929, and undated Madden memorandum, CAB 27/407, TNA.

77. FS (29) 22, MacDonald memorandum, 31 December 1929, CAB 27/407; CP 2 (30), TNA.

78. Board of Admiralty minute 2676, 9 January 1930, ADM 167/81, TNA; Madden memorandum, "Naval Construction Programme 1929: Report of Fighting

Services Committee," appendix to cabinet conclusions 4(30), 22 January 1930, CAB 23/63, TNA. Roskill depicts Madden's letter as a protest against the decision to accept fifty cruisers, but it was actually a protest against the government's failure to live up to its part of their deal by approving all the new cruisers in the 1929 building program. Roskill also mistakenly claims that Madden objected to the new position adopted on battleships, but the letter is dated 8 January, nearly a week *before* the government's policy was changed. Madden's letter contains no reference to capital ships. Roskill, *Naval Policy between the Wars*, II:53.

79. LNC (29) 3: Jellicoe memorandum, 3 January 1930, CAB 29/117, TNA.

80. Henderson to R. H. Campbell (Paris), 26 November 1929, *DBFP II*, I:149–50.

81. Bellairs minute, 27 November 1929, ADM 116/2689, TNA.

82. Fisher minute, 27 November 1929, ADM 116/2689, TNA.

83. Fisher minute, 12 December 1929, ADM 116/3372, TNA.

84. Madden memorandum, 20 December 1929, CAB 29/117, TNA.

85. "Naval Conference, 1930: Draft Memorandum respecting British Proposals to Be submitted to the Conference," 13 December 1929, CAB 29/117, TNA.

86. LNC (29) 5th Mtg, 9 January 1930, CAB 29/117, TNA.

87. Barry D. Hunt, *Sailor-Scholar: Admiral Sir Herbert Richmond 1871–1946* (Waterloo, Ont.: Wilfrid Laurier University Press, 1982), chap. 10.

88. LNC (29) 5th Mtg, 9 January 1930, CAB 29/117, TNA.

89. GC Upcott, "Naval Conference," 10 January 1930, T 172/1693, TNA.

90. Snowden to MacDonald, 12 January 1930, appendix to cabinet conclusions 1(30), 14 January 1930, CAB 23/63, TNA.

91. Japanese delegation, London to Japanese foreign minister, Tokyo, 14 January 1930, HW 12/127, TNA.

92. MacDonald diary, 15 January 1930, PRO 30/69/1753, TNA.

93. Cabinet conclusions 1 (30), 14 January 1930, CAB 23/63, TNA.

94. *Times*, 16 January 1930, 12.

95. Dalton diary, 15 January, cited in David Carlton, *MacDonald versus Henderson* (London: Macmillan, 1970), 122. See also Kitching, *Britain and the Problem of International Disarmament*, 121.

96. MacDonald to Dawes, 23 September 1929, *DBFP II*, I:95.

97. MacDonald memorandum, 25 June 1929, *DBFP II*, I:10–11.

98. Hankey to MacDonald, 11 October 1929, PREM 1/99, TNA.

99. CP 510 (29): memorandum by Parmoor, "Belligerent Rights," CAB 24/206, TNA; cabinet conclusions, 45 (29) 3, 6 November 1929, CAB 23/62, TNA.

100. MacDonald to Hoover, 19 November 1929, PREM 1/99, TNA.

101. B. J. C. McKercher, *Transition of Power: Britain's Loss of Global Preeminence to the United States, 1930–1945* (New York: Cambridge University Press, 1998), 44.

102. MacDonald conveyed his acceptance of the American position on battleships to Stimson at their pre-conference meeting on 18 January. Stimson to Cotton, 19 January 1930, *Papers Relating to the Foreign Relations of the United States 1930* [hereafter cited as *FRUS 1930*] (Washington: U.S. Government Printing Office, 1945), I:4.

103. LNC (29) 5th Mtg, 9 January 1930, CAB 29/117, TNA.

104. MacDonald memorandum, 2 Sept 1929, *DBFP II*, I:63–64.

105. Plans Division memorandum, "The Japanese Ratio Question," and minutes by Bellairs and Fisher, 14 January 1930, ADM 116/3372, TNA; MacDonald diary, 29 November 1929, PRO 30/69/1753, TNA.

106. Henderson to Sir J. Tilley (Tokyo), 16 and 20 November 1929, *DBFP II*, I:139–40, 143–44.

107. Japanese delegation, London to Japanese Foreign Minister, Tokyo, 10 January 1930, HW 12/127, TNA.

108. Henderson to Howard, 20 December 1929, *DBFP II*, I:171.

109. Stimson to Joseph Cotton, 19 January 1930, *FRUS 1930*, I:2–3; O'Connor, *Perilous Equilibrium*, 62.

110. Stimson to Cotton, 4 February 1930, *FRUS 1930*, I:13–14; LNC 11, statement by Stimson, 6 February 1930, CAB 29/120, TNA; *FRUS 1930*, I:19–20.

111. Notes of a meeting of the British delegation, 9 February 1930, CAB 29/128, TNA.

112. Notes of a meeting with American delegates, 11 February 1930, CAB 29/128, TNA.

113. Notes of a meeting of the British delegation, 12 February 1930, CAB 29/128, TNA.

114. Madden memorandum, 17 February 1930, ADM 116/3624, TNA.

115. On the problem of war debts in Anglo-American relations, see Robert Self, *Britain, America and the War Debt Controversy* (London: Routledge, 2006).

116. Craigie memorandum, 13 February 1930, CAB 29/129, TNA.

117. Stimson to Cotton, 28 February 1930, *FRUS 1930*, I:32.

118. Notes of a meeting of the British delegation, 28 February 1930, CAB 29/128, TNA.

119. The British were reading the diplomatic traffic of all the participants of the London Conference. See John Ferris, "Commentary: Communications

Intelligence and Conference Diplomacy, London, 1930," *Exploring Intelligence Archives,* ed. R. Gerald Hughes, Peter Jackson and Len Scott (London: Routledge, 2008), 45–49, and chapter 5 in this volume.

120. Henderson to Tilley, 15 March 1930, *DBFP II,* I:249–51.

121. Craigie memorandum on MacDonald's meeting with Matsudaira, 4 March 1930, CAB 29/129, TNA.

122. Stimson to Cotton, 12 and 13 March 1930, *FRUS 1930,* I:58, 60.

123. For example, Naval Conference (NC) 240, Admiral Sakonji, London to Japanese admiralty, 17 March 1930 (decoded 21 March 1930); NC 294, Admiral Sakonji, London to Japanese Vice Minister of Marine, 25 March 1930 (decoded 29 March 1930), HW 12/126, TNA.

124. Henderson to Tilley, 15 March 1930, *DBFP II,* I:251.

125. Henderson to Tilley, 19 March 1930, *DBFP II,* I:261.

126. Notes of a meeting of the British and Japanese delegations, 2 April 1930, *DBFP II,* I:282–89.

127. Craigie memorandum, 18 December 1929; French government memorandum, 20 December 1929, *DBFP II,* I:167–70, 173–77.

128. Henderson to Howard, 29 December 1929; Howard to Henderson, 31 December 1929, *DBFP II,* I:183, 186–87.

129. Memorandum communicated to the French ambassador, 10 January 1930, *DBFP II,* I:195–98.

130. Note by Tyrrell, 11 January 1930, *DBFP II,* I:198–99.

131. Meeting with French delegates, 11 February 1930, CAB 29/128, TNA.

132. Madden Memorandum, "Figures Communicated by the French Delegation," February 1930, CAB 29/128, TNA. Madden proposed that more reasonable figures for the French would be six 8-inch-gun cruisers and 40,000 tons of submarines (as against 60,000 tons or less for Britain and the United States).

133. MacDonald diary, 12 February 1930, PRO 30/69/1753, TNA.

134. Notes of a meeting of American, French and British delegations, 13 February 1930, *DBFP II,* I:211–18.

135. Note by Craigie of a conversation with Massigli, 25 February 1930, *DBFP II,* I:236.

136. *DBFP II,* I:237–38.

137. Stimson to Cotton, 10 March 1930, *FRUS 1930,* I:55.

138. On the divergent views of Henderson and MacDonald, see in particular Carlton, *MacDonald versus Henderson.* Also Kitching, *Britain and the Problem of International Disarmament,* 121–22.

139. MacDonald diary, 16 and 18 February 1930, PRO 30/69/1753, TNA; meeting of British delegation, 16 February 1930, CAB 29/128, TNA.

140. *Times*, 10 March 1930, 13.

141. Meeting of American and British delegations, 24 March 1930, *DBFP II*, I:266; Stimson to Cotton, 25 March 1930, *FRUS 1930*, I:80–81.

142. Record of a conversation between Henderson and Briand, 27 March 1930, *DBFP II*, I:276–79.

143. Meeting of British delegation, 30 March 1930, CAB 29/128, TNA.

144. Cabinet conclusions 19 and 20 (30), 7 April 1930, CAB 23/63, TNA.

145. Meeting of French and British delegations, 8 April 1930, *DBFP II*, I:295.

146. Memorandum setting forth the position of the Italian delegation at the London Naval Conference, 19 February 1930, CAB 29/120, TNA.

147. Craigie note of a conversation with Rosso, 19 February 1930, *DBFP II*, I:235–36.

148. Record of an interview between MacDonald and Grandi, 24 March 1930, *DBFP II*, I:274–76.

149. MacDonald diary, 30 March 1930, PRO 30/69/1753, TNA.

150. Henderson to Graham, 15 March 1930, 251–52; Graham to Henderson, 16 and 18 March 1930, *DBFP II*, I:257–58.

151. NC 275, Mussolini to Grandi, 20 and 21 March 1930 (decoded 27 March 1930), HW 12/126, TNA.

152. Meeting of French, British and Italian delegations, 10 April 1930, *DBFP II*, I:309–11.

153. Correlli Barnett, *The Collapse of British Power* (London: Eyre Methuen, 1972), 288–91.

154. Paul Kennedy, *The Rise and Fall of British Naval Mastery*, 3rd ed. (London: Fontana, 1991), 336–38; Roskill, *Naval Policy between the Wars*, II:67.

155. McKercher, *Transition of Power*, 60–62; Gregory C. Kennedy, "The London Naval Conference and Anglo-American Maritime Strength, 1927–1930," *Arms Limitation and Disarmament: Restraints on War, 1899–1939*, ed. B. J. C. McKercher (Westport, Conn.: Praeger, 1992), 149–71; O'Brien, *British and American Naval Power*, 215–18. Orest Babij also considers the London Conference a success both for Britain and the Admiralty, for the latter because it secured a new cruiser program. See Babij, "The Second Labour Government"; and Orest Babij, "The Making of Imperial Defence Policy in Britain, 1926–1934" (PhD dissertation, Oxford University, 2003), 117–19.

156. John R. Ferris, "'It Is Our Business in the Navy to Command the Seas': The Last Decade of British Maritime Supremacy, 1919–1929," in *Far Flung Lines*, ed. Keith Neilson and Greg Kennedy (London: Frank Cass, 1996).

157. Ferris, "Last Decade"; G. A. H. Gordon, *British Seapower and Procurement between the Wars* (Annapolis, Md.: Naval Institute Press, 1988).

158. See for example Keyes to Beatty, 1 December 1930; Beatty to Keyes, 6 December 1930; and Richmond to Keyes, 7 December 1936; Chatfield to Keyes, 3 January 1938; all *Keyes Papers*, II:284–85, 356, 373.

159. Babij, "The Second Labour Government"; and Orest Babij, "The Royal Navy and the Defence of the British Empire, 1928–1934," in *Far Flung Lines*, ed. Neilson and Kennedy, 171–89; Nicholas Tracy, "Admiral Sir Charles E. Madden (1927–1930) and Admiral Sir Frederick L. Field (1930–1933)," in *The First Sea Lords*, ed. Malcolm Murfett (Westport, Conn.: Praeger, 1995), 141–56.

160. Barnett, *Collapse of British Power*, 289.

161. B. J. C. McKercher, "From Enmity to Cooperation: The Second Baldwin Government and the Improvement of Anglo-American Relations, November 1928–June 1929," *Albion* 24, no. 1 (Spring 1992), 84–87. For example, at p. 84: "*All* the Conservatives under Baldwin had to do was to win the election, then resolve the belligerent rights question, as well as the remaining technical differences over the 'yardstick' [emphasis added]. Also see McKercher, *Second Baldwin Government*, 198–99; McKercher, "Belligerent Rights," 974; and B. J. C. McKercher, "The Politics of Naval Arms Limitation in Britain in the 1920s," 35–59, in *Washington Conference, 1921–22*, ed. Goldstein and Maurer. The latter article asserts that a Conservative government could have secured a comparable improvement in Anglo–American relations but without making as many harmful concessions on naval matters. However, a later article suggests that the settlement did not in fact involve the surrender of any British interests. See B. J. C. McKercher, "'A Certain Irritation': The White House, the State Department, and the Desire for a Naval Settlement with Great Britain, 1927–1930," *Diplomatic History* 31, no. 5 (November 2007), 829–63.

162. The blueprint argument is also rejected in Babij, "Making of Imperial Defence Policy," 106.

CHAPTER 3

The London Conference and the Tragedy of the Imperial Japanese Navy

Sadao Asada

T
he London Naval Conference of 1930 was a crucial milestone, marking the midpoint between the Washington Conference of 1921–22 and
the outbreak of the Pacific War in December 1941.[1] The present study
reexamines the naval decision making over the London Treaty in the context
of Japanese-American relations; the major efforts of the Japanese delegation
at London were directed at the United States, its hypothetical enemy across
the Pacific.

Existing works on the London Conference from the Japanese perspective
are based mainly on records and accounts left by the "moderate" leaders of
the Navy Ministry who strove for the treaty.[2] This study capitalizes on hitherto
unused records of the "hawks" in the Japanese delegation and the Navy General
Staff, highlighting the internecine splits within the navy that erupted at the time
of the London Conference and indeed continued to plague the navy well into
the late 1930s.[3]

In the face of very heavy opposition of the Navy General Staff, the moderate leaders of the Navy Ministry succeed in steering the London Treaty safely
to its conclusion. Walter LaFeber calls this "the Foreign Minister and Prime
Minister's greatest diplomatic triumph," but actually it was nothing of the sort.
It turned out to be a Pyrrhic victory.[4] In the tumultuous aftermath of the conference, the enemies of the treaty gained control of the navy and took steps that

would foredoom the next naval conference, scheduled for 1936, thus leading to an incipient naval race that one American historian has called the "race to Pearl Harbor."[5] It is in this sense that a contemporary naval journalist, Ito Masanori, wrote, "The London Conference was the greatest tragedy in the history of the Imperial Japanese Navy," becoming "one of the remote causes of the war with the Anglo-American powers."[6]

Opposition to the Washington Treaty

Outwardly, the Washington Conference of 1921–22 seemed a high-water mark of naval limitation during the interwar period, but within the Japanese navy a sharp clash of views had already emerged, a clash that was to reach a climax at the London Conference.

The key to Japan's success at the Washington Conference had been the magnificent leadership of Admiral Kato Tomosaburo, the head delegate and navy minister. He was a charismatic figure, towering above all others and exercising unquestioned authority in the naval establishment. He was chosen by Prime Minister Hara Kei as head delegate because he was regarded as the only leader capable of controlling and containing unruly naval subordinates, advocates of a "big navy." In the absence of any constitutional provision, Kato may be said to have exercised "civilian control by proxy."[7]

In Washington, Kato Tomosaburo decided to accept the American proposal that assigned to Japan a 60 percent ratio in the capital-ship strength vis-à-vis the United States. He opted for this compromise ratio because he gave the highest priority to improving relations with the United States. Keenly aware of Japan's financial limitations, he subordinated military-strategic needs, however imperative, to broader political considerations. His basic policy was that "avoidance of war with the United States through diplomatic means constitutes the essence of national defense."[8] In the age of total war, he declared, "national defense is not the monopoly of the military."[9]

Kato Tomosaburo, however, was vehemently opposed by his chief naval adviser, Vice Admiral Kato Kanji (no relation). Representing blue-water navalism and Mahanian sea-power doctrine, Kanji (the junior Kato) demanded that a 70 percent ratio was the absolute minimum requirement for Japan's security. Behind the American proposal he saw an ulterior motive to "deprive the Imperial Japanese Navy of its supremacy in the Far East" and replace it with American "hegemony."[10]

On the day Japan accepted the 60 percent ratio, the junior Kato was seen shouting with tears of chagrin in his eyes: "As far as I am concerned, war with America starts now. We'll get our revenge over this!" In the end, however, the junior Kato was squelched and forced into silence by the senior Kato.[11] On 4 December, Kato Kanji wrote in his diary, "A totally unprecedented event. What will Japan's future be?" On the following day, he wrote, "Spent a whole day seething with agonies." On the 6th, Kanji even hinted at hara-kiri, saying he had written a will.[12] It is no exaggeration to say that to Kato Kanji and his colleagues the Washington Treaty was to become a source of something akin to post–traumatic stress disorder (PTSD).

The two opposite stands on naval limitation sketched above were to set the pattern of confrontation at the London Conference of 1930: Kato Kanji versus the heirs of the late Kato Tomosaburo.[13]

As long as Tomosaburo (appointed prime minister in June 1922) remained in command, he powerfully controlled dissident elements. But after his untimely death in August 1923, nobody could restrain Kanji's meteoric rise as vice chief of the Navy General Staff. With the hindsight of history, it is possible to trace the navy's road to Pearl Harbor from the gradual breakdown of Kato Tomosaburo's legacy from the mid-1920s into the 1930s. Kato Kanji set out to reverse Tomosaburo's policy of "avoidance of war with America" and his support for the "Washington system," an interrelated system of treaties providing for naval limitation, the status quo in the Pacific, and the Open Door in China.[14]

In 1923 Kanji played a crucial role in revising the Imperial Defense Policy, a top-level document sanctioned by the highest council of the state. For the first time, the United States was designated the hypothetical enemy number one for both the navy and the army. The policy's fixation with inevitable war projected Mahanian economic determinism: "The United States, following the policy of economic invasion in China, menaces the position of our Empire and threatens to exceed the limits of our endurance. The long standing embroilments, rooted in economic problems and racial prejudice, are extremely difficult to solve. . . . Such being the Asiatic policy of the United States, an armed clash will become inevitable with our Empire sooner or later."[15]

It is an irony of history that obsession with inevitable war with America seized Kato Kanji and his followers just at a time when a measure of stability and equilibrium had come into being and neither navy could wage an offensive war across the Pacific. The new dispensation of the Washington naval system, which had in effect facilitated Japan's command of the western Pacific and supremacy in the Far East, made no difference to Kato Kanji. To the contrary, he saw naval treaties as merely a humanitarian veil to hide America's hegemonic design in East Asia.

As the decade of the 1920s drew toward the end, the Washington Treaty and the reputation of Kato Tomosaburo came under increasing attacks from the fleets. For example, the chief (1929–31) of the Combined Fleet, Yamamoto Eisuke (no relation to Yamamoto Isoroku), later wrote, "As the nation's first line of defense, the fleets were conducting day and night relentless drills to overcome the deficiencies in armaments [brought about by the Washington Treaty]. But the top leaders of the Navy Ministry were all too ready to make political compromises when confronted with budgetary difficulties. These moderate leaders in Tokyo resembled 'civilian desk officers' rather than real 'sailor-warriors.'" Yamamoto traced this "deplorable condition" to the Washington Conference. The root of all evils, he said, was Kato Tomosaburo, who "castrated" the navy by cashiering stalwart officers and replacing them with soft-spoken officers who obediently followed him and were too ready to compromise.[16]

Such strong feelings bespoke a deep division within the navy. One group may be called the "sea warriors," or "old sea dogs," led by Kato Kanji and centering in the Navy General Staff. Having built their careers as line or staff officers, these officers were "big-navy" men, Mahanians all, preoccupied with strategic considerations and vehemently opposed the Washington Treaty. Convinced that the "inferior" proportion of 60 percent had been "imposed" on Japan, they were determined at London to offset the "grave deficiencies" by obtaining, no matter what, a 70 percent ratio in auxiliary ships. The other group, derisively called (by their opponents) "desk officers," were elite leaders of the Navy Ministry who excelled in administrative and political tasks. Navy Vice Minister Yamanashi Katsunoshin and head of the Naval Affairs Bureau Hori Teikichi, who had both ably assisted Kato Tomosaburo at the Washington Conference, were his "disciples" and took a flexible view of naval ratios, fully aware of political, financial, and international factors. These divergent backgrounds of the two groups accentuated their differences at London. The London Conference of 1930, then, was bound to smack of a replay of the confrontation at Washington—this time over the auxiliary ship.

Pacific Strategy and Naval Ratios

In January 1929 Kato Kanji was appointed chief of the Navy General Staff. Upon assuming office, he later recollected, he was "greatly surprised" to realize that in any war with the United States the navy would be virtually helpless to defend Japan's sea lines of communications and that it would have no chance of success.[17] Kato was to be the most belligerent leader of the navy at the time of the London Conference.

After Admiral Takarabe Takeshi became navy minister in July 1929, the Navy General Staff declared it was essential to gain a 70 percent ratio in auxiliary ships.[18] The navy took it for granted that the United States (and Britain) would attempt to extend the Washington ratio of 60 percent to all classes of auxiliary ships. To counter such a move, the navy formulated "three basic principles" that would become instructions to the delegates to the London Conference. They were: (1) an overall 70 percent ratio vis-à-vis the United States in total auxiliary tonnage; (2) the special importance attached to the 70 percent ratio with regard to the ten-thousand-ton, 8-inch-gun cruiser (the heavy cruiser); and (3) the vital importance of a total submarine strength of 78,000 tons. Premiums were attached to the heavy cruiser and the submarine, on which overall auxiliary ships were to be predicated.[19]

As Raymond O'Connor puts it, "the Japanese request for a higher ratio was based on reasons as sound from her point of view as they were unsatisfactory to Britain and America."[20] Underlying the strategic outlooks of the two navies was the "security dilemma." A Japanese navy powerful enough to control the western Pacific and protect Japan's vital sea-lanes would inevitably appear as a menace to the United States. Conversely, an American fleet powerful enough to protect the Philippines and compel respect for U.S. Far Eastern policy would just as inevitably appear to Japan as a menace.[21] Each party, regarding itself as "defensive" and interested solely in its own security, failed to see how its own "defense" might be regarded as "aggressive" and threatening to the other.[22]

The 70 Percent Ratio

Japan's demand for a 70 percent ratio had surfaced for the first time at the Washington Conference in 1921–22. This ratio rested on the premise that "an approaching enemy armada needed a margin of at least 50 percent superiority over the defending fleet." It spelled out a 70 percent ratio for Japan; with it Japan would have a good chance or even a slight advantage. This 70 percent ratio would ensure "a strength insufficient for attack but adequate for defense."[23] The hawkish leaders of the Navy General Staff, led by Kato, were convinced that a 70 percent ratio was an "absolute" requirement to prepare for the "inevitable" war with the Unites States.

To Japanese naval planners, the seemingly minor margin between 60 and 70 percent made the difference between victory and defeat. Kato Kanji appealed to assembled commanders, "This goal for a 70 percent ratio has stiffened our navy's morale and sustained its determination through unspeakable hardships ever since the Washington Conference."[24] The idea of a 70 percent ratio crystallized into a firmly held naval consensus, even an obsession, that governed Japanese naval policy and strategy to the eve of the Pearl Harbor attack.

Regarding naval strategies and the ratio question, a "mirror image" could be noted between the two navies. The U.S. Navy also required a 70 percent ratio as a precondition for transpacific offensive operations against Japan. Traditionally, as a rule of thumb, the U.S. Navy had estimated that its fighting strength would erode by 10 percent for each thousand miles from its major base.[25] As applied to the Pacific, the U.S. fleet's combat strength would be reduced to roughly 70 percent by the Japanese submarines' "attrition attacks," wearing it down during the transpacific passage.

Japan's claim for a 70 percent ratio was also predicated on the premise of a "quick engagement, quick showdown" (Kato Kanji's favorite words).[26] Upon the opening of hostilities the Japanese navy would quickly annihilate America's much smaller Asiatic Fleet and seize the Philippines and Guam. Japanese planners expected that the American people would be so enraged as to force the U.S. fleet to make a "quick westward dash" to recapture the Philippines. The Japanese navy would wait and ambush it, seeking a classic line-to-line decisive battle between the Bonins and Marianas.[27]

But did Japan have the means to compel the U.S. fleet to steam to the western Pacific? Kato's answer was, "The fundamental guideline of American strategy is the principle of the quick-and-decisive battle. The U.S. Navy is bent on promptly forcing an early encounter with the Japanese fleet and deciding the issue in one stroke."[28] In fact, the 1923–24 version of the U.S. Navy's War Plan Orange envisaged "an offensive war, primarily naval," with a view to establishing "at an earliest date American sea power in the west Pacific in strength superior to that of Japan."[29] Kato never doubted that any war with the United States would be one of short duration. Although the age of total warfare had dawned with the First World War, waging a protracted conflict was never in Kato's mind.[30] In such a war Japan's naval ratio would lose all its meaning, for

America's shipbuilding capacity was estimated during the 1920s to be three or four times that of Japan.[31]

Kato took special note that "Japanese navy's strategic studies tallied with their American counterpart." He explained, "It was natural that strategic planning for any nation, even that bearing on the most secret aspects of national defense, should lead to identical conclusions, if based on the same premises and reliable data. . . . This is precisely the reason why the United States tries to impose a 60 percent ratio on us and we consistently demand a 70 percent ratio."[32] It was precisely because of such a "mirror-imaging" that a fundamental conflict arose and intensified between the two navies over naval ratios. The mirror image noted by Kato reflected the shared Mahanian dicta of supremacy of the battleship, warfare of short duration, offensive operations, early and decisive fleet engagement, and the underlying inevitability of war.[33] Based on these strategic principles and the fact that Japan's auxiliary strength, in the estimate of its navy, had surpassed 70 percent of the U.S. Navy's, the Japanese navy would "absolutely" demand a 70 percent ratio at London.

Seventy Percent Ratio for the Heavy Cruiser

The heavy cruiser—a ten-thousand-ton cruiser mounting 8-inch guns—was built in large numbers in the late 1920s to compensate for the "shortage" of capital ships under the Washington Treaty. (The ten-thousand-ton cruiser was the maximum allowed by the Washington Treaty and hence was called the "treaty cruiser.") Deemed as a "quasi-capital ship," it was held by the Japanese to be absolutely imperative to obtain a 70 percent ratio of them at the forthcoming conference. Japan took the world lead in heavy cruiser design.

In a lengthy report in December 1929 the Operations Division emphasized the "formidable power" of the heavy cruiser as the main prop of auxiliary strength: first, it exceled in speed (more than thirty-three knots); second, it was equipped with great firepower (8-inch guns had 2.5 times the range of 6-inch guns); and third, and most important, it had great cruising radius, a vital element in transoceanic operations (eight thousand miles at twenty-four knots).[34]

To the U.S. Navy, the heavy cruiser was crucial because of the five thousand miles of water between the Philippines and Hawaii.[35] It was regarded as vitally needed for transpacific operations—defense of the Philippines, trade-route protection, and the carrying of a war into the western Pacific.[36] Here again, one notes mirror-imaging between the two navies.

Although during the 1920s the United States had fallen behind the other major naval powers in this category, Japanese planners were alarmed that the

U.S. Navy, if in possession of sufficient numbers of ten-thousand-ton cruisers, would be able to link its hitherto remote strategic outposts in the Pacific—the Philippines and Guam in the west, Hawaii at the center, Samoa in the south, and the Aleutians in the north. This would mean a radical shortening of Japan's geographic depth, which had hitherto been to its advantage. And if American heavy cruisers were to join in the decisive fleet engagement, they could threaten Japan's vital sea communications. In short, the ten-thousand-ton cruiser was seen as a formidable offensive weapon, a weapon that would make it easier for the attacker, the U.S. Navy, to conduct operations against Japan.[37] In a memorandum to Makino Nobuaki, Lord Keeper of the Privy Seal, Kato stated, "The United States is determined to construct eighteen ten-thousand-ton cruisers precisely because it is preparing for offensive operations against Japan."[38] (Kato perhaps felt it necessary to "educate" Makino, who was close to the emperor.) For all these reasons, Japanese planners regarded the heavy cruiser as the "substitute" for the battleship. In "interceptive operation," it was to damage the U.S. fleet before it could reach the western Pacific.[39] In retrospect, however, the actual performance of the heavy cruiser during the Pacific War betrayed the great expectations the Japanese navy held. The roles of the light cruiser and the destroyer turned out to be far more important.

The Submarine

With regard to the submarine, total tonnage (irrespective of ratios) was what mattered. All other naval powers deployed the submarine for commerce destruction; the Japanese navy was unique in planning to use it for attrition, to whittle down the enemy fleet. As David C. Evans and Mark R. Peattie point out, "the Japanese navy aimed at transforming the submarine from a weapon of passive, short-range defense to one of long-range, offensive, and strategic operations." Regarding the submarine as "a weapon for the weak," the Japanese navy had placed on it great importance, as offsetting the "deficiency" in capital ships ever since the Washington Conference.[40]

For attrition attacks, the Japanese navy built large, high-speed, oceangoing submarines (surface speed of from twenty to twenty-three knots, eight knots submerged) with a radius of 20,000 miles (sufficient to reach California and return without refueling). From 1928, Japan led the world in the construction of 1,800-ton submarines.[41] Because the fastest American battleship could command a maximum speed of only twenty knots, Japan's fleet submarines were believed capable of scouting and attacking the U.S. fleet. According to the 1930 plan, submarines were to engage in the surveillance, chasing, and attrition of the American main fleet advancing from Hawaii to Japan's mandate islands and to scout it from the Marianas to the Philippines.[42] It was Rear Admiral Suetsugu Nobumasa, known as "the father of submarine strategy," who worked out the attrition strategy, as commander of the 1st Submarine Squadron in 1923–25. He declared that the outcome of any war would depend on the success of the attrition strategy. To support such a strategy, Japan would "absolutely" demand at the London Conference a total submarine strength of 78,000 tons, which would be Japan's tonnage upon completion of the current building program at the end of fiscal 1931.[43] Looking back, it is ironic that when it actually came to the test during the Pacific War, Japanese submarines made a very poor showing. They could not sink even a single American battleship, whereas American submarines played havoc with Japanese shipping.

The "Never-Again" Syndrome: The "Lessons" of Washington

There was a strong feeling that Japan, having backed down at Washington in 1921–22, had to stand firm the next time, whatever the risk. Its naval leaders, as they began preparations for the London Conference, carefully reviewed the perceived "lessons of the Washington Conference" so that the same "mistakes" should not be committed.[44]

The first "lesson" was that Japan had attended the Washington Conference without adequate preparations and had been utterly surprised by the American initiative, getting off to a bad start. This time, Japan had to set forth "a firm, concrete and clear-cut policy."

Second, the navy had come to fear that the Anglo-American powers would collude to impose a 60 percent ratio on auxiliary vessels.[45] Kato anticipated that these powers would ask: "If a 60 percent ratio was acceptable at Washington, why not at London?" His response would be that, on the contrary, precisely because the ratio of 60 percent had been imposed on capital ships at Washington, it was all the more necessary now to obtain a 70 percent ratio in auxiliary strength. One way to forestall Anglo-American collusion would be to reach separate understandings by preliminary negotiations at Washington and London.

The third and most important "lesson" for Kato was derived from his own bitter experience. At Washington he and naval advisers had keenly felt "the lack of domestic support."[46] Therefore, the Navy General Staff under Kato mobilized a vociferous nationwide campaign to inflame public opinion, appealing to the press, business circles, and political right-wing organizations.[47] This virulent propaganda campaign greatly annoyed Wakatsuki Reijiro, soon to be the head delegate, who felt his hands were being tied. The American ambassador, William R. Castle, observed, "The [70 percent] ratio has become a political doctrine of major importance.... A large portion of the [Japanese] people have been taught to look upon this [70 percent] ratio as essential to national safety.... The fact that the United States refused to consider this is seen as an indication that we foresee the possibility of war."[48] Even after the conference had commenced, Kato was sending a letter to Admiral Abo, the highest naval adviser in London, requesting him to send home more and more telegrams about Anglo-American "oppression" of Japan that could be used to stir up public sentiment and "spur the government to stiffen its attitude."

The Worldview of Admiral Kato Kanji

Admiral Kato Kanji is said to have been an emotional, hot-blooded, and impetuous, as well as a simple-minded, man. He himself admitted that "eighty percent of my behavior is governed by emotion."[49] Admiral Suzuki Kantaro, Kato's immediate predecessor as chief of the Naval General Staff, said that he was "headstrong and emotional, thus hard to deal with." But simple-minded he was not. His stated position on a 70 percent ratio was not lacking in ideological content, although it was often clothed in convoluted doctrines. In this respect, his beliefs stood in sharp contrast to the "rational" views held by Kato Tomosaburo at the Washington Conference. To understand Kato Kanji's *Weltanschauung*, it is necessary to look at his convictions about national defense and national prestige as well as the emotional baggage they carried. These ideas revealed a remarkable continuity since the days of the Washington Conference.

The most striking features about his views were the doctrines of "equality of armament" and the "point of Japan's national honor." He held that Japan as a sovereign nation was inherently entitled to parity—a ratio of 10:10. From this viewpoint, a 70 percent ratio, was an extreme concession, "the rock bottom demand."[50] Anything less would jeopardize Japan's naval defense and infringe on its national honor.[51] At heart, Kato would have preferred a higher ratio. In a letter of January 1930 he wrote, "Rather than being restricted to a 70 percent ratio, it is better to be flexible, free, and independent to suit our expanding naval power." He argued that the breakup of the conference would be preferable; Japan would then be enabled to build an independent navy that would accommodate its growing power. From this viewpoint, a 70 percent ratio, even if it could be achieved, would still carry the stigma of "inferiority to the Anglo-American powers."[52]

Kato was totally opposed to the use of existing strength as the basis for naval limitation. He argued that imposition of the existing ratio would permanently shackle weaker nations on the basis of temporary power configurations.[53] Specifically, Kato attacked the "stop-now" formula applied by Charles Evans Hughes at the Washington Conference. While seemingly fair, this formula had been designed to freeze the status quo, which had been favorable to the United States.

Kato presented a case for "a have-not" nation (Japan) as against a "super-have" nation (the United States). Since the latter nation had incomparable war potential—wealth, resources, and industrial power—it did not actually need great peacetime armaments. American security could be assured with peacetime armaments equal to or even smaller than those of less favored nations.[54] Conversely, Japan needed large peacetime armaments.

Unlike most navalists who shunned continental entanglements, Kato linked the 70 percent ratio issue to the China question. Even at the time of the Washington Conference, he had told the American attaché that "[Japan] must have opportunity to expand, and America must not endeavor to restrict Japan expansion on the continent of Asia."[55] In 1930, Kato, reflecting Mahanian brand of economic determinism, was convinced that America's "economic penetration" of the China market was destined sooner or later to bring about a Japanese-American war. Kato warned that the real intention of the United States at the London Conference was to relegate Japan to such an inferior naval position that the United States could freely pursue its "domination" of China.[56]

Throughout the 1920s, Kato gave much thought to how the war would come about. Again projecting the Mahanian idea of inevitable war, Kato said the United States, as the leading capitalistic-imperialistic nation, then at the pinnacle of its power under a business-conscious Republican administration, was bound to seek in China an outlet for its surplus production. (Like turn-of-the-century American imperialists, Kato ignored the fact that Japan offered a greater market than China.) Kato warned Foreign Minister Shidehara Kijuro that economic conflict would bring about political clash, that "diehards" in America would demand that the China question be resolved by naval force.[57] To prepare for such a war, Kato warned, the United States was building a powerful navy "for offensive operations against Japan."[58]

Holding that commercial rivalry was bound to cause armed conflict, then, Kato Kanji believed in the inevitability in war with America "sooner or later."[59]

Opposed to such a conviction were Yamanashi, the navy vice minister, and Hori, chief of the Naval Affairs Bureau, who were self-conscious heirs of Kato Tomosaburo; to them the navy was no more than "a silent power" to deter the United States from naval actions in the western Pacific.[60] Kato Kanji's conviction about unavoidable war was a background against which he "absolutely" demanded the "three basic principles" at the London Conference.

The Failure of Preliminary Negotiations

When the British invitation to the London Conference arrived in Tokyo on 7 October 1929, the navy was reluctant to participate. The government, however, did not wish to offend the United States by rejecting it. So the navy demanded that the "three basic principles" be accepted by the United States and Britain prior to the main conference. On 11 October, Kato told Foreign Minister Shidehara, "It is a most urgent matter to obtain from the Anglo-American powers a commitment to the 'three basic principles' before our delegates depart for London." Further, to pressure Shidehara, Kato quoted Fleet Admiral Togo Heihachiro as saying that "we should not refrain from rupturing the conference as the last resort."[61]

Shidehara, known as a pro-American diplomatist committed to cooperative approach, had difficulties in coping with Kato's demands, so he sent his ambassadors in Washington and London unusually stiff instructions to get the 70 percent demand accepted.[62] At times Shidehara seemed almost as adamant as Kato; the foreign minister was afraid that the navy was intent on boycotting the conference unless prior understanding was reached. In November, Kato stepped up his pressure on the government. He told Shidehara that there was absolutely no room whatsoever for compromising the 70 percent demand: "Not even a 70 percent was sufficient, so the 70 percent was the rock bottom and constituted a matter of life or death for our navy. . . . We must be prepared to break up the conference if our demands are not accepted."[63] Powerfully backing Kato was Fleet Admiral Togo, the eighty-three year-old hero of the battle of Tsushima, a naval demigod venerated as "the Nelson of Japan." On 18 November, Kato told Prime Minister Hamaguchi Osachi that "the 70 percent ratio was the rock bottom ratio, a matter of life or death for our navy," and he conveyed Togo's declaration: "Not even an inch should be yielded on the ratio question. If England and America do not accept our demand in the preliminary negotiations, we will simply refuse to participate in the main conference."[64]

In Washington, Ambassador Debuchi Katsuji made no headway in his efforts to persuade Secretary of State Henry L. Stimson (soon to be the head delegate) about the 70 percent ratio. Parallel efforts were being made in London by Ambassador Matsudaira Tsuneo (soon to become one of the delegates), with equally negative results. On 11 December, Matsudaira warned Tokyo that the coming conference would break up if Japan absolutely persisted in the 70 percent demand. He argued that it would be to Japan's advantage to accept a compromise settlement and asked whether the government was prepared for such a proposal.[65] He frankly stated, "If it is the policy of the government not to make the slightest concession, I believe there is no way out but to break up the conference."[66] In closing the preliminary negotiations in December, Wakatsuki Reijiro (the head delegate, who stopped in Washington on his way to London) advised the government, "If we were to push the matters to the extreme, we must be prepared for an angry parting."[67] Foreign Minister Shidehara rejected these recommendations as "counsels of despair." He feared that the navy would refuse participation in the conference.

Leaders and Delegates

For the Japanese government, the most pressing issue of the day was a severe financial crisis that had struck the nation in 1927, two years before the U.S. market crash precipitated the Great Depression. Prime Minister Hamaguchi Osachi's foremost tasks were financial retrenchment and cooperation with the Anglo-American powers. His cabinet was committed to the view that Japan's future lay in peaceful economic development based on multilateral trade expansion.[68] He was for not only naval limitation but naval reduction.

To implement this policy, Hamaguchi chose Wakatsuki as head delegate to the London Conference. Wakatsuki, outwardly an affable man, was a powerful senior statesman with exceptional brainpower, mathematical ability, cool judgment, and strong determination. He had served twice as finance minister (1912–13 and 1914–15) and once as prime minister (1926–27). In 1921–22 he had welcomed the Washington Conference. Acutely aware of Japan's financial limitations, he had ruled out a naval race. His "broad view" of national defense, emphasizing the importance of "friendly international relations and enhancement of national resources," reminds one of Kato Tomosaburo's outlook.[69] Wakatsuki felt it would be "unwise to persist uncompromisingly in a 70 percent ratio." Rather, he would conclude a treaty "within negotiable limits, say 65 or 67 percent." In his memoir he recalled, "At bottom my conviction was that it was to Japan's advantage to stop competitive building by naval limitation."[70]

Another distinguished civilian delegate was Matsudaira Tsuneo, ambassador to Britain. A suave and liberal-minded diplomat with perfect command of English, he had attended the Washington Conference as the director of general affairs and in that capacity had assisted Kato Tomosaburo, acquiring in the process a broad knowledge of naval limitation. His diplomatic credentials were such that he was superbly suited as a delegate to the London Conference.[71] He was to negotiate with an American delegate the crucial compromise plan that would become the basis of the London Treaty.[72]

The choice of the naval delegate fell to Navy Minister Takarabe Takeshi. His rise in the navy had been meteoric, thanks, it was said, to the clout of his influential father-in-law, former navy minister Yamamoto Gonbei. He had served as navy minister intermittently in 1923–24 and 1929–30. But in naval circles he had the reputation of being "unreliable," "irresolute," and lacking in leadership. Why such a man was chosen as the naval delegate remains unclear. It would appear that the navy unthinkingly followed the precedent set by having sent Navy Minister Kato Tomosaburo as head delegate to Washington. But there was a world of difference between a vacillating Takarabe and a charismatic Kato. At the London Conference, Takarabe could never determine whether he should act as navy minister or naval delegate, and this uncertainty made him vulnerable to criticism from both civilian delegates and hawks in the naval delegation. Besides, Takarabe had a hard time resisting pressure from the diehard middle echelons of the naval delegation. Perhaps what tied Takarabe's hands most was a pledge he had given twice before his departure, once to Imperial Prince Fushimi Hiroyasu (the most senior naval officer and a member of Supreme Council) and again to Fleet Admiral Togo, that he would never retreat even an inch from the "three basic principles." Fushimi, a leading hawk and Kato's former classmate at the Naval Academy, was later to remember this and hold him to make good this promise.[73] At London, Takarabe seldom participated in top-level meetings of the delegates. Nor did he keep in close contact with the members of naval delegation. He seldom sent telegrams to the naval leaders in Tokyo, and those he did send were drafted and telegraphed by his chief naval adviser, Sakonji Seizo. Vice Admiral Sakonji, former head of the Naval Affairs Bureau, seems personally to have favored naval limitation, but since his assigned task was to draft his chief's telegrams, he found himself agreeing with Takarabe most of the time.

What infuriated Fleet Admiral Togo most was Takarabe's taking his wife to London. To Togo a naval conference was a battlefield in peacetime, not an occasion for international socializing. (Cosmopolitan-minded Admiral Saito Makoto and Foreign Minister Shidehara, regarding the naval conference as a diplomatic gathering, had advised Takarabe to take his wife.) Takarabe and his wife had plenty of free time to enjoy sightseeing and shopping.

Kato had feared that Admiral Takarabe would be outsmarted by the brainy civilian delegate Wakatsuki.[74] Upon consultation with Fleet Admiral Togo, Kato decided to send Admiral Abo Kiyokazu to London as "the highest naval adviser." Kato's childhood crony, a Naval Academy classmate, and a member of the Supreme Military Council (composed of the highest-ranking admirals and generals), Abo represented the hard-line stance of the Navy General Staff. He was expected to be Kato's spokesman in London and also to keep close watch on Takarabe's behavior. (Some called Abo a "deputy naval delegate.") Abo sent telegrams to Kato supporting an intransigent policy.

The second-ranking naval member, Rear Admiral Yamamoto Isoroku, was decidedly a hawk. Kato could count on him to take a strong stand. Yamamoto repeatedly told the delegates that Japan should never make a "political retreat." A popular biography, *The Reluctant Admiral,* makes him out to be a supporter of naval limitation;[75] however, it was only after the London Conference that he became converted to it. The U.S. embassy in Tokyo reported, "Yamamoto is well known in Washington; is a good mixer; speaks excellent English, and is rated a smart, capable naval officer."[76] Among the younger members of the delegation Kato took care to include Capt. Nakamura Kamesaburo, chief of Operations Section and a belligerent mouthpiece of the middle echelons in the Navy General Staff.

In Tokyo, Kato Kanji worked in tandem with Suetsugu, vice chief of the Navy General Staff. Kato was impetuous and hot-blooded, but he was, as Admiral Okada Keisuke, who would later emerge as a crisis manager, commented, "at least honest in his single-minded opposition so it was rather easy to handle him." Suetsugu, in contrast, was a schemer, calculating and harboring political ambitious, so it was much harder to deal with him.[77] As early as the Washington Conference, Suetsugu had acted as Kato's eminence grise, drafting his intransigent telegrams to the Naval General Staff behind the back of head delegate, Kato Tomosaburo. Some said at the time of the London Naval Conference that Suetsugu was manipulating Kato behind the scenes.[78]

During Navy Minister Takarabe's absence, Prime Minister Hamaguchi assumed the titular portfolio of navy minister, but he left Vice Minister Yamanashi to assume the onerous task of controlling the naval establishment. A brilliant graduate of the Naval Academy, second in his class, Yamanashi was a superb naval administrator. Though mild mannered and modest, he had firm convictions and took "a large view" of naval policy. In Wakatsuki's words, Yamanashi was "a man of sharp brain and a strong sense of responsibility." After the conference the superintendent-general of the Tokyo Metropolitan Police whispered to Yamanashi, "You were in such physical danger [of assassination] that I feared for the worst. You are indeed lucky to be alive!"[79] The American naval attaché once described Yamanashi as "extremely well read, particularly on American naval history (Mahan) . . . as non-militaristic as any naval officer of his rank."[80]

Ably assisting Yamanashi was Rear Admiral Hori, head of the Naval Affairs Bureau. Celebrated as the finest brain ever to have graduated from the Naval Academy, Hori was known for his sound judgment, broad outlook, and logical thinking. Yamanashi and Hori had faithfully assisted Kato Tomosaburo at the Washington Conference and inherited his philosophies of naval limitation and "no war with the United States." However, they simply did not possess the great Kato's charisma. And they were no match for Chief of the Navy General Staff Kato Kanji, who outranked them.

In 1930, the leaders of the Navy General Staff comprised men who prided themselves on being "old sea dogs," having built their careers as line or afloat staff officers. Their views were rigidly operational. Neither Kato nor Suetsugu had held a Navy Ministry post to speak of, while Yamanashi and Hori, "desk officers," had experienced few tours of duty in the fleet. With regard to naval limitation, the unwritten tradition of the navy, à la the British, held that it was the responsibility, and within the jurisdiction, of the government (the Navy Ministry) to decide on the size of armaments.[81] As navy vice minister, Yamanashi took a flexible position: armament plans, drafted by the Navy General Staff from strategic-operational viewpoints, were not something absolute; they must be agreed upon with the Navy Ministry. Hori asserted that decisions on armaments, involving budgetary matters, were political and that hence responsibility for them lay with the government.[82]

For his part, Kato Kanji contended that the chief of the Navy General Staff, in charge of strategic plans, was responsible for deciding on the size of armaments. He and his subordinates argued that they were only performing their duty in absolutely demanding the 70 percent ratio. But there was a hitch—there was no constitutional provision in case the two branches disagreed.

The Rift between Civil and Naval Delegates

On 21 January 1930, an exceptionally foggy morning, the opening ceremony of the conference was held in the Royal Gallery of the House of Lords. As had become clear from the abortive preliminary negotiations in Washington and London, Japan's chance of obtaining the "three basic principles" was practically nil, but its delegates were directed by Tokyo to persist. The main target of their negotiations was, of course, the United States. However, as one contemporary observer noted, the Japanese delegates directed their "diplomatic" efforts more toward navy diehards in Tokyo than toward the American delegates.

Shortly after the conference opened, a very serious rift developed between Japan's civilian and naval delegates. As early as 25 January, Wakatsuki and Matsudaira reaffirmed that gloomy conclusion, drafting a telegram to Tokyo: "We are at our rope's end; the time has come now for us to request the government to apprise us of the terms of compromise." Wakatsuki said that as the chief delegate he was responsible for the proposed telegram, but Takarabe and his naval advisers strenuously objected, so the draft telegram was shelved.[83] On 20 February, when the conference floundered on Japanese-American differences, Wakatsuki sent a most confidential message to Foreign Minister Shidehara. Prefaced by a request "to please burn this upon reading," this telegram warned Shidehara that there was no prospect whatsoever of having Japan's demands being accepted and that "the breakup of the conference would place it [Japan] in an extremely inimical position internationally."[84] In Tokyo, however, Shidehara had great difficulties coping with Kato and the Navy General Staff. Powerless, he turned to Takarabe, asking him to take the initiative in London and work out an acceptable settlement. "If we at this time try to draft in Tokyo a concrete compromise plan, it will be extremely difficult to obtain an agreement within the navy." So Shidehara asked Wakatsuki "to follow the logical step of first consulting with Navy Minister Takarabe and jointly working out some appropriate measures. It is earnestly hoped that you will get assistance from Admiral Abo with a view to persuading the navy."[85] By this time, however, relations between Wakatsuki and Takarabe had so deteriorated that it was no longer possible for them to jointly "work out" a settlement. The civilian and naval delegates had become locked in irreconcilable differences. But of this Shidehara was blissfully unaware.

Later, when Japanese-American issues reached a critical point, Wakatsuki, in a telegram to Shidehara, bitterly criticized Takarabe's intransigence: "Although I have urged delegate Takarabe to rise resolutely to the occasion as would befit a statesman and take broad-minded measures to save the situation, he disagrees with me in every instance and has instead aligned himself with Admiral Abo and other naval advisors. . . . To my great distress, it has proved beyond my power to persuade Takarabe."[86]

The Reed-Matsudaira Compromise

On 5 February, the American delegates publicly proposed a plan that provided for a 60 percent ratio both for overall and heavy-cruiser tonnages. Suddenly a very tense atmosphere pervaded Japan's naval delegation, and the situation became "a very grave one."[87] Chief naval adviser Sakonji reported that the American proposal "almost totally disregards Japan's position, which had been so painstakingly explained by chief delegate Wakatsuki during his recent visit to the United States. . . . Of course, there is no room whatsoever for accepting the 'selfish' American proposal."[88] In Tokyo, the worried Yamanashi visited Prime Minister Hamaguchi for a long consultation. In his diary Hamaguchi wrote, "The problem of naval limitation is getting more serious than ever. We must carefully watch the situation."[89] Kato wired naval advisers in London that the Naval General Staff was "firmly resolved" to oppose the compromise proposal.[90] Naval adviser Yamamoto urged Takarabe that "no political retreat" must be made and cabled to Hori, his friend and head of the Naval Affairs Bureau, that he was pessimistic about the future of the conference.[91]

With Japan firmly refusing to yield, the conference came to a deadlock. To find a way out of the impasse, Wakatsuki and Stimson arranged on 25 February for Matsudaira and the American delegate, Senator David A. Reed, to enter into private, informal, free-talking, high-level discussion. The two men had known each other since 1924, when they had been on opposite sides of the controversy over the Immigration Act of that year. It was understood that the agreement to emerge from the Reed-Matsudaira talks would not be binding on either party.[92] Talks between admirals, it was feared, would only aggravate the situation, by focusing on strategic and technical differences, as had been the case with the Geneva Naval Conference of 1927.[93]

Cdr. Sato Ichiro, a junior hawk in the naval delegation, was worried: "An always a smiling Matsudaira will not be up to his task. The tough negotiations will require deadly confrontations that would be fiery and almost bloodletting."[94] On his part, Reed complained, "The negotiations with the Japanese are very tedious, as the Japanese evidently in an endeavor to satisfy internal dissentions in their delegation, are bringing to us recurrent propositions which they know we will refuse."[95] Chief delegate Stimson was more understanding: "Negotiations are rendered delicate and difficult by Japanese political situation at home."[96] Because of "the free and nonbinding nature" of the talks, Japanese civilian delegates decided not to report to Tokyo or consult with the leading naval members. Success, they felt, required strict secrecy.

Naval leaders in Tokyo, kept in the dark about the progress of the Reed-Matsudaira talks, had become "gravely apprehensive" that these talks might sow the seeds of discord with the delegates.[97] Indeed, unknown to the navy the Reed-Matsudaira talks had come to a head. On 11 March, after nearly two months of patient exploration, the two negotiators reached a bilateral agreement that came to be known as the "Reed-Matsudaira compromise."[98] In presenting this plan, Reed categorically stated and repeated that "further concession would be absolutely impossible."[99] It gave Japan an overall ratio of 69.75 percent, in effect meeting Japan's demand. However, with respect to the heavy cruiser, it provided eighteen for the United States and twelve for Japan. This gave Japan only a 60.2 percent ratio in principle, but to mollify the Japanese, the United States was in practice not to launch the last three of its eighteen heavy cruisers until 1933, 1934, and 1935.[100] This meant that although in theory Japan was assigned only a 60 percent ratio, it actually could keep a de facto 70 percent ratio during the life of the treaty—that is, until the next conference, scheduled to be held in 1935.[101] What hindered acceptance by the Japanese navy, however, was that Japan, already in possession of eight heavy cruisers and four more nearly complete, would not be allowed to build a single new ship, whereas the United States was free to build fourteen vessels between 1930 and 1936.

As for the submarine, Japan fared worse. The Reed-Matsudaira compromise provided for parity in total tonnage, set at 52,000 tons combined. This would allow Japan to have one-third of the 78,000 tons it demanded. It meant Japan could not construct a single new submarine to replace outdated ships, thus retarding its submarine technology and construction capacity. However, Wakatsuki was quite satisfied with the Reed-Matsudaira compromise; he honestly believed that the purport of the "three basic principles" had been fulfilled. Did it not provide an overall ratio of 70 percent? With regard to the submarine, had not the United States made "a great compromise" by receding from the initial demand for 60 percent?[102]

The prudent course for Wakatsuki, of course, would have been to keep at least Abo, Sakonji, and Yamamoto informed about of the progress of the Reed-Matsudaira talks. To the naval members, instead, the compromise plan came as a "bolt from the blue." It was all the more galling since Wakatsuki had assured them that the compromise formula would merely be a "private plan with no binding force." Had he not promised to decide on the compromise plan "only after consulting with the naval advisers"? But the turn of the Japanese-American negotiations had forced the civilian delegates to commit themselves to a compromise plan that was purely civilian in origin and unacceptable to the naval members, not to mention the naval authorities in Tokyo.[103]

The naval advisers in London—Rear Admiral Yamamoto, Captains Nakamura and Toyoda Teijiro—held that only Takarabe's "determined opposition" could undo the Reed-Matsudaira compromise.[104] The naval advisers' opposition notwithstanding, Wakatsuki proceeded on 14 March to draft a telegram to Tokyo, to be jointly signed by the four delegates. It requested final instructions from the government directing the delegates to accept the Reed-Matsudaira compromise. Wakatsuki warned that there was no prospect whatsoever of obtaining more favorable terms, pleading for the government "to make the final determination to accept the compromise plan." At nine o'clock that night the Japanese delegates met at Grosvenor House, where they were staying, to discuss the draft telegram. Takarabe demurred, anticipating that Kato and the Navy General Staff would violently oppose. However, after a meeting that lasted four hours, Takarabe was most reluctantly brought to consent to the telegram. However, the vacillating Takarabe was soon to reverse his position.[105]

The jointly signed telegram was sent to Tokyo on the morning of 15 February. It urged the government to accept the Reed-Matsudaira compromise: "If we continued haggling as *we have been doing,* there is no prospect for the moment of making Japan's position more advantageous." (The italicized words were inserted upon Takarabe's demand to tone down the telegram.) Just to ensure that Tokyo would understand the full implications of the joint telegram, Wakatsuki followed it with another to Shidehara. It warned, "Unless new situation arises, it will be difficult to obtain further compromises." If Japan persisted in its inflexible position, the conference would break up and bring about "most serious consequences."[106] Later on the same day, Wakatsuki sent Shidehara another confidential telegram, stating, more explicitly than Takarabe would have approved, "Now the time has come to finally make up our minds. The only course left is to conclude the conference on the basis of the Japanese-American [Reed-Matsudaira] compromise."[107]

Wakatsuki's open and frequent expressions of his "resolve" only enraged naval advisers. He told them, "If we can reach a settlement with the Reed-Matsudaira compromise, what happens to my life and honor will not matter." Again, he declared, "I am staking not only my position as chief delegate but my life itself."[108] Later, he repeated that on the acceptance of the Reed-Matsudaira compromise, he staked not only "his position as chief delegate but his life itself." To the naval aides he asserted, "No matter what new instructions I receive from Tokyo, I am determined to stick to my conviction. If the Reed-Matsudaira compromise is disapproved by the government, there will be no choice but for me to resign as chief delegate."[109] Uppermost in his mind was, of course, the importance of avoiding a clash with the Anglo-American powers and preventing a naval race.

Alarmed that the delegates' joint telegram to Tokyo might indeed constitute their final recommendation, the naval advisers decided to cable the naval authorities that there was no room whatsoever for considering the Reed-Matsudaira compromise.[110] From the experts' professional viewpoint, Wakatsuki's thinking was "amateurish"; the naval advisers were quick to point out that the compromise plan did not comply with the "three basic principles." They vigorously protested that it gave Japan only a "token" of an overall ratio of 70 percent while rejecting the crucial demands on heavy cruisers and submarines.[111]

As to heavy cruisers, Japan would be stuck with old vessels (planned in 1921), while the United States would be free to build new ships. More important, the submarine strength provided by the Reed-Matsudaira compromise was meant to "suppress" the Japanese force in the name of parity. Japan could not build a single new ship, and the plan "will severely cripple our submarine strength almost to the point of uselessness." It would jeopardize Japan's operations in Philippine waters and in connection with the attrition strategy.[112] To Kato and Suetsugu, these were excruciating conditions, seriously undermining Japan's entire strategy and destroying its morale.

In London, the Reed-Matsudaira compromise had stirred up a hornet's nest among naval members of the delegation. Admiral Abo accused Takarabe of succumbing to civilian delegates, bitterly attacking his failure to consult the naval experts. Agonized, he said that he would have to resign from the Supreme Military Council if the delegates' joint telegram were sent as it stood. He insisted there was still room for carrying through Japan's original demands.[113] When Sakonji and other naval advisers found out that that the delegates had already committed themselves to the Reed-Matsudaira compromise, they were enraged and warned that it would precipitate "an unprecedented domestic crisis, destroy the unity of the delegation, and incur the contempt of other powers."[114] (Sakonji's counterproposal, cabled to Yamanashi and Suetsugu, called for one additional heavy cruiser and the submarine strength of 70,000 tons.)[115] On 17 March, the naval members of the delegation pressured Takarabe, demanding that he repudiate the joint telegram of 14 March, which he himself had signed. But Takarabe equivocated, saying he had to consider also his position as a member of the Hamaguchi cabinet.[116] Two days later, Abo sent a most confidential telegram to Kato, suggesting that that the government send an instruction that would firmly reject the Reed-Matsudaira compromise.[117] On 19 March, Takarabe (through Abo) received a top-secret message from Kato stating: "As one responsible for strategic plans for national defense, I [Kato] am absolutely opposed to the compromise plan. There is no room for concession."[118] Within the delegation the most agitated were younger officers like Captain Nakamura. On 16 March, he appealed directly to head delegate Wakatsuki and on the following day urged Takarabe to maintain "a firm and resolute stand." Disappointed with Takarabe's equivocation, the younger officers proposed to cable Kato and Yamanashi directly. Their aim was to wrest from Tokyo "drastic" new instructions that would reverse Wakatsuki's "defeatist policy."[119] To mollify these unruly young officers, Yamamoto wired his friend Hori, head of the Naval Affairs Bureau, warning him of the volatile situation in London.[120]

In Tokyo, Prime Minister Hamaguchi tersely wrote in his diary, "The situation is extremely serious. I ordered the navy vice minister to come to an agreement about the telegram [the Reed-Matsudaira compromise]."[121] But coming to an "agreement" within the navy would be a Herculean task.

Naval Opposition in Tokyo

The Reed-Matsudaira compromise, by creating consternation and indignation, had brought about a crisis in Tokyo. In the words of the late Kiyoshi Ikeda, a distinguished naval historian, "With the arrival of the delegates' telegram on 15 March requesting the government's final instructions, began a turmoil unprecedented in the history of the Japanese Navy."[122] Kato led the diehards, marshalling both tangible and emotional arguments. On the one hand, he stated that Japan already possessed a 74 percent overall ratio in auxiliary ships and an 80 percent ratio in heavy cruisers. On the other hand, he emphasized intangible factors of national prestige and credibility: "The more humbly Japan acquiesces despite its sovereign right of equality, the more flagrant the United States would become in flaunting its high-handed and coercive attitude."[123] In a letter to Abo, Kato wrote, "the real issue at stake is no longer our naval power per se but our national prestige and credulity."[124] Equally serious would be the baneful effects on the navy's morale.

Admiral Suetsugu, "the father of submarine strategy," was especially unsparing in his attacks on the drastic reduction of submarine strength. He warned that it would cause grave deficiencies in submarines to be deployed in Philippine operations and in scouting Hawaiian waters. It would also cripple the attrition strategy against the approaching American fleet. The compromise plan, he declared, would necessitate "fundamental overhauling of our operational plans."[125]

The navy's opposition mounting, Kato cabled to Takarabe on 17 March: "There is no room for considering the American proposal [as he misleadingly called the Reed-Matsudaira compromise]. . . . It is an imposition of American terms on Japan."[126] To increase the pressure on Takarabe, Kato forwarded what Fleet Admiral Togo had told him the previous day:

> The United States refuses to make the slightest concession in the heavy cruiser. There is no way left but for us to withdraw from the conference. Even if we withdraw, it will not lead to great naval expansion, so there will be no financial worry. Since we have taken the position that our national defense cannot be assured with anything less than the 70 percent ratio, there is no haggling over one or two percent. . . . Even if the conference breaks up because of our position, it will be better than concluding a disadvantageous treaty.[127]

Prince Fushimi recalled that Takarabe had promised him twice before his departure that he would not retreat a single step from the "three basic principles." Fushimi, Emperor Hirohito's cousin, said that he intended to appeal to the emperor to stand firmly by that position. (He did not know then that Hirohito actually supported the treaty.) On 19 March, Kato called Prime Minister Hamaguchi at his official residence and harangued him for more than an hour. Insisting that he was the one in charge of naval defense and strategic planning, as chief of the Navy General Staff, he "absolutely" opposed the compromise plan.[128]

The Navy Ministry's ranking officials, Yamanashi and Hori, endeavored to bring about the treaty. As naval officers, wearing naval uniforms, they as a matter of course supported the "three basic principles" and agreed that the Reed-Matsudaira compromise would cause deficiencies in naval defense, but they did not regard ratios in absolute terms. Above all, they took a "large" view of national defense, one that carefully took into consideration diplomatic, political, and financial factors, in the best tradition of Kato Tomosaburo. On 22 March, Yamanashi frankly warned Takarabe that the time would soon come when "political and diplomatic imperatives" might override the navy's demands.[129]

The delay in the government's instructions was placing the Japanese delegates in a tight place. In a confidential dispatch to Tokyo, Wakatsuki made a passionate appeal to the government to come to a decision promptly: "If we continue to be unyielding, an agreement will become impossible, posing great difficulties for Japan's international position. If the government does not desire the breakup of the conference, please make that point very clear to us in your return instructions. It is because of my anguish for the future of our Empire that I ask special considerations before the matter reaches extremity." Shidehara did not respond to Wakatsuki's desperate appeal but merely confessed that the government's decision making was paralyzed by the Navy General Staff's intransigence: "For the moment, the navy ministry will have difficulties in reaching an agreement within the navy. If we decide too hastily on our final instructions, it would cause grave domestic consequences." So Shidehara (through a most confidential telegram to Wakatsuki) turned to naval delegate Takarabe, asking him to help mollify the Navy General Staff. Shidehara solicited him as navy minister to create a naval consensus in London in favor of acceptance of the Reed-Matsudaira compromise. Takarabe could then advise the naval authorities in Tokyo that it was impossible to obtain further concessions from the Anglo-American powers, so the navy would have to accept the compromise plan.[130]

Forsaking his role as a policy coordinator in Tokyo, Foreign Minister Shidehara at this late hour solicited assistance from Takarabe and Abo in softening the Navy General Staff and creating consensus in favor of the Reed-Matsudaira compromise. Of course, Takarabe turned down Shidehara's request, saying that deciding on the size of armaments was the province of the Navy General Staff.[131] If Shidehara had really counted on Takarabe to soften Kato Kanji, he was deluded. The irony is that Shidehara was imploring support and help precisely from those in London who opposed the compromise plan. In fact, Abo was sending a telegram to the naval authorities in Tokyo recommending a diametrically opposed course: "A good case can be made for breaking the negotiations at the present time when there still remain such great discrepancies between both parties."[132] Although Shidehara has received high marks from historians for his adroit diplomacy with the Anglo-American powers, he utterly failed in the "crisis management" of naval politics.

At this juncture, who could control Kato and Suetsugu? In need of a reliable mediator between the pro- and anti-treaty forces, as well as between the navy and the government, ministry leaders turned to the naval elder, Admiral Okada Keisuke. As navy minister (1927–29) and a member of the Supreme

Military Council, he was the most senior naval officer aside from Prince Fushimi. Hailing from Kato's native province of Fukui, Okada was considered the only man to whom he would listen. Okada was ideally qualified as an intercessor and troubleshooter. A man of common sense and great political tact, he knew how to handle the treacherous politics of naval limitation. Fancying himself a "disciple of Kato Tomosaburo," Okada used to say, "I have learned much from Admiral Kato about arms limitation. . . . He could fix the 10:10:6 ratio at the Washington Conference and yet no difficulty arose at home."[133] As early as 17 March, Okada had intimated to Navy Vice Minister Yamanashi, "If unavoidable, we will in the end have to swallow the whole proposal [the Reed-Matsudaira compromise] as it stands. We must not be responsible for breaking up the conference."[134]

In London, Takarabe was caught in the crossfire. He was ever mindful of the violent opposition of Kato and Suetsugu, backed by Fleet Admiral Togo and Prince Fushimi. Also, the naval advisers in London had been urging the view that if Japan doggedly persisted, the United States would retreat.[135] But at the same time, Takarabe as navy minister was responsible for controlling the navy.[136] On 21 March, Vice Minister Yamanashi cabled Takarabe to ascertain what precisely his real views were as navy minister, not as naval delegate. Yamanashi explained that since Kato was "absolutely opposed" to the Reed-Matsudaira compromise, it was "extremely difficult to work out an agreement within the navy."[137] In response, Takarabe warned Tokyo that if the government should decide to accept the Reed-Matsudaira compromise, "this would lead to most serious disturbances in the navy." He added, "Even if the conference breaks up, we can find ways of coping with it."[138] And he opined to Wakatsuki that Japan must "fight to the last" to carry through its demands.[139]

The clash between Wakatsuki and Takarabe reached a climax on 26 March. No longer able to contain their differences, the naval and the head civilian delegates decided to send Tokyo two separate telegrams urging two conflicting policy recommendations. On the one hand, Takarabe assured Yamanashi that if Japan were willing to risk rupture of the conference, there still would be room for negotiating for better terms: "Let us express our determination to withdraw [from the conference] and say that we wish to wait patiently until the time is ripe. If they [the Anglo-American powers] show they are sincere in their wish to conclude a new agreement, we will confront them with our final proposal [salvaging some features of the 'three basic principles']. . . . If we handle it this way, we surely will not have much to fear from the breakdown of the conference."[140] This telegram flatly contradicted—in fact, repudiated—the joint telegram of 15 March, which Takarabe himself had signed. But the naval advisers from Sakonji and Yamamoto on down supported Takarabe.[141]

On the same day, Wakatsuki sent a long telegram to Shidehara. He rejected Takarabe's contention that if only Japan would give one more push, the United States would yield: "If we present a counterproposal to improve our position, we must be prepared to withdraw from the conference in case it should be rejected. [However] Japan could not risk breakup of the conference, which would lead to a naval race it cannot financially withstand."[142] The arrival of the two radically irreconcilable telegrams from Takarabe and Wakatsuki bewildered the government and brought about a major crisis.

The Final Instructions to the Delegates

Prime Minister Hamaguchi and Shidehara were all the more anxious to conclude the treaty without further delay because they knew the United States would expeditiously conclude a bilateral Anglo-American treaty if Japan rejected the compromise plan. Indeed, Stimson had cabled Washington, "Should Tokyo repudiate [the Reed-Matsudaira compromise] the United States would have difficulty in continuing to negotiate. . . . If the so-called counterproposal is sent we will immediately commence preparations of a two-power agreement with Great Britain."[143]

Late March was a tense, incredibly hectic, and climactic time in Tokyo. Confrontational meetings took place between the government and naval leaders. It was now Prime Minister Hamaguchi's turn to make good his professed international vision, courage, and leadership. He and Foreign Minister Shidehara were convinced that "if Japan's harmonious relations with the Anglo-American powers collapsed, the stability of the international political situation would be jeopardized." It would be "extremely dangerous to be overoptimistic about a naval race with the United States."[144] At a meeting with naval leaders on 25 March, Hamaguchi said that the government had decided not to risk breaking up the conference. "Though I lose prime ministership, though I lose my life itself, this decision is unshakable."[145]

On 27 March, Hamaguchi had an audience with Emperor Hirohito, who was twenty-eight years of age. The emperor told the prime minister, "Make every effort to conclude speedily [the London Treaty] in the interest of world peace."[146] On the same day Hamaguchi called Okada, Kato, and Yamanashi to his official residence and explained his decision in detail.[147] Hamaguchi emphatically stated that good relations with the Anglo-American powers far outweighed any conceivable losses from accepting the Reed-Matsudaira compromise. "In the light of America's peculiar national character and conditions," Hamaguchi warned, "it is most dangerous" to take an optimistic view of naval race. He reaffirmed his position that "the question of whether or not to conclude the treaty is a matter that the government, not the chief of Navy General Staff, must decide.[148]

The first of April was a historic day. At long last, the government's final decision was made. At 8:45 in the morning, before the instructions were presented to the cabinet, Hamaguchi met the key naval leaders—Kato, Okada, and Yamanashi—in order to obtain the navy's consent.[149] Hamaguchi stated that "from the military, diplomatic, and financial angles," he had decided to conclude the treaty. He believed that world peace rested on a good relationship among Japan, Britain, and the United States. "If Japan should break up this relationship and place itself in isolation to the detriment international relationship, Japan would find itself in an unspeakable predicament in the world."[150]

Speaking for the navy, Okada responded that if the government had decided to send the final instructions to London, the navy accepted it as inevitable and would "do everything in its power to devise a means of adjusting to the decision." At this point, Kato interjected, "From a strategic viewpoint, there are difficulties."[151] But he did not unequivocally oppose the draft instruction, as he later insisted he had. On the contrary, at the meeting he gave the impression that he passively acquiesced in them.[152]

In London, even at this late hour, Takarabe, under strong pressure from his advisers, still vacillated. Wakatsuki had warned Shidehara that Takarabe had difficulty in deciding his view because he was swayed by his hard-line advisers, who insisted that "one final thrust" would wrench concessions from the United States.[153] Even as the government's "final instructions" were being cabled, Navy Vice Minister Yamanashi was deeply worried as to whether Takarabe would faithfully follow the instructions. So he sent an extraordinary telegram urging on his chief the "utmost prudence" and "circumspection":[154]

> It is feared that in the event that you should take actions at odds with Wakatsuki, they will divide our delegation in London to the detriment of its negotiating power, and at home such actions will cause grave political difficulties, driving the navy into a most inimical and self-damaging predicament. Furthermore, such a situation will bring about most serious consequences to the future of our Empire. I earnestly beg you to act from the standpoint of the

overall interest of the nation. I implore you to prudently bear with these difficulties and fulfill your duty as a delegate.[155]

This finally put a stop to Takarabe's indecision. In his reply he pledged, "I will
not err with respect to the great work of the nation by reckless insistence on my
own narrow views. I will refrain from behavior that might create difficulties
for the future."[156] In his diary, Takarabe wrote that he was "overwhelmed with
shame."[157] At last, he had come around to accepting the treaty.

Tokyo's instructions, arriving in London on 1 April, produced an uproar
among the naval representatives. Some were moved to tears. Younger staff
officers denounced Wakatsuki and plotted to storm Takarabe's suite in the
Grosvenor Hotel. On their behalf, Yamamoto rushed to Takarabe's suite to convey their overheated views. However, Yamamoto himself was not immune to
the uproar. He felt that "the government, unmindful of the distress of the naval
authorities and disregarding the navy minister's views, sent a telegraph that the
navy could hardly consent [to]. Tokyo's decision caused great indignation and
disappointment among all the naval members." He continued: "It came as a
shock to the entire navy and will have an adverse effect on its morale."[158]

When the representative of the finance ministry, Kaya Okinori, supported the government instructions, Yamamoto thundered, "Say another word,
Kaya, you will get a smack in the face!" That night the naval aides gathered
in Yamamoto's room and had an all-night session, vehemently denouncing the
instructions "as if they were demented."[159] Indeed, such was their excitement
that they forgot themselves and gave a bloody nose to a civilian member of
the delegation.[160]

On 2 April, Yamamoto admonished his subordinates "not to commit a
breach of service discipline," but he contradicted his own order when in fire-eat-
ing words he demanded that Takarabe take responsibility by resigning at once:
"The last and the only way left for you as the navy minister to preserve honor
after this defeat at the conference is for you to resign in protest as befits the occasion to prove to the Japanese people that 'the navy has not betrayed their trust.'"[161]
Several days later, Yamamoto went against the government's final instructions,
urging Takarabe to demand the raising of submarine strength to 65,000 tons.
Taking this opportunity, Yamamoto warned Takarabe that acceptance of the
Reed-Matsudaira compromise would "greatly shock our entire navy, destroy its
morale, and bring about some untoward incidents that would have grave consequences on Japan's domestic and external policies."[162] This ominous warning was
to be fulfilled in the tumultuous aftermath of the conference.

British prime minister Ramsay MacDonald (left) and U.S. president Herbert
Hoover, in Washington, D.C., 5 October 1929. The two leaders were determined
not to allow naval special interests to impede an arms-control agreement.
The final obstacles to an Anglo-American accord were worked out during
MacDonald's visit to the U.S. in the autumn of 1929. *Library of Congress*

Japanese delegates arrive in London. L–R: Matsudaira Tsuneo, Wakatsuki Reijiro, Admiral Takarabe Takeshi. *National Digital Archives, Poland*

French delegates arrive in London. L–R: Vice Admiral Louis-Hippolyte Violette, Jacques-Louis Dumesnil, and Aristide Briand, with British foreign secretary Arthur Henderson. *National Digital Archives, Poland*

The Italian delegation giving the fascist salute at the Cenotaph in Whitehall. *National Digital Archives, Poland*

Delegates meeting informally in the garden of 10 Downing Street. L–R: Italian foreign minister Count Dino Grandi, Secretary of State Henry Stimson, French foreign minister Aristide Briand, British prime minister Ramsay MacDonald, and French prime minister André Tardieu. *National Digital Archives, Poland*

Henry Stimson (foreground) and other delegates addressing journalists and newsreel cameras in the garden at 10 Downing Street. In the background, L–R: Wakatsuki Reijiro, Dino Grandi, Ramsay MacDonald, Aristide Briand, André Tardieu, James Ralston (Canada), Timothy Smiddy (Ireland), Atul Chatterjee (India). *National Digital Archives, Poland*

Sir Robert Craigie, the head of the American section at the British Foreign Office, was MacDonald's chief adviser on naval arms control. He later served as British ambassador to Japan, 1937–1941. *Library of Congress*

Britain's King George V opening the Naval Conference in the Royal Gallery in the House of Lords, London, 21 January 1930. His speech was broadcast worldwide. *National Digital Archives, Poland*

British prime minister Ramsay MacDonald makes the opening speech at the conference. *National Digital Archives, Poland*

Banquet given by the Lord Mayor of London (William Waterlow, center) in honor of the Naval Conference participants. Head table, L–R: German ambassador Friedrich Sthamer, Archbishop of Canterbury Cosmo Gordon Lang, Ramsay MacDonald, André Tardieu, Waterlow, Spanish ambassador Alfonso Merry del Val, Dino Grandi, Cardinal Francis Bourne, Henry Stimson, Lord Chancellor John Sankey, Aristide Briand. *National Digital Archives, Poland*

Delegates photographed on the grounds of St. James Palace prior to signing the treaty, 22 April 1930. *National Digital Archives, Poland*

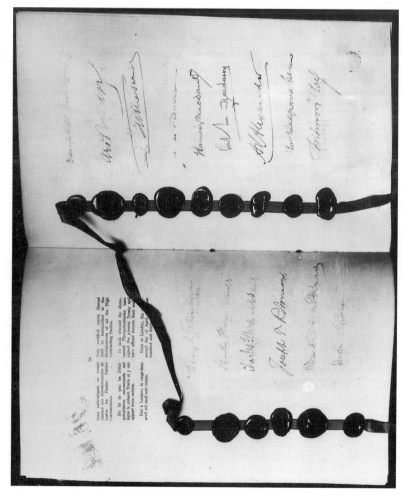

The final pages of the treaty. *National Digital Archives, Poland*

Northampton (CL 26) on a full-power speed trial in Penobscot Bay, near Rockland, Maine, on 17 April 1930. The fast *Northampton* class of six light cruisers—reclassified as heavy cruisers in 1931—easily met the displacement requirements set by the treaty regime. They incorporated a main battery of three turrets with three 8-inch guns each, two turrets forward and one aft, which became the standard arrangement in subsequent classes of U.S. heavy cruisers. *U.S. Naval Institute Photo Archive*

Louisville (CL 28), the third unit of the *Northampton* class, is fitting out at Puget Sound Navy Yard, Washington, on 27 August 1930. The ship was commissioned in January 1931. The graceful lines of the "clipper bow," an improvement introduced by the Navy in battleships some fifteen years earlier, are evident.

U.S. Naval Institute Photo Archive

USS *Houston* (CA 30) at Shanghai in 1933. After Japan invaded Manchuria in 1931, *Houston*, in duty typically performed by such warships during peacetime, was dispatched to China to protect U.S. interests. The interwar heavy cruisers were lightly armored, and three of the *Northampton* class, including *Houston*, succumbed to damage caused by Japanese torpedoes during the Pacific War.

U.S. Naval Institute Photo Archive

USS *Pensacola* (CL 24) photographed from the Manhattan Bridge on 6 March 1930, as the new cruiser steamed from New York City to begin a series of speed, stability, and gun tests. Owing to their high speed, the interwar heavy cruisers proved to be suitable escorts for the fast aircraft carriers during the Pacific War. *U.S. Naval Institute Photo Archive*

In Tokyo, a depressed Kato wrote in his diary, "I have been agonizing days and nights; there are moments when I feel like committing suicide. Yet I must pluck up my courage."[163] Hearing about Kato's intent, Okada sarcastically observed, "Those who go around telling people about committing hara-kiri seldom do."[164] On 2 April, Kato went to the palace and submitted his memorial to the Throne. He stated that as the chief of the Navy General Staff, solely responsible for national defense, he could not concur with the government's final instructions: "They would create serious operational deficiencies and would necessitate major changes in the Imperial Defense Policy [of 1923]."[165] The rupture between the Navy General Staff and the Navy Ministry (and also the government) was now complete.

On 22 April 1930, the London Treaty was signed at the Court of St. James's, but a major domestic crisis in Tokyo was ahead. Public reception of the London Treaty in Japan was overwhelmingly favorable, in contrast to that among the majority of naval men. When the delegates arrived at the Tokyo Station on 19 June, an enthusiastic crowd greeted them with deafening shouts of "Banzai!" Yamamoto was so astounded that he began to reconsider his hawkish position and soon would join his friend Hori as a staunch supporter of naval limitation.

The Tragic Consequences of the London Treaty

At the meeting of 1 April, Kato, far from objecting to the final instructions, had implicitly acquiesced. Suddenly, on 21 April, the opposition party tried to overthrow the government by attacking the London Treaty. A major domestic turmoil erupted. The issue revolved around article 12 of the constitution, which stipulated that the organization and peacetime standing of military forces were "imperial prerogatives."[166] The conventional interpretation held that these matters rested with the navy minister. But the Navy General Staff violently objected, ruling that any decision relating to the size of armaments rested with the high command. Soon Kato jumped on the bandwagon, claiming that the "right of supreme command" had been infringed upon when the Hamaguchi government decided on its final instructions to London without his consent. The resulting controversy shook the entire nation. The first victim was Prime Minister Hamaguchi, who was shot on 30 November by a crazed ultranationalist youth disgruntled with the treaty. The prime minister was to die of the wound on 26 August the following year—the first of political assassinations that was to occur in the 1930s.

As the result of the London Treaty embroilment, the navy, which had hitherto prided itself on internal unity and harmony, became violently split into two
hostile groups: the "fleet faction," led by Kato, which opposed the treaty, and the
"treaty faction," which supported it. One highly placed officer observed, "When
we go to the navy ministry, they deride the Navy General Staff as demented and
when we go to the Navy General Staff, they call the navy ministry traitors."[167]
The internecine struggle was to last through the 1930s.

The London Treaty was doomed to be short-lived. Emperor Hirohito, sur-
mising the navy's intent, tried to obtain an assurance that the navy "would not
bind its position at the next conference scheduled for 1936." This caveat notwithstanding, the Supreme Military Council replied to the Throne on 23 July,
"It will be most disadvantageous from the viewpoint of national defense to be
compromised by this treaty. We must complete our naval defense immediately
upon expiration of this treaty."[168] The navy thus made clear that it would oppose
continuation of the London Treaty after 1936.

Just as the majority in the navy's leadership had suffered from an acute
case of PTSD relative to the Washington Treaty, so was it afflicted by this syndrome in the aftermath of the London Conference. Kato, who resigned in
protest as chief of the Navy General Staff, retained his influence as a vocal
member of the Supreme Military Council. He operated behind the scenes
to strengthen the "fleet faction" and undermine the London Treaty. The first
step was to install the hawkish Prince Fushimi in the high place as chief of
the Navy General Staff in February 1932. This appointment decisively strengthened the fleet faction. Fushimi was to remain in that position until April 1941,
pursuing hard-line policies that would lead to Pearl Harbor in December 1941.
As the second step, in 1933 Fushimi ordered Navy Minister Osumi Mineo, an
opponent of naval limitation, to revise the Navy General Staff regulations to
establish its primacy over the Navy Ministry, especially regarding decisions on
armaments. As a distinguished naval historian Nomura Minoru has remarked,
this revision was "an important milestone on the navy's road to the war with
the United States."[169]

The third step to decimate the treaty faction and strengthen the fleet faction was the so-called Osumi purge, engineered behind the scenes by Prince
Fushimi and Kato. During 1933–34, senior officers who had worked for and
supported the Washington and London Treaties were systematically cashiered
from the navy. Among the victims were some of its ablest leaders, most notably Yamanashi and Hori.[170] Yamanashi was reputed to be future commander
in chief of the Combined Fleet. Yamamoto Isoroku, then attending the

preliminary naval talks in London, was so mortified at the loss to the navy of his friend Hori that he called it more costly than that of a division of cruisers would be.[171]

By 1933–34 the navy, deciding that it must no longer be fettered by the "humiliating treaties" of Washington and London, came out for their abrogation and in October 1934 demanded that parity be sought at the forthcoming London naval talks. Kato Kanji was the most outspoken advocate of this view.[172] Emperor Hirohito, highly skeptical of the parity demand, told Prince Fushimi that it would only kindle a naval race.[173] But the Osumi purge had made such a clean sweep of the treaty faction that few voices of caution remained. London naval talks in 1934 failed, although Japan's representative Yamamoto Isoroku, now a supporter of naval limitation, tried his best to avoid a breakup. In December 1934, the Japanese government notified Secretary of State Cordell Hull of its unilateral abrogation of the Washington Treaty. At the Second London Conference, in 1935–36, the navy inflexibly insisted on "the common upper limit" (parity). Predictably, the conference broke up, when on 15 January 1936 the Japanese delegation walked out, thus nullifying the interwar achievements in naval limitation.[174] This signaled the resumption of naval race, which some Japanese officers would later feel constituted a major proximate cause of the Pacific War.

American Perceptions of the Japanese Situation

To turn to the U.S. Navy, one could, again, note a mirror image. Its naval officers were as opposed to the London Treaty as their Japanese counterparts were—for precisely opposite reasons. American naval men were convinced that Japan had obtained concessions that "made it practically impossible for the United States to support its policies in the Far East." The benefit already accruing to Japan from the Washington Treaty was now "tilted farther to her advantage."[175] The U.S. Navy's General Board held that Japan at London had obtained "indisputable naval supremacy in the western Pacific" and "the absolute dictation in the affairs in the western Pacific."[176]

However, American foreign policy leaders did not share the navy's Mahanian views. Adhering to their traditional Far Eastern policy, Secretary of State Stimson (America's head delegate) dismissed as a "fantastic fear" the admirals' talk about war with Japan, because he knew that no force lay behind the Open Door policy. Ambassador William Castle, sympathetic to Japan, wrote, "Japan believes—not the government perhaps—that we are building our navy with the thought in mind that we shall have to fight Japan on account of China." On 25 January 1930, he urged Washington to make Japan "understand that we have no plans in regard to China which might conceivably lead to war."[177] Of course, no such assurance was made, and Japanese naval officers continued to listen nervously to American admirals' war talk. Ambassador Castle reported that "the Japanese navy, public, and the mass media believe that we are building our navy with the thought in mind that we shall have to fight Japan on account of China." Castle emphatically told Japanese Foreign Ministry officials, "I could conceive of no circumstances in which America would go to war with Japan over China."[178]

The U.S. government complacently expected that the London Treaty would bring about rapprochement with Japan based on cooperation with its moderate-liberal leaders. During the London negotiations, Stimson had become aware of the internal struggle going on between the pro-treaty and anti-treaty forces. He perceived "a real controversy between Japanese civil government and the naval party there." But he honestly believed that the United States was making substantial concessions to Japan, with an eye to supporting the moderate-liberal forces represented by Hamaguchi, Wakatsuki, and Shidehara— men whom he hoped would restrain Japan's rabid navalists. He wrote President Hoover on 17 February 1930 that "the Japanese Delegation is hampered by political conditions at home of a very serious character. . . . I feel it would be unwise to do anything which would weaken Wakatsuki's independent power in the meanwhile."[179] Just as Theodore Roosevelt three decades earlier found in Japan a stabilizing factor in East Asia, so did Stimson, stating at a meeting of the head American, British, and Japanese delegates in London that he regarded Japan as "a great stabilizing force in the Far East, and such an existence was to the advantage of the United States." He further said, "Since Japan is in a position to make the Orientals understand the Western civilization in the Far East, we have nothing to worry about Japan's superior position in the Far East; rather we believe it is to our advantage."[180]

Reed, the coauthor of the Reed-Matsudaira compromise, went even farther: "The United States fully understands that Japan, in possession of certain naval force, is the protector of peace in the Far East, just as the United States plays the same role in the Western Hemisphere."[181] The United States had sent troops into Nicaragua, Haiti, the Dominican Republic, and Panama. President Herbert Hoover, pro-Japanese and anti-Bolshevik, expressed himself as in sympathy with the view that "Japan is our first line of defense in the Far East; and I am certainly glad they are fairly well armed."[182] Contrary to his

Mahanian colleagues, Admiral William V. Pratt—Commander in Chief, U.S. Fleet, and a veteran of the Washington and London Conferences, and friendly to Japan—even declared, "The London Treaty has been the most potent factor in eliminating friction between ourselves and Japan. . . . It may be said, with assurance, that in the course of a few years the mistrust, lack of confidence and suspicion will be partially allayed through the medium of treaties for limitation of competitive armaments."[183]

However, neither Stimson, Hoover, nor Admiral Pratt could fathom the depth of the resentment harbored by most Japanese navy men. Nor did these American leaders understand the seriousness of the dissention that was wracking Japan. Stimson later wrote in his memoirs that "the essential difficulty was one of Japanese pride, which had been seriously offended by the Washington ratio of ten-ten-six."[184] But the domestic turbulence caused by the London Treaty went much farther than mere wounded pride. The American delegates failed to see its long-term implications in Japan. Stimson and company never realized that the aftermath of the conference would fatally weaken Japan's moderate leaders committed to the Washington-London system of naval limitation. Actually, Stimson's greatest preoccupation in London was the betterment of Anglo-American relations. Stimson had closed the London Conference with the roseate prediction that the treaty established America's naval relationship with "our good neighbor across the Pacific and [that it] insures the continuous growth of our friendship with that great nation toward whom we have grown to look for stability and progress in the Far East."[185] Robert Ferrell remarks, "No one saw into the future, and it was possible to believe with Stimson and his contemporaries that the London Conference helped secure world peace, reinforcing the treaties of 1921–22."[186]

Success or Failure?

Most American historians have assessed the London Conference as "a partial success." But in light of its aftereffects (the PTSD syndrome) in Japan and their impact on Japanese-American relations, the conclusion is unavoidable that as far as the Japanese navy (and also Japanese-American relations) was concerned, the conference spelled a tragedy, marking a significant milestone on the road to Pearl Harbor.

Recently, it has become fashionable, especially among American political scientists, to argue that the London Conference failed because the Anglo-Saxon powers did not address themselves to "political sources of instability" in

East Asia and instead confined themselves to narrowly "military-based strategies of arms control." For example, Emily O. Goldman contends, from a post–Cold War perspective, that although Japan accepted an unpopular compromise at London, it received "no political compensations" and the conference "failed to address" Japanese fears about a unified Nationalist China.[187] In arguing this way she follows political theorists, like Hedley Bull, who argue that "arms control systems depend for their survival on the continuance of those wider areas of political agreement of which they are a part."[188]

The theory is only partially applicable to London naval limitation. The Washington Conference succeeded because it was a part and parcel of "the Washington system," a cooperative framework that defined naval, political, and economic relations among Japan, the United States, and Great Britain in East Asia and the Pacific.[189] This does explain the success of the Washington Conference, the only naval gathering to succeed between the wars, but it assuredly does not explain the "failure" of the London Conference. As Tokyo and Japan clearly realized, introducing political issues, be they China or the Immigration Act of 1924 (otherwise known as the Japanese Exclusion Act), would have only complicated the negotiations.[190] Neither was an outstanding issue at that time.

The Washington Conference had dispelled an acute war scare preceding it between the United States and Japan, but no such nightmare existed before the London Conference. For example, in September 1929 Ambassador Debuchi telegraphed to Tokyo that "today relations are in a very excellent shape. Past misunderstandings about China are almost gone."[191] Ambassador Castle too wired Washington: "Both countries wanted a China which was substantially and politically sound." He said that there was "no quarrel on the subject of China and that I foresee none in the future." He explained that there had been "a radical change in Japanese policy toward China and it is clearly recognized that friendly assistance must be the basis for their relations." In his reply, Acing Secretary of State Joseph Cotton agreed that "it is also the desire of Japan to see China achieve economic and political stability."[192] Neither Japan nor the United States attempted to treat the issue of naval limitation in the broader political context, because they perceived no serious bilateral differences aside from the Immigration Act, and neither country saw the London Conference as a fitting occasion for raising this issue.[193]

No study of interwar attempts at naval limitation can leave out the conflict within the most dynamic and volatile actor, the Imperial Japanese Navy. In 1933, Prime Minister and Admiral Saito Makoto (Kato Tomosaburo's former superior and navy minister in 1912–14) said, "The present commotions have their roots in Admiral Kato Kanji's antipathy toward [the policy of] Admiral Kato Tomosaburo, the chief delegate at the Washington."[194] No one was better qualified to make this statement. The study of the Japanese and American navies and their roles in naval limitation between the wars must go back to the revolt against the Washington Treaty, personified by Kato Kanji.[195]

NOTES

1. Individual Japanese names are given in the usual Japanese order—that is, the family name preceding the given name, except for my name when publishing abroad. A superb survey of Japanese naval history is provided by Mark R. Peattie and David C. Evans, "Japan," in *Ubi Sumus? The State of Naval and Maritime History,* ed. John B. Hattendorf (Newport, R.I.: Naval War College Press, 1994), 213–21.

2. There is only one Japanese monograph: Kobayashi Tatsuo, "Kaigun gunshuku joyaku (1921–1936)," in *Taiheiyo senso e no michi* (Asahi Shimbunsha, 1963). Its English translation is contained in James Morley, ed., *Japan Erupts: The London Naval Conference and the Manchurian Incident, 1928–1932* (New York: Columbia University Press, 1984).

3. The 259 volumes of naval records relating to the three interwar naval conferences were preserved by Enomoto Juji, who participated in all of them as a senior counselor to the Navy Ministry and a specialist in naval limitation. His papers are now deposited at the National Institute of Defense Studies, Defense Ministry of Japan, Tokyo [hereafter NIDS]. A smaller but extremely valuable collection left by Vice Admiral Hori Teikichi, mostly on the London Conference, are deposited at the library of the National Maritime Self-Defense Staff College [hereafter cited as MSDSC]. Since I examined them some thirty-five years ago, they have been closed; only portions of them have been photo-copied and are available at the NIDS.

4. The present chapter is based on materials used for chapters 4–6 of my study *From Mahan to Pearl Harbor: The Imperial Japanese Navy and the United States* (Annapolis, Md.: Naval Institute Press, 2006). See also my "From Washington to London: Imperial Japanese Navy and the Politics of Naval Limitation, 1921–30," in *The Washington Conference, 1921–22: Naval Rivalry, East Asian Stability and the Road to Pearl Harbor,* ed. Erik Goldstein and John Maurer (London: Frank Cass, 1994). The quotation is from Walter LaFeber, *The Clash: U.S.-Japanese Relations throughout History* (New York: W. W. Norton, 1997), 157.

5. Stephen E. Pelz, *Race to Pearl Harbor: The Failure of the Second London Naval Conference and the Onset of World War II* (Cambridge, Mass.: Harvard University Press, 1974).

6. Ito Masanori, *Dai kaigun o omou* (Bungei Shunju, 1956), 365. (The place of publication for all Japanese-language sources, unless otherwise noted, is Tokyo.)

7. See Sadao Asada, *From Mahan to Pearl Harbor: The Imperial Japanese Navy and the United States* (Annapolis, Md.: Naval Institute Press, 2006), 69.

8. See ibid., 73–84. A theoretical and comparative analysis of Kato Tomosaburo's leadership appears in Asada, "Washington Kaigi o meguru Nichi-Bei no seikaku kettei katei no hikaku," in *Taigai seisaku kettei katei no Nichi-Bei hikakku*, ed. Hosoya Chihiro and Watanuku Joji (Tokyo Daigaku Shuppakai, 1977), 444–51.

9. Kato's thoughts on naval limitation and philosophy of national defense were articulated in the now famous "Kato's message" to Navy Vice Minister Ide Kenji. Its full text is printed in Ooita kenritsu Sentetsu Shiryokan, ed., *Hori Teikichi shiryoshu* (documents) (Ooitaken kyoiku iinkai, 2006), I:68–77.

10. Correctly, his name was Hiroharu, but popularly he went by Kanji. Kato Kanji to navy vice minister and chief of the Naval General Staff [NGS], 4 December 1921 (no. 52), strictly confidential; 4 December 1921 (no. 53), NIDS. Unless noted otherwise, all the naval telegrams are deposited at NIDS.

11. For comparison of the two Katos regarding their personalities, career backgrounds, and views on naval limitation, see my "Japanese Admirals and the Politics of Naval Limitation: Kato Tomosaburo and Kato Kanji," in *Naval Warfare in the Twentieth Century*, ed. Jerald Jordan (London: Croom Helm, 1977), 141–66.

12. Mori Shozo, *Senpu 20-nen* (Kojinsha, 1968), 50; Ito Takashi et al., eds., *Zoku gendaishi shiryo (5): Kaigun (Kato Kanji nikki)* (Misuzu Shobo, 1994), 49.

13. For the Japanese navy's opposition of the Washington Treaty, see my "Revolt against the Washington Treaty: The Imperial Japanese Navy and Naval Limitation, 1921–1927," *Naval War College Review* 46, no. 3 (Summer 1993), 82–97.

14. For the emergence of the "Washington system," see my "Old Diplomacy and the New: The Washington System and Origins of Japanese-American Rapprochement, 1918–1922," *Diplomatic History* 30 (April 2006).

15. The document is fully quoted in Shimanuki Takeji, "Daiichiji sekai taisen igo no kokubo hoshin, shiryo heiryoku, yohei koryo no hensen," *Gunji shigaku* 9 (June 1973), 65–74. Previously, in the Imperial National Defense Policy of 1907, the United States had been designated as the navy's hypothetical enemy.

16. Kido nikku kenkyukai, ed., *Kido Koichi kankei bunsho* (Tokyo Daigaku Shuppankai, 1966) 1:263–66.

17. Kato Kanji, "Rondon Kaigun Joyaku hiroku" [The Secret Record about the London Naval Treaty], in *Eiketsu Kato Kanji*, ed. Sakai Keinan (Noberu Shobo, 1983) [hereafter cited as Kato Kanji hiroku], 143.

18. Yamanashi Katsunoshin, *Rekishi to meisho* (Mainichi Shinbunsha, 1981), 169 (memoir); *Hori Teikichi shiryoshu*, 1:100–101, 170. Admiral Suzuki Kantaro later (when he was chief of the Navy General Staff, April 1925–January 1930) told Yamanashi that there was no such thing as the "three basic principles."

19. The "three basic principles" are printed in Gaimusho [the foreign ministry, hereafter cited as JMFA], *Nihon gaiko bunsho: 1930 Rondon Kaigun Kaigi* [Documents on Japanese Foreign Policy: London Naval Conference]) (1984) [hereafter cited as NGB, *Rondon Kaigun Kaigi*], 1:106–9.

20. Raymond G. O'Connor, *Perilous Equilibrium: The United States and the London Naval Conference* (Lawrence: University of Kansas Press, 1962), 53.

21. Harold Sprout and Margaret Sprout, *Toward a New Order of Sea Power: American Naval Policy and the World Scene, 1918–1922* (Minnetonka, Minn.: Olympic, 1946), 102–103; Hedley Bull, "The Objectives of Arms Control," in *The Use of Force*, ed. Robert J. Art and Kenneth N. Waltz (Boston: Little, Brown), 357.

22. Glenn H. Snyder and Paul Diesing, *Conflict among Nations* (Princeton, N.J.: Princeton University Press, 1977), 29.

23. Boeicho Senshishitsu [War History Office, Defense Agency], ed., *Senshi sosho, Daihon'ei kaigunbu: Rengo Kantai* (Asakumo Shinbunsha, 1975), 1:156–59 [hereafter cited as *Rengo Kantai*]; Nomura Minoru, "Tai-Bei-Ei kaisen to kaigun no tai-Bei 7 wari shiso," *Gunji shigaku* 9, no. 3 (1973), 26.

24. Kato Kanji to Makino Nobuaki, 29 January 1930, Makino Papers, National Diet Library, Tokyo [hereafter cited as DL].

25. Edward S. Miller, *War Plan Orange* (Annapolis, Md.: Naval Institute Press, 1991), 32–35, indicates that there were debates about alternative routes. Robert E. Love, *History of the U.S. Navy*, vol. 1, *1775–1941* (Harrisburg, Pa.: Stackpole Books, 1992), 529.

26. The Japanese navy's "Annual Operational Plan" of 1926 estimated that the main fleet encounter would take place about forty-five days after the outbreak of hostilities. This estimate remained the same until 1939.

27. The Japanese navy estimated that most likely the U.S. fleet would advance along the "central route," through the Marshalls, Guam, the Carolines, then on to the Philippines. William Reynolds Braisted, "On the United States Navy's Operational Outlook in the Pacific, 1919–1931" (paper presented to the

Conference on Japanese-American Relations, 1918–1931, Kauai Island, Hawaii, 5–9 January 1976).

28. Kato Kanji's memo, "Gunshuku shoken" [My Views on Naval Limitation], January 1930, Saito Makoto Papers, DL. (The titles of particularly important naval documents are translated.).

29. Office of the Chief of Naval Operations, "Strategic Survey of the Pacific," 10 May 1923; Joint Board, "Estimate of the Orange Situation Joint Army and Navy," 25 May 1923; Joint Board, "Estimates of the Orange Situation," 7 July1923; Joint Board, "Estimates of the Orange Situation," 15 August 1924; all National Archives and Records Administration (NARA), Washington, D.C.

30. *Rengo Kantai,* 175–76, 201.

31. The U.S. capability for building submarines was estimated at twice that of Japan, for cruisers ten times. Fukui Shizuo, *Nihon no gunkan* (Shuppan Kyodosha, 1956), 230.

32. Kato Kanji, "Gunshuku shoken."

33. For Mahan on naval strategy and its influence on the Japanese navy, see Asada, *From Mahan to Pearl Harbor,* chaps. 1, 2.

34. Operations Division, memorandum on the power of ten-thousand-ton, 8-inch-gun cruisers, 1 December 1929, BBKS; "The Value of 10,000-Ton Cruisers and the Need to Secure 70 Percent Ratio," Saito Makoto Papers, DL; Kaigun Daijin Kanbo, ed. *Kaigun gunbi enkaku* (reprint Gannando, 1979), 162, 177.

35. Ernest Andrede Jr., "The Cruiser Controversy in Naval Limitations Negotiation, 1922–1936," *Military Affairs* 48, no. 3 (July 1984), 114, 117.

36. Gerald Wheeler, *Prelude to Pearl Harbor: The United States Navy and the Far East, 1921–1931* (Columbia: University of Missouri Press, 1963), 174.

37. Navy General Staff (Kato Kanji), "Kojutsu oboegaki," top secret, n.d. [1930], BBKS.

38. Kato Kanji to Makino, 29 January 1930, Makino Papers.

39. BBKS, *Rengo Kantai,* 1:218.

40. Dave Evans and Mark Peattie, *Kaigun* (Annapolis, Md.: Naval Institute Press, 1997), 214–15.

41. These submarines could cruise for 24,000 miles without refueling.

42. Kaigun Rekishi Hozonkai, ed., *Nihon kaigun rekishi* (Daiichi Hoki Shuppan, 1995), 3:152–53.

43. It is ironic that when it came to the actual test in the Pacific War, the performance of Japanese submarines was deplorable; they did not sink even a single American battleship. In contrast, the U.S. submarine force was amazingly

effective throughout the war. Carl Boyd and Akihiko Yoshida, *The Japanese Submarine Force and World War II* (Annapolis, Md.: Naval Institute Press, 1995), 158, 179, 183, 189.

44. Gunbi Seigen Kenkyu Iinkai, "A Study of a Second Arms Limitation Conference," 18 February 1925, BBKS. The "never-again" phenomenon is analyzed in Snyder and Diesing, *Conflict among Nations*, 189.

45. Kato to Makino Nobuaki, 29 January 1930, Makino Papers.

46. Kato Kanji Taisho Denki Hensankai (eds), *Kato Kanji Taisho den* (Tokyo: Kato Kanji taisho denki hensankai, 1941), 750.

47. Yamanashi, *Rekishi to meisho*, 141; Harada Kumao, *Saionjiko to seikyoku* (Iwanami Shoten, 1950), 1:9.

48. U.S. Embassy (Tokyo) to Stimson, 22 October 1929, confidential, *FRUS 1930*, 1:24; NGB, 1930 *Rondon Kaigun Kaigi*, 2:151.

49. Harada, *Saionjiko to seikyoku*, 1:33, 151.

50. Kato Kanji Taisho den, 890–92, 747–50.

51. *Zoku gendaishi shiryo*, vol. 5, *Kaigun: Kato Kanji nikki* (Misuzu Shobo, 1994) [hereafter cited as *Kato Kanji nikki* (Kato Kanji's diary)], 540.

52. Ibid., 890.

53. Ibid., 749–50.

54. Ibid., 756–57.

55. Director of Naval Intelligence, memorandum for Chief of Naval Operations, 11 October 1921, NARA.

56. "Kahu Kaigi go ni okeru Beikoku no gunbi" [U.S. Armaments since the Washington Conference], 14 December 1929, presented by Kato Kanji to Saito Makoto, Saito Papers, DL; Ikeda Kiyoshi, "Rondon kaigun joyaku ni kansuru Gunreibu gawa no shiryo 3-pen," *Osaka Shiritsu Daigaku, Hogaku zasshi* 13 (December 1968), 103–104.

57. Kato Kanji Taisho den, 823–34, 831; Kato Kanji's memo, "Gunshuku shoken"; *Kato Kanji nikki*, 464–65.

58. Navy General Staff (Kato Kanji), "Kojutsu oboegaki."

59. For Mahanian determinism, see my *From Mahan to Pearl Harbor*, 38–41 and passim.

60. Navy Minister's secretariat, ed., *Kaigun gunbi enkaku*, 220.

61. *Kato Kanji nikki*, 465.

62. Telegrams to attaches in Washington and London, 25 July 1929.

63. Kato Kanji hiroku, 142–44.

64. Ibid., 145–47.

65. Matsudaira to Shidehara, 30 August, 1929, strictly confidential; Shidehara to Matsudaira, 16 September 1929, confidential, JMFA.

66. Matsudaira to Shidehara, 11 December, 1929, JMFA; NGB, *Rondon Kaigun Kaigi,* 1:325.

67. Wakatsuki (London) to Shidehara, 14 January 1930, JMFA; State Department to Castle, 26 December 1929, USFR, 1929, 1:307–10.

68. Morley, *Japan Erupts,* 9.

69. Wakatsuki Reijiro, *Kofuan kaikoroku* (Tokyo, 1950), 262–63, 334–35; Yamanashi Katsunoshin sensei ihoroku (Tokyo: Suikokai, 1968), 122; Harada, *Saionjiko to seikyoku,* 1:19.

70. Wakatsuki, *Kofuan kaikoroku,* 263.

71. Ko-Matsudaira Tsuneo tsuioku Kai, ed., *Matsudaira Tsuneeo tsuiokushu* (Editor, 1961).

72. Ibid., 530–32. The other delegate, the ambassador to Belgium, Nagai Matsuzo, played no role in the Japanese-American naval negotiations.

73. Okada Keisuke, *Okada Keisuke kaikoroku* (Mainichi Shinbunsha, 1977), 44.

74. Enomoto Shigeharu, interview, August 1975.

75. Hiroyuki Agawa, *The Reluctant Admiral: Yamamoto and the Imperial Navy,* trans. John Bester (Tokyo: Kodansha International, 1979), 20, 32–33.

76. American Embassy (Tokyo) to Stimson, 9 November 1929, 500/17/1844, Papers of Henry L. Stimson, Yale University Library (microfilm).

77. Harada, *Saionjiko to seikyoku,* 1:63; Enomoto Juji, interview, August 1975.

78. Okada, *Okada Keisuke kaikoroku,* 47; Harada, *Saionjiko to seikyoku,* 1:63.

79. Yamanashi ihoroku, 129; Wakatsuki, *Kofuan kaikoroku,* 365.

80. Report of Naval Attache in Tokyo, 10 October 1921, RG 45 QY-Japanese, ONI Reg. 14746-B c-10–1, NARA.

81. See Asada, *From Mahan to Pearl Harbor,* 135.

82. Hori, Memo on the London Conference and the right of the supreme command, 11 July 1946; Ito Takashi, Showa shoki seijishi kenkyu (Tokyo Daigaku Shuppankai, 1969), 141; Harada, *Saionjiko to seikyoku,* 1:62.

83. Takarabe diary, entry of 25 January 1930; Sakonji, "Report on the 1930 London Naval Conference [hereafter cited as Sakonji report], JDA, 1, 22, 41–42. This revealing report was a day-to-day record of the naval advisers. Although the report was considerably toned down by Kobayashi, it was never submitted to the higher naval authorities, for fear of aggravating "domestic political unrest" by inflaming the controversy over the London Treaty and complications within the navy. The Sakonji report is supplemented by Capt. Nakamura Kamesaburo's "Report on Circumstances Leading to Request for the Final

Instructions from the Government" [hereafter cited as Nakamura report], 25 January 1930.

84. Wakatsuki and Matsudaira to Shidehara, 20 February 1930, JMFA.

85. Shidehara to Matsudaira, 21 February 1930, JMFA.

86. Matsudaira to Shidehara, 24 March 1930, JMFA; Takarabe diary (entry of 4 March 1930); Koga Mine'ichi diary, entry of 6 March 1930, Hori Papers.

87. Sakonji report, 31, 34–35.

88. Ibid., 28, 34–35.

89. Ikei Suguru, Hatano Masaru, and Kurosawa Fumitaka, eds., *Hamaguchi Osachi: Nikki, ziusoroku* (Misuzu shobo, 1991) [diary], entry of 7 February, 207.

90. Kato Kanji hiroku, 152.

91. Yamamoto's oral proposal to Wakatsuki, 10 March 1930; Abe to Kato, 6 March 1930, Kato Papers.

92. NGB, *Rondon Kaigun Kaigi,* 2:102.

93. For the Geneva Conference of 1927, see Asada, *From Mahan to Pearl Harbor,* 111–23.

94. NGB, Rondon Kagun Kaigi keika gaiyo [A Summary Account of the Developments at the London Naval Conference] (1979), 277; Sato Shintaro, ed., *Chichi Sato Ichiro ga kakinokoshita gunnshuku kaigi hiroku* (Bungeisha, 2001), 176–77.

95. Stimson to Cotton, 10 March 1930, *FRUS,* 1930, 1:56.

96. Stimson to Cotton, 16 February 1930, *FRUS,* 1930, 1:26.

97. Hori to Sakonji, 10 March 1930; Yamanashi to Abo, 12 March 1930, Papers of Hori Teikichi, NIDS.

98. Wakatsuki, *Kofuan kaikoroku;* O'Connor, *Perilous Equilibrium,* 77–81.

99. Nihon Kokusai Seiji Gakkai [Japan Association of International Relations] ed., *Taiheiyo Senso e no michi: Bekkan shiryoyhen* [The Road to the Pacific War: Supplementary Volume of Documents] (Tokyo: Asahi Shinbunsha, 1963). Hereafter cited as *TSM,* Shiryohen.

100. This meant Japan would retain the proportions of 72.2 percent in 1935, 67.8 percent in 1936, 63.8 percent in 1937, and 62 percent in 1938.

101. For the Reed-Matsudaira compromise, see *TSM,* Shiryohen, 11–12.

102. Wakatsuki to Shidehara,14 March, 1930, NGB, *Rondon Kaigun Kaigi,* 2:131–32.

103. Sakonji report, 46–47.

104. Nakamura report, entry of 13 March 1930.

105. Sato Naotake, *Kaiko 89-nen* (Jiji Tsushin, 1964), 245–59.

106. Hori bunsho, 1:178; Wakatsuki, *Kofuan kaikoroku*, 355–57.

107. Kobayashi Tatsuo and Shimada Toshihiko, eds., *Gendaishi shiryo, 7, Manshu jihen* (Misuzu Shobo, 1967), 35.

108. Ibid., 356.

109. Wakatsuki, Kohuan kaikoroku, 357.

110. Nakamura report, 15 March 1930.

111. Yamamoto to Hori, 17 March 1930, Hori Papers.

112. Navy General Staff, Measures to Cope with the Reed-Matsudaira Compromise, n.d., NIDS.

113. Takarabe diary (entry of 15 March 1930); Sato Naotake, *Kaiko 80-nen*, 245–50.

114. Ibid., 101.

115. Nakamura report, 28 March 1930.

116. Ibid., 16 March 1930; Sakonji report, 15–16; Nomura Minoru, *Yamamoto Isoroku saiko* (Chuo Koron, 1996), 179.

117. Abo to Kato, 19 March 1930, Library, Institute of Defense Studies, Japanese Defense Agency.

118. From Yamanashi to Abo, 21 March 1930, NIDS.

119. *TSM*, Shiryohen, 15; Nakamura report, 13–16 March 1930; Yamamoto to Hori, 17 March 1939, Hori Papers; Abo to Kato Kanji, 15 and 19 March 1930.

120. Yamamoto to Hori, 17 March 1930, Hori Papers.

121. Hamaguchi Osachi, *Hamaguchi nikki* [diary], ed. Ikei Masaru, Hatano Masru, and Kurosawa Fumitaka (Mizuzu Shobo, 1991), 312 (entry of March 15, 1930).

122. Kiyoshi Ikeda, *Nihon no kaigun* (Shiseido, 1967), 2:67.

123. Kato Kanji hiroku; Kato, "My Views on Arms Limitation: Memo for an Oral Presentation"; Navy General Staff, memorandum on the present state of American armaments since the Washington Conference.

124. Kato Kanji to Makino Nobuaki, 29 January 1930; Kato Kanji Taisho en, 890–92.

125. NGS, "Rondon kaigi kosho gaiyo narabini Beikoku teian no naiyo kento." [Summary of the Negotiations at the London Naval Conference and an Analysis of the Contents of the American Proposal], in Ikeda Kiyoshi, "Rondon kaigun joyaku ni kansuru Gunreibu gawa no shiryo 3-pen," Osaka Shiritsu Daigaku, *Hogaku zasshi* 13 (December 1968).

126. Kato to Takarabe, 17 March 1930, *TSM*, Shiryohen, 17; *Hori Teikichi shiryo-shu*, 1:186.

127. *TSM*, Shiryohen, 17.

128. Nihon Kokusai Seiji Gakkai (ed.), *Taiheiyo Senso e no michi* (Tokyo: Asahi Shinbunsha, 1962-63), 1:80–81.

129. Yamanashi to Takarabe, 22 March, 1939, *TSM*, Shiryohen, 22; *Hori Teikichi shiryoshu,* 1:196.

130. JMFA, NGB, *Rondon Kaigun Kaigi,* 2:412.

131. Ibid., 161; Matsudaira to Shidehara, 24 March 1930, JMFA.

132. Abo to Kato Kanji, 26 March 1930; Sakonji to Yamanashi, 25 March 1930, NIDS; *Kato Kanji nikki,* 609.

133. Okada Keisuke, *Okada Keisuke kaikoroku* (Mainichi Shinbunsha, 1977), 40–42.

134. Ibid., 43.

135. Matsudaira (for Wakatsuki) to Shidehara, 22 March 1930.

136. Sakonji to Yamanashi, 25 March 1930.

137. Yamanashi to Takarabe, 22 March 1930, NIDS; Yamanashi to Abo, 21 March 1930, Hori Papers, NMSDC.

138. *TSM*, Shiryohen, 22.

139. Takarabe's draft memorandum to Wakatsuki, 24 March 1930, NIDS.

140. Takarabe to Yamanashi, 26 March, 1930, NGB, *Rondon Kaigun Kaigi,* 2:163–63; Sakonji to Yamanashi, 26 March 1930.

141. Sakonji report, 109.

142. Wakatsuki to Shidehara, 24 March 1930; NGB, 1934-nen *Rondon Kaigun Kaigi,* 1:160–61.

143. *FRUS 1930,* 1:171; NGB, *Rondon Kaigun Kaigi,* 2:151.

144. *TSM*, Shiryoshu, 25, 318, 444–45.

145. Kobayashi and Shimada, *Gendaishi shiryo,* 7:37; *TSM*, Shiryohen, 25.

146. *Hamaguchi nikki,* 318 (entry of 27 March, 1939); "Heika no okotoba" [The emperor's words], Hori Papers, no. 30, NMSDC.

147. Yamanashi to Takarabe, 31 March 1930, *TSM*, Shiryohen, 36–37; *Hori Teikichi shiryoshu,* 1:209.

148. Kobayashi Seizo, *Kaigun taisho Kobayashi Seizo oboegaki* [Memoranda of Admiral Kobayashi Seizo], ed. Ito Takashi and Nomura Minoru (Yamakawa Shuppansha, 1981), 55; Hori Teikichi shiryoshu, 209.

149. *TSM*, Shiryohen, 37–38.

150. Ibid., 44.

151. Okada Keisuke, *Okada Keisuke kaikoroku* (Mainichi Shinbunsha, 1977), 174.

152. Ibid., 49–50, 174; *Okada Taisho Kiroku Hensan Kai, ensankai,* ed. Okada Keisuke (Editor, 1956), 81; *Hori Teikichi shiryoshu,* 1:219; *TSM*, Shiryohen, 43–46.

153. NGB, *Rondon Kaigun Kaigi*, 2:159.

154. *TSM*, Shiryohen, 36–37. The final instructions are printed in JMFA, *Nihon gaiko nenpyo narabini shuyo monjo*, 2:155–57.

155. Sakonji report, 101–5, 111; *TSM*, Shiryohen, 22, 37; Kobayashi and Shimada, *Gendaishi shiryo*, 7:4.

156. Ibid., 49; Takarabe diary (entry of 31 March 1930).

157. Takarabe diary (entry of 31 March 1930); *TSM*, Shiryohen, 49.

158. Yamamoto's oral presentation to Takarabe, 2 April, Hori Papers, NMSDC.

159. Wakatsuki, *Kofuan kaikoroku*, 362.

160. Nakamura report, 1 April 1930; Sakonji report, 114; Yamamoto's oral presentation to Takarabe, 2 April 1930, Hori Papers, NMSDC; Sorimachi Eiichi, Ningen Yamamoto Isoroku no shogai (Kowado, 1964), 301–302; Nakamura Takafusa et al., *Gendaishi o tsukuru hitibito* (Mainichi Shinbun, 1971), 3:51.

161. Yamamoto's oral presentation to Takarabe, 9 April, 1930, Hori Papers, NMSDC.

162. Ibid.

163. *Kato Kanji nikki*, 93.

164. Okada Keisuke, *Okada Keisuke kaikoroku* (Mainichi Shinbunsha, 1977), 48–49.

165. *TSM*, Shiryohen, 46–48.

166. The best treatment is found in Kobayashi, "Kaigun gunshuku joyaku," 100–40.

167. Takahashi Shin'ichi, ed., *Waga kaigun to Takahashi Sankichiki* (Editor, 1970), 82.

168. "Heika no on hito kotoba" [His Majesty's Word], Hori Papers, NMSDC.

169. Terashima Ken Denki Kanko Kai, ed., *Terashima Ken den* (Editor, 1973), 146.

170. After the Pacific War, Wakatsuki told Yamanashi that if he had not been "purged," he would have become commander in chief of the Combined Fleet or navy minister. Agawa *Naoyuki, Umi no yujo* (Chuo Koron, 2001), 78.

171. Agawa, *Reluctant Admiral*, 45.

172. *Kato Kanji nikki*, 540–41.

173. BBKS, *Rengo Kantai*, 1:281–82.

174. For details on these developments, see Asada, *From Mahan to Pearl Harbor*, 195–204.

175. Quoted in Elting E. Morison, *Turmoil and Tradition: A Study of the Life and Times of Henry L. Stimson* (repr. n.p.: History Book Club, 2003), 260; Love, *History of the U.S. Navy*, 561.

176. Castle to acting secretary of state (Cotton), 25 February, 1930; Japanese Relations throughout History, 58; JMFA, *1930-nen Rondon Kaigun Kaigi* (1983–84), 2:87–88.

177. Cited in James B. Crowley, *Japan's Quest for Autonomy: National Security and Foreign Policy, 1930–1938* (Princeton, N.J.: Princeton University Press, 1966), 65, cited in LaFeber, *Clash,* 158.

178. Castle to Secretary of State, 31 January 1930 (relayed to the delegation), Stimson Papers, Yale University (microfilm).

179. Stimson to Cotton, 19 March 1930, *FRUS,* 19 March 1930, 1:67. During the negotiations in London Stimson had written to the president, "I feel it would be unwise to do anything which would weaken Wakatsuki's independent power." Stimson to Hoover 17 February 1930, Stimson Papers.

180. Matsudaira to Shidehara, 17 March 1930, JMFA.

181. NGB, 1930-nen *Rondon Kaigun Kaigi,* 2:87–88, cited in LaFeber, *Clash,* 58.

182. Cited in O'Connor, *Perilous Equilibrium,* 160.

183. Quoted in Gerald E. Wheeler, *Admiral William Veazie Pratt, U.S. Navy: A Sailor's Life* (Washington, D.C.: Navy History Division, 1974), 341.

184. Stimson felt "a satisfactory agreement" was necessary to "save Japan's face." Stimson memorandum with Ramsey MacDonald, 17 January 1930, Stimson Papers.

185. Cited in Gerald E. Wheeler, *Admiral William Veazie Pratt, U.S. Navy: A Sailor's Life* (Washington, D.C.: Navy History Division, 1974), 178.

186. Robert H. Ferrell, *The American Secretaries of State and Their Diplomacy: Frank B. Kellogg and Henry L. Stimson* (New York: Cooper Square, 1963), 197.

187. Emily Goldman, *Sunken Treaties: Naval Arms Control Between the Wars* (University Park: Pennsylvania State University Press, 1994), 11, 14–15, 134.

188. Bull, "Objectives of Arms Control," 354.

189. See Asada, *From Mahan to Pearl Harbor,* 62–63.

190. At the time of the London Conference, Stimson and Reed promised each other to make all their efforts to put an end to the exclusion of Japanese immigration, but the time did not seem propitious for such a proposal. Charles E. Neu, "American Diplomats in East Asia" (paper presented to the Conference on Japanese-American Relations, 1918–31, Kauai Island, Hawaii, 5–9 January 1976).

191. NGB, *Rondon Kaigun Kaigi,* 1, 205.

192. Castle to acting secretary of state (Cotton), 31 January 1930; Cotton to Castle, 1 February 1930, *FRUS 1930,* 1:11–12.

193. "Decision on our policies regarding the Washington and London treaties," 14 October 1933, JMFA, NGB, 1935 *Rondon Kaigun Kaigi* (Gaimusho, 1986), 8–9.

194. Harada, *Saionjiko to seikyoku,* 3:147. To be sure, at the Washington Conference, Kato Kanji harbored personal animosity, even venom, toward Kato Tomosaburo. He wrote in his diary, "Now I know how crafty he is. He is not the kind of person one can work with"; *Kato Kanji nikki,* 53, 55. But it was, of course, their diametrically opposed views on naval limitation that determined the course of Japanese naval policy.

195. See Asada, "The Revolt against the Washington Treaty," pp. 82–97.

CHAPTER 4

The French and Italian Navies

Paul G. Halpern

T he French and Italian navies at the London Naval Conference of 1930 can easily appear to be spoilers. Their failure to agree over the issue of parity between France and Italy necessitated division of the treaty concluded at the conference into two parts, with one part agreed to by only Great Britain, the United States, and Japan. French-Italian rivalry may have appeared as a noisy distraction to the larger navies, but that rivalry was very real and had a long history, and the fears it created were also very real. France and Italy by the end of the nineteenth century were members of rival blocs, the Italians in the Triple Alliance and therefore allied to Austria-Hungary and Germany. They had entered this alliance in 1882 at least partially to safeguard their position in the face of rivalry with the French over Mediterranean issues, notably Tunisia. The naval component was likely to be small as long as Italy's ally—and rival—Austria-Hungary had what was a navy suitable largely for coast defense. An early Triple Alliance naval convention was largely moribund and forgotten.

The situation changed after the turn of the century, when Austria-Hungary began to build truly modern and powerful warships, culminating with the laying down in 1908 of what would be a squadron of four dreadnoughts. This was matched by an Italian building program that included dreadnoughts. At the same time there was a weakening of British strength in the Mediterranean, in favor of a concentration against the German fleet in northern waters. The

French, who had enjoyed a comfortable superiority over the Italians and certainly over the Austrians, now found themselves with a serious challenge. Furthermore, their own fleet had, as a result of French internal politics and conflicting technical strategies, begun to fall behind. There was now a serious prospect that the combined Italian and Austrian fleets might match that of the French. The same possibility was apparent to the Italians, who in 1913 took the initiative in bringing about a Triple Alliance naval convention calling for the union in Sicilian waters of the Austrian and Italian fleets, to be joined by whatever German ships were in the Mediterranean. On the outbreak of the world war in 1914, the Triple Alliance naval convention proved to be a mirage. The Italians declared their neutrality at first and subsequently joined the war on the side of Britain and France, in May 1915.[1]

The French navy in 1914 was behind in the naval competition despite the *Statut Naval* of 1912, calling for a fleet by 1920 that would include twenty-eight battleships, ten light cruisers, fifty-two destroyers, and ninety-four submarines.[2] Unfortunately, the French navy was behind the technical curve in regard to capital ships. The first French dreadnoughts were inferior to their British and German contemporaries. They were less powerfully armed and slower. The French had also deferred the building of fast light cruisers until the later years of their program and were thus caught when the war broke out lacking in a type of warship that soon proved its worth. (At least they were encumbered by a large number of armored cruisers. This type of warship, large and expensive to man and maintain, proved highly vulnerable to dreadnoughts and battle cruisers in the encounters between the British and Germans.) French destroyers also left much to be desired, and many of the comparatively numerous French submarines were also deficient from a technical point of view.[3] Nevertheless, the fact that Great Britain and eventually Italy were allies meant that the command of the sea was never really in doubt, the most serious challenge coming from submarines. In these circumstances the French suspended construction of the majority of large ships in their naval program. The resources freed were turned toward fulfilling the immense needs of the army. The French navy even had twelve badly needed destroyers built in distant Japan. The five *Normandie*-class dreadnoughts under construction were never completed, although one—the *Bearn*—was eventually converted into an aircraft carrier.

The French suffered losses among their large ships during the war, mostly to submarines and mines at the Dardanelles or in the Mediterranean. The losses were generally older or obsolete warships, but they were not replaced during the war. Many of the destroyers were also worn out through hard use. The

Italian navy also suffered losses to large ships—some to sabotage—during the war.[4] However, the bulk of the Italian battle fleet was carefully preserved in the main base at Taranto, to be used only in the unlikely situation that the Austrian battle fleet attempted to come out of the Adriatic. The Italian naval commanders were quite frank about preserving the fleet for the future balance of power in the Mediterranean, and the French were well aware of this. Italian light craft were more active, and this meant many of these too ended the war thoroughly worn out. Nevertheless, the Italians built a number of new ships during the war that might be classed as flotilla leaders and destroyers. They were well suited for Adriatic or Mediterranean conditions. The French were also aware of this. They claimed the Italians had built 48,000 tons during the war, compared to none for themselves, conveniently omitting the twelve destroyers acquired from Japan.[5] Moreover, the conduct of the war had resulted in considerable friction between the two nations. The Italians had insisted that only an Italian should command in the Adriatic, and the result was a waste of resources, with two battle fleets facing the much smaller Austrian fleet when one would have sufficed. There was little real fraternity of arms between the two erstwhile allies.[6]

The stage had been set for the postwar rivalry. At the end of the war the French were, by their own calculations, far ahead of the Italians in tonnage. In ships in service, the French navy had a total tonnage of 695,000, compared to 353,000 for the Italians.[7] A good portion of the French tonnage was, however, obsolete, and the French were worried about the future. The Italians also had reason to worry about the future. They were conscious of their present inferiority and potential vulnerability. Moreover, the threat of the Austrian navy may have been removed, but in place of the Austrian empire there was now the new South Slav state—subsequently named Yugoslavia—as a rival in the Adriatic. The Yugoslavs might not possess much of a navy, but they were eventually allied with France.

The Italians gained a significant victory at the Washington Naval Conference, when they were granted parity in battleships with the French. This meant 175,000 tons in the well-known ratio for Britain, the United States, Japan, France, and Italy of 5:5:3:1.75:1.75; for Italy this translated into five battleships, at the maximum allowable tonnage of 35,000 tons per ship.[8] The French saw this as a great humiliation and were adamant that the same ratio should not be applied to cruisers and destroyers (*bâtiments légers*) or submarines. These proportions would have reduced the French and Italian allocation to 150,000 tons for destroyers and 30,000 tons for submarines. The Italians indicated they would have been ready to accept 31,500 tons as the maximum for submarines—they actually had only 21,000 tons at the time—but only if they were put on a parity with France. The French insisted, however, that their requirements for cruisers and destroyers were 330,000 tons and for submarines 90,000 tons. The latter figure was particularly difficult for the British to accept, and with further agreement impossible, the treaty was restricted to battleships and aircraft carriers. The French continued to emphasize the point and in the exchange of treaty ratifications on 1 August 1923 made the reservation that the French government had always maintained that the total tonnage of battleships and aircraft carriers attributed to each of the contracting powers did not express the relative importance of the maritime interests of those powers and could not be extended to other categories of ships beyond those expressly stipulated.[9]

Battleships in the early 1920s were not the major priority for the French, who had no immediate plans to build the quota allotted them under the Washington Treaty. They did not need expensive battleships as much as they needed other types. Their immediate requirement was to rebuild their fleet with the types of warships that had proved so valuable during the war, notably cruisers, destroyers, and submarines. French plans immediately after the war had been to lay down in 1920 six scouts *(éclaireurs d'escadre)* and twelve flotilla leaders of 1,800–2,000 tons *(torpilleurs éclaireurs).* Vice Admiral Henri Salaun, then *chef d'état-major général,* did not consider this number sufficient, and after considerable discussion the Conseil Supérieur de la Marine decided that the minimum program for the French navy would be a fleet of eleven battleships, fifteen 12,000-ton cruisers, fifteen eight-thousand-ton cruisers, nineteen destroyers, ninety-two torpedo boats, and one hundred submarines, plus auxiliary vessels. The first *tranche,* or installment, of this program was voted by the French parliament in March of 1922.[10] The objective of what was termed the "normal program" of the French navy was clear. It was a French version of a "two-power standard"—superiority over both the Italians in the Mediterranean and a now weakened Germany in the north.[11]

The Washington arms control treaty restricting the French to 175,000 tons in battleships and 60,000 tons in aircraft carriers brought about further revision, and a series of laws enacted in 1924 and 1925—usually referred to by the French as the "*Statut Naval* of 1924"—expressed the French program regarded as necessary for their security as in metric tons: battleships, 177,800 tons; aircraft carriers, 60,960 tons; light vessels *(bâtiments légers),* comprising cruisers and destroyers, 390,000 tons; high-seas submarines, 96,000 tons; special ships (minelayers, tenders, etc.), 51,774 tons; and coastal submarines, 28,800 tons. The French estimated that the 390,000 tons of *bâtiments légers* would result in twenty-one ten-thousand-ton cruisers and between sixty and eighty destroyers. The French parliament declined, however, to adopt the *Statut Naval* as a full naval law, and the French navy had to be content with an annual *tranche*.[12]

The Italians were determined not to be eclipsed, and after October 1922 they had in Mussolini a leader who was not reticent to use the rhetoric of power, force, and the need for naval expansion. However, as some Italian historians have pointed out, on the question of naval expansion there was little to distinguish Mussolini and the Fascists from their predecessors of liberal Italy.[13] The Italians, like the French, had suspended work on four super-dreadnoughts during the war. Three were canceled outright, and a fourth was launched but never completed; the Italians simply could not afford them. They also scrapped numbers of obsolete warships. The Italian navy did complete seven destroyers and five submarines laid down during the war and also laid down an additional ten destroyers and two scouts *(esploratori leggiere)*.

On the eve of the Washington Naval Conference, the *capo di Stato Maggiore,* Vice Admiral Giuseppe De Lorenzi, even claimed that Italian maritime requirements were actually superior to those of the French and that the Italian navy must therefore have absolute equality. The claim was based on the size of Italy's merchant marine, its population, and the necessity of maintaining contact with the colonies of Italian emigrants abroad. In addition, the Italian coastline was long and vulnerable, too extensive to be protected by fixed installations. Communications with the islands of Sardinia and Sicily also had to be maintained. Moreover, the Italian Peninsula was situated in a closed sea—the Mediterranean—and Italy had to import food and raw materials by sea. The French, De Lorenzi claimed, were better situated. They had a smaller Mediterranean coastline, protected by the major base at Toulon. The Italian minister of marine, as well as by the civilian delegates to the Washington Conference, hoped to obtain an allowance of 90 percent of the French total and would even have settled for 80 percent. The award of parity with the French in battleships and carriers therefore came as a surprise.[14] The Italians, like the French, refrained from filling their Washington quota of battleship tonnage and concentrated instead on cruisers, destroyers, and submarines.[15]

By the end of 1929 the French had recognized that the Italians had two new ten-thousand-ton, 203 mm–gun cruisers in service and another four under construction and were building six 5,270-ton light cruisers, making a total of 92,600 tons of new cruisers. At this moment, and by way of comparison, the French had three new ten-thousand-ton, 203 mm–gun cruisers in service, another three under construction, and one authorized. They had also built three new light cruisers armed with 155 mm guns, making the total tonnage of new cruisers either built or under construction 93,000 tons.[16] After the Washington treaties, the ten-thousand-ton cruiser had in many respects become the upper limit of new naval construction in the Mediterranean, and in total tonnage of new cruisers the French and Italians seemed fairly close, although the French light cruisers were larger than their Italian counterparts.

At the Preparatory Commission formed by the Council of the League of Nations to prepare the way for a general disarmament conference, the French continued to diverge widely from the British on the method of calculating naval strength. In March 1927, at the third session of the commission, the British and French presented draft conventions that put their differences in sharp relief. The British proposed limitations on the number of ships, individual tonnage, caliber of gun, and total tonnage of each type. They proposed nine categories, ranging from battleships and battle cruisers down to river gunboats, with no subdivision of cruisers or submarines by size. The French, in contrast, proposed limitation by total tonnage, or "global tonnage," in two categories—home defense and defense of overseas territory—with free allocation of tonnage among different types as each nation thought necessary. The only limitation would be a maximum tonnage and gun caliber for any individual vessel. They contended the British plan by establishing mathematical scales like those of the Washington Treaty would create an arbitrary hierarchy between navies. The French proposal, in contrast, would allow nations to allocate tonnage according to their individual resources and needs and thereby respected the sovereignty of each.

This concept could also be linked to article 8 of the Covenant of the League of Nations, by which members of the League were to recognize that the maintenance of peace required the "reduction of national armaments to the lowest point consistent with national safety." The French spoke of the interdependence of different types of armaments in achieving that security and of the necessity of taking into account the war potential of each country. The French draft for limitation by global tonnage secured the agreement of eleven nations, including the Italians. The British draft, one of limitation by categories, secured the assent of the United States, Japan (with reservations), Argentina, and Chile. The British nevertheless were inclined to minimize the larger number in favor of the French draft: "The only countries to support France were Italy and such insignificant naval Powers as Serbia, Roumania, Holland and Sweden."[17]

In March 1927 the French attempted to reach a compromise on the question of limitation by total tonnage or category with what they termed a *"projet transactionnel."* Each of the high contracting parties would declare the total tonnage it considered indispensable for it security and national interests, accompanied by a declaration of the total tonnage it agreed not to exceed during the duration of the treaty. This would be followed by a declaration of the allotment of this tonnage between four classes: battleships, aircraft carriers, surface ships *(bâtiments légers de surface)*, and submarines. Each nation would remain free to transfer tonnage from one category to another, within a limit to be determined and subject to one year's prior notice before laying down a ship. The French hoped this would guard against the possibility of surprise, which the British feared, yet retain the subtlety of a limitation by total tonnage and thereby preserve national sovereignty. The British thought that the "compromise amounted to very little," for although recognizing a subdivision into categories, it still "provided for unlimited tonnage transfer between those categories." This would fail to put an end to competitive building, as there would be no limit on unit tonnage or armament in the categories not covered by the Washington Treaty.[18]

The Admiralty also suspected that the real reason behind the French proposal to have the two categories of home defense and overseas defense was probably the hope of obtaining by that method a greater combined tonnage than Italy. Others, including the Italians, thought the same, and in the final version of the French proposal the division into home and overseas categories was dropped. The Admiralty still viewed the probable effect of the first part of the French proposal—the declaration of the tonnage necessary for security—as leading to an all-round increase in naval armaments, because each nation would feel compelled to legislate for its requirements in terms of the largest permissible ship in each class. Moreover, the maximum displacement of destroyers would not be determined. This meant that "total tonnage must be agreed upon without knowing its composition."[19]

The Italian delegate at Geneva, Gen. Alberto De Marinis, pointed out in his public rejection of the French proposal that Italy could not accept the distinction between naval force destined for home defense and the defense of colonial territory, since naval force by its nature and that of naval warfare had to be considered in its entirety, because the nation to whom it belonged was completely free to use it in the place and manner it judged most useful. The Italians also had no desire, on the question of tonnage considered necessary for security, to ask for either a higher or lower figure for themselves, but they deemed it indispensable to reserve the right to reach the global tonnage of any other continental European power.[20] The Italians did agree with the French on the question of global tonnage rather than tonnage by categories.

In the summer of 1927, the French and Italians declined to attend the naval conference at Geneva that met at the invitation of President Coolidge of the United States primarily because it excluded the principle of limitation by global tonnage. The conference was therefore limited to three powers—Great Britain, the United States, and Japan—and it failed, largely because of unbridgeable Anglo-American differences over parity in the cruiser question. The French and Italian reasons for declining the invitation were similar. The French maintained that the conference should not be limited to five nations. This might have been acceptable at the Washington Conference, when limitations on only battleships and aircraft carriers had been imposed; only the major navies had these costly ships. In contrast, cruisers, destroyers, and submarines were of interest to most navies in the world. The French insisted on the interdependence of land, sea, and air armaments, as well as on the principle of limitation by global tonnage.[21] The Italians also found it unacceptable that the Mediterranean and other powers who had not signed the Washington treaties—notably Russia, Spain, Yugoslavia, and Greece—were not equally limited. The Italians further insisted on the interdependence of land, sea, and air armaments.[22]

In July 1928, after lengthy and intricate negotiations, the French and British reached a compromise agreement on limitation.[23] There would be four classes of ships: (1) capital ships, meaning ships of over ten thousand tons or armed with guns of greater than 8-inch (203 mm) caliber; (2) aircraft carriers over ten thousand tons; (3) surface vessels of or below ten thousand tons, armed with guns greater than 6-inch (155 mm) and up to 8-inch caliber; and (4) oceangoing submarines over six hundred tons. In the first two classes, capital ships and aircraft carriers, the only change would be to extend the limitations to powers that had not signed the Washington treaties. In regards to classes (3) and (4), a final disarmament conference would fix maximum tonnages applicable to all powers, and no power would be allowed to exceed the total of vessels in each of these categories during the period of the convention. At the final conference, each power would indicate for each category, within this maximum limit, the tonnage it proposed to reach and not exceed for the period covered by the convention.[24] The French felt they could accept this departure from the system of total tonnage and the dropping of their transactional proposition, because it involved only a restriction in the number of units in a category of cruisers, in which individual displacement and armament were already limited. Battleships and aircraft carriers were already limited by the Washington treaties. However, this concession to what the French regarded as the cause of disarmament was dependent on two essential conditions, notably the nonlimitation of other surface ships or coastal submarines and the establishment of a common ceiling in the two categories for all nations. This would safeguard the fundamental principles of the French thesis, the independence of nations and the free exercise of their sovereignty.[25]

The compromise failed, largely because of the firm opposition of the Americans to any limitation on cruisers mounting guns of over 6-inch caliber when there was no limitation on cruisers with 6-inch guns or below. The Americans claimed this would constitute a limitation "on the only class of vessel suitable to American needs while imposing no restriction on the type most suitable to the requirements of others."[26] The Japanese seemed inclined to accept, but the Italians reiterated their familiar positions: the impossibility of separating naval from aerial and land armaments; their preference for global limitation and their willingness to accept any figure, no matter how low, in limitation of their own naval armaments provided those armaments were not exceeded by any other continental European power—meaning, of course, France. The Italians also proposed a naval holiday in the construction of battleships—that is, the five signatories of the Washington treaties should postpone laying down until after 1936 the battleships they would have been allowed to start in the years 1931 to 1936. The Italians had initially been inclined to make some concession in regard to global tonnage in the interests of securing general acceptance of the Anglo-French compromise, but the American rejection of the proposals made it unnecessary for them to make "this sacrifice."[27]

There may also have been more practical reasons behind the initial readiness of the Italians to accept. Ammiraglio di Squadra Ernesto Burzagli, *capo di Stato Maggiore* since December 1927, told the British naval attaché that the Italians were not anxious to build more of the ten-thousand-ton *Trento*-class cruisers beyond the four already built or projected and that submarines of over six hundred tons "were not of special interest to Italy." Burzagli claimed that he did not like the *Trentos*—already under construction when he assumed office—because they lacked armor, and he had tried to introduce two 12,500-ton cruisers with additional armor but less speed. The Ministry of Marine had supposedly vetoed his proposal because of their concern that the French would reply by increasing their individual cruiser tonnage, thereby leading to constant increase of tonnage by both nations in future programs. Burzagli's other proposal, to eliminate two of the projected cruiser's 8-inch guns in order to increase armor, was also frustrated, when naval constructors were unable to offer an efficient design that would satisfy all Italian requirements. Needless to say, the British could hardly have been pleased at the prospect of cruisers larger than the ten-thousand-ton Washington type, but they must have found nonthreatening Burzagli's description of the four *Condottieri*-class light cruisers under construction as "the ideal type of general utility Mediterranean cruiser at reasonable cost." They could also take comfort at the *capo di Stato Maggiore*'s admission that finances would not permit the construction of battleships at the moment or in the immediate future. Burzagli wanted three battleships of relatively modest dimensions—23,000 tons instead of the permitted 35,000 tons—but, perhaps less comfortingly to the Admiralty, to be armed with 15-inch guns.[28]

In April 1929, the U.S. government indicated it was willing to reconsider the French *"projet transactionnel"* it had rejected in 1927. Moreover, to meet British objections, it suggested devising a "yardstick"—that is, a method of estimating equivalent naval values that would take account of factors other than displacement tonnage alone. Those factors producing variations might include age, unit displacement, and caliber of guns. The proposal was a means of overcoming the deadlock between the British and Americans over parity in cruisers. The compromise would be roughly along the lines of a greater number of 8-inch-gun cruisers considered essential for American needs by the U.S. Navy Department and a larger number of 6-inch-gun cruisers for the Royal Navy. The major price was the reduction by the British of their minimum requirements from seventy to fifty in cruisers and in all categories smaller tonnages than they had been prepared to accept in 1927. The end result of long and complicated negotiations was the sending of invitations in October 1929 to the five powers to meet at a naval conference in London in the third week of January 1930.[29]

The Italians accepted. The Stato Maggiore della Marina believed the Kellogg-Briand Pact of 1928 had altered the international climate and that Italian maintenance of the principles of parity with France, interdependence of armaments, and refusal to accept the naval status quo as a point of departure would not prevent participation. The forthcoming conference might actually allow them to affirm their aspirations and right to parity. In addition, the potential results of the conference would be subordinated to the more comprehensive framework of a general disarmament conference, thereby maintaining the principle of interdependence of arms. The Italians might also obtain limits that did not prevent their navy from reaching a better ratio in comparison with other navies, thereby breaking the status quo. There was likewise the possibility of indirectly obtaining a reduction of the construction foreseen in the French *Statut Naval*. They might not be in a position to catch up with future French construction, for they recognized that from the financial point of view France was inherently stronger and therefore in a better position. The Italian naval staff was also conscious of political realities—that it would be difficult to give an a priori refusal to attend, given the current tide of international optimism created by the combined political action of President Herbert Hoover of the United States and Prime Minister Ramsay MacDonald of Great Britain.[30]

By the eve of the naval conference, all the powers were well aware that the question of parity between the French and Italians was likely to be one of the more difficult ones to solve at the conference. At a cabinet meeting on 8 November 1929, Mussolini emphasized the importance of naval parity with France given that the Italians were enclosed in the Mediterranean and could not remain voluntarily imprisoned. The question of supply by sea was most difficult for Italy, and the Italians could go to the London Conference with a secure conscience even if they had to provoke a rupture.[31] Preliminary talks aimed at reaching agreement before the conference led nowhere, although a sudden Italian proposal for the abolition of submarines was interpreted by the British as "a shrewd bid" for American and British support. The French were inclined toward the same view, noting the "remarkable variations" in Italian statements on the subject, as well as apparent inconsistencies between recent statements of Mussolini and a recent diplomatic note, and regarding the whole proposal as a means of winning British and American support and exerting pressure on France on the question of parity. The French added a complication of their own when they proposed that other Mediterranean powers not signatory to the past treaties be invited to participate in a treaty of mutual guarantee and nonaggression. The proposal was directed particularly at Spain.[32]

As the question of parity with Italy was one that was to remain deadlocked, it would be useful here to see exactly why the French naval staff was so opposed to any extension of parity to categories of warships other than battleships and aircraft carriers—the bitterly resented concession that had been extracted from them at Washington. The French considered two cases: one where either France or Italy was at war with a third nation, the other remaining neutral, and a second case where France and Italy were in opposing camps. In the first case, French maritime requirements were to ensure the integrity of French territory and maintain military and economic communications. However, the separation of the French coast into Mediterranean and Atlantic portions complicated reinforcement of threatened areas. An Italian concentration, in contrast, was rapid and easy, and so from the point of view of the defense of its own coast, France had a right to claim a fleet superior to that of Italy. In addition, the French had to provide for the defense of their colonies. The Italian need for colonial defense, the French claimed, was reduced to the coasts of Eritrea and Italian Somaliland, while French obligations extended to numerous colonies far beyond Europe. The lessons of the Seven Years' War in the eighteenth century showed those that colonies made tempting objectives for a potential enemy. The defense of these colonies required minesweepers, torpedo boats, and submarines, supported by larger warships, which could not be diverted from metropolitan forces. The French therefore had need of dedicated additional warships to defend their colonies; the Italians had only a feeble need for such forces.[33] The French naval staff made no mention of Libya, possibly because of its proximity to Sicily or, more likely, to strengthen their argument.

The French navy was also obligated to ensure as quickly as possible the transport of troops from North Africa and the colonies to metropolitan France. Furthermore, should the war extend to French colonies, reinforcements had to be transported to those colonies. Consequently, the French had considerable need for transport of troops and war materials, an obligation they claimed the Italians did not have. The extensive French interests around the globe potentially required protection from enemy surface ships or submarines. Enemy surface ships had to be matched by ships of similar power, but France did not have enough to provide each convoy with direct protection against possible attackers. Therefore, the French would have to use light forces for escorts and rely on indirect protection of convoys by means of mobile groups of warships capable of repelling and destroying assailants—on the condition that they could arrive in time. Submarines were best countered by light escorts, notably *avisos* and *chasseurs,* backed up by a certain number of *torpilleurs.* These were the ships classified in the disarmament talks as *bâtiments spéciaux.* France's dispersed assets, whether they be mobile in the form of convoys or fixed in the form of colonies, therefore required significant forces, particularly light craft and torpedo boats. The combination of colonies and vital lines of communication required the French to reject clearly the idea of parity with Italy.

These considerations, which applied even when France and Italy did not find themselves on opposing sides, would only be magnified when they were— and they were not likely to be alone in the struggle. French concerns about the Atlantic and distant waters would oblige the French to divert forces to these areas, from where they could not intervene in the Mediterranean theater. To admit Italian parity with France would be to concede that in a struggle not limited to the two powers, the French would be inferior in the Mediterranean, very inferior if an ally of Italy had a fleet even the size of Germany's, the latter supposedly limited by the Treaty of Versailles. The limitation of the conflict to France and Italy at the beginning of hostilities would not absolve the French of the obligation to guard against the intervention of a third party outside the Mediterranean. Once again, parity with Italy would put France in a state of inferiority. Even if France and Italy were alone in the struggle, with all external threats removed, the French would still be in a state of inferiority if they accepted parity. Not all French forces would be in the Mediterranean in time of peace, because French general policy required naval forces overseas and on the Atlantic coast. These forces could not immediately reach the Mediterranean, and as a result in the first weeks of a conflict the French would be in a clear state of inferiority. Moreover, while the Italians had all their bases and yards in the Mediterranean, the French had only a portion of theirs in that sea and so might not be able to repair battle damage as quickly as the Italians.

The French naval staff now proceeded to demonstrate how even with all French naval forces concentrated in the Mediterranean and with equality in means of support, the geography of the Mediterranean still made them inferior to the Italians. The argument ran along these lines. The Italians were in a position to threaten all of the French coastline, from Provence to Languedoc to the North African coast. The Italians could discreetly deploy their forces in the Tyrrhenian, exit either in the north or the south, and unexpectedly attack all the exposed French ports. The French, in contrast, were limited in the portions of the Italian coast they could attack to the Ligurian and Tuscan coasts, between the island of Elba and the Franco-Italian frontier. This was only the upper portion of the Tyrrhenian; the lower part of the Tyrrhenian was shielded by the islands of Sicily and Sardinia. The French could not think of attacking in the Adriatic and Ionian, whereas Sicily and Sardinia, while directly accessible, did not have important ports. The French were also obliged to maintain, on their longer coastline and at the entrance of their more numerous ports, coastal-defense forces, notably minesweepers, gunboats, submarines, and torpedo boats. In geographic terms, the inability of the French to use interior lines also made difficult the timely intervention of their main fleet.

The French could not neglect their colonies either. They themselves might have no interest in attacking the Italian colonies of Eritrea and Somaliland, but the Italians might find it advantageous to attack French colonies in the Far East or the Indian Ocean. The Italians could easily move forces through the Suez Canal, thereby obligating the French to provide some level of naval defense, even if reduced, for their colonies. The situation in regard to French military communications with their colonies was particularly unfavorable. The Italians, in the opinion of the French naval staff, did not have military communications of their own to secure, because the French would probably not think of attacking Tripolitania, and even if the Italians were uneasy, it would be easy for them to send reinforcements from Augusta to Tripoli in a few hours without the French being able to stop them. Troop movements between the Italian Peninsula and Sardinia could also be accomplished in less than a night, in a zone where the French could not act. The French navy, in contrast, had to secure significant troop movements between North Africa and France. The French had the double disadvantage of having first to accomplish a series of troop movements requiring the use of their main fleet, thereby preventing it from being employed elsewhere, and subsequently to protect a nearly continuous flow of transports.

Turning to the subject of economic communications, the French saw equal dangers. From the beginning of hostilities the Italians would be compelled to renounce the use of Italian-flagged merchant ships in the western basin of the Mediterranean on the routes to Gibraltar, but the French would be forced to do the same with their merchant ships in the eastern basin. Both nations would consequently attempt to ensure the flow of supplies on the abandoned routes by means of neutral ships. While a good proportion of French commercial communications would be diverted to the Atlantic, all food supplies from North Africa would pass through the Mediterranean, and because of the constraints of the French network on land, it was necessary to terminate an important part of this traffic at Marseille. The geographical situation was more favorable to the Italians, because the closest point to French bases on the Italian lines of communication from the eastern Mediterranean was the southern entrance to the Strait of Messina. French forces attempting to attack this point would have little chance of avoiding detection, being obliged to travel 360 miles through a region under the control of the Italians. Moreover, the French attack would take place near the Italian bases of Messina and Augusta. The French would then have to return by a single route through the Sicilian Channel, and their line of retreat would be easily intercepted by Italian light forces based in Sicily. Conversely, French lines of communication were much more accessible to the Italians. Cap Creus was 260 miles from Maddalena, and Marseille was 220 miles—barely one night's steaming—while Bône was only 150 miles from Cagliari. The threat of Italian attack on French communications was therefore more serious; Italian light forces could emerge from three different exits from the Tyrrhenian and pass outside the zones of effective French surveillance. They also did not depend on a single line of retreat but could choose between three routes. These considerations all led to the conclusion that the Italians would have to devote fewer forces to the direct protection of their lines of communication and could more easily combine naval forces to attack lines of communication or oppose enemy raids, achieving a concentration that would obtain more decisive results. All these considerations meant that if the French conceded parity to the Italians it would be much more difficult to maintain French communications.

The French naval staff sought to demonstrate how the perceived Italian advantages might play out in different scenarios. In one case, the French would have two convoys of around a dozen ships each at sea at the same time, one in the Gulf of Lyon proceeding southward toward Algeria and the other in the neighborhood of Algiers proceeding north. To completely protect them against a raiding force, estimated at perhaps two cruisers and six *torpilleurs,* one would have to assign each convoy a force of at least the same strength, plus around eight ships for protection against submarines. This would be an extremely costly procedure, depriving the main French force of useful ships for several days. The French would therefore be led to adopt a mixed system— that is, assigning a small force to the immediate protection of each convoy and deploying another force for indirect protection, by which it might, if possible, stop the enemy before an attack or at least punish him afterward. The escort to be assigned each convoy would be, for example, eight ships, perhaps two *torpilleurs* and six *avisos.* The group employed for indirect protection would be at least the same strength as the enemy—say, two cruisers and six *torpilleurs.* However, since the Italians might come out of any of three possible exits from the Tyrrhenian, this group would have little chance of success. To give indirect protection a reasonable prospect of success, it would be necessary to have two groups of the same strength, one on alert at Toulon and the other in Tunisia or eastern Algeria. While one of these groups would be close to the primary French naval force, the other would be distant and would have difficulty in participating in an action against the primary Italian force.

Taking the case of eastbound Italian convoys and using naval forces of the same size, the Italians had an easier task, since the danger of French raids would be limited to the approaches of the Strait of Messina. An Italian force at Augusta, if alerted shortly after the French departure from Bizerte, would be able to reach the convoy before the French and prevent their attack. If the Italians had not been warned of the French departure and were alerted only at the moment of the attack on the convoy, they would nevertheless be between the French and Bizerte and in a favorable position to cut the French line of retreat. An Italian force stationed at Palermo would be less well placed to prevent an attack on the convoy but in an excellent position to cut the line of retreat in the Sicilian Channel. In addition, the Italian forces at Augusta could discreetly and rapidly move through the Tyrrhenian in order to rejoin the primary Italian force, and it was therefore easy for the Italian high command to regroup all its forces for an impending major action. This hypothetical exercise also demonstrated why French needs for cruisers and torpedo boats were more severe than those of Italy.[34]

There is the possibility that memorandum by the naval staff that laid out all this was in the nature of a lawyer's brief produced to buttress the arguments of the navy and French diplomats against the principle of parity by invoking what today would be called a "worst-case scenario." While this might have been true to at least a certain extent, it was also an attempt to go beyond the artificial formula and numbers of the naval treaties. Warships in the treaties became invisible, merely part of abstract tonnages and ratios. There was no attempt to translate those tonnages and ratios into terms of actual warships in service or how they might be employed. The naval staff in this case performed a useful function in seeking to point out exactly what in terms of real ships would be needed in certain likely scenarios in the event of an actual war.

But did the French really believe a war was likely? The Kellogg-Briand "peace pact" of 1928 should have created an atmosphere in which bellicose considerations of this sort played no part. Georges Leygues, the veteran minister of marine whose name is associated with much of the renewal of the French fleet following the First World War, admitted that the pact of 1928 had most certainly diminished the chances of conflict. Nonetheless, there were still multiple and grave difficulties that the navy had to foresee before the pact made its beneficent influence felt. These included: the need sooner or later to put back into discussion the Versailles Treaty; the movement for the *Anschluss* of Germanic people in Central Europe; what Leygues perceived as a marked tendency toward an Italo-German entente, coupled with Italian efforts toward a rapprochement with Spain; the internal situation of Yugoslavia; and the imperialism of the Soviet Union. The navy had to prepare for the most dangerous hypothesis, that of a war against an Italian and German coalition, and then had to enjoy a certain margin of strength in case Spain joined that coalition. On the other hand, Leygues argued, the French navy at no time envisaged the possibility of conflict with the two largest naval powers in the world—Great Britain and the United States—and French naval programs had been conceived in the most objective spirit and with the greatest moderation.[35]

According to Leygues, the tonnage necessary to meet these needs would be "a strict minimum" of 800,000 tons, but he insisted that the division of that tonnage had to remain subtle, taking into account the development of naval technology and the various circumstances to be foreseen in the event of war. For example, one might give more importance to light craft as opposed to battleships, or to destroyers and torpedo boats as opposed to cruisers. Leygues insisted the navy still considered battleships to be the backbone of the fleet, but because of their cost the navy was waiting until naval technology became fixed before adopting a new type. This uncertainty alone explained why the French had not yet used the quota allowed to them in the Washington treaties. Eight capital ships would constitute the minimum, but because of the progress of naval art the French navy at present would be content with a displacement of 20–25,000 tons, less than the maximum fixed at Washington. The greatest freedom of action was necessary for *bâtiments légers,* and therefore a total tonnage of only 390,000 was mentioned for this type in the *Statut Naval.* This figure included ten-thousand-ton cruisers and below that destroyers and torpedo boats of any tonnage and armament.

French operational planning had also demonstrated that it was indispensable to reserve at least twelve cruisers with the maximum permitted armament (203 mm) for the defense of French lines of communication. The present state of aeronautical technology made 60,000 tons the indispensable minimum acceptable for aircraft carriers, and approximately 60,000 tons were necessary for minelayers, seaplane carriers, and school ships—types generally given the designation *bâtiments spéciaux.* The French needed no less than 125,000 tons for submarines, divided into 29,000 tons for small, coastal submarines and 96,000 tons for large, high-seas submarines. These figures were calculated on the basis that one could have one only submarine out of three at sea at any given time. In making his arguments, Leygues also stressed that submarines were necessary for the defense of France's metropolitan or colonial coast as well as for the protection of its principal convoys. He made no mention of possible offensive operations by submarines. It went without saying that the French could not accept any suppression of submarines or that, finally, the limitation by categories not already included in the Washington treaties, as opposed to limitation by global tonnage, must be formally discarded as "incompatible to the vital interests of France."[36]

Leygues amplified his views to the Conseil Supérieur de la Défense Nationale, in a tone that was if anything even harsher. To accept limitation by categories according to the coefficients analogous to those in the Washington treaties would be the definitive French abdication at sea and would leave the "Anglo-Saxons" free to exercise to their own profit control of maritime communications. Such limitations would leave French overseas possessions at the mercy of any action undertaken by one of the powers that had profited from the Washington treaties and would gravely compromise French security. Leygues affirmed that France must remain the judge of the strength and composition its fleet needed.[37] Limitation by categories without a common ceiling would also establish an arbitrary hierarchy among navies and would deliberately place certain navies in a situation of inferiority in all classes of ships, injuring the principle of sovereignty and destroying that of equality of rights. It was therefore unacceptable, and the French *"proposition transactionnelle"* was a means to respect the principle of sovereignty by letting each power deem what it considered necessary for its needs and responsibilities, as well as the tonnage it would agree not to exceed for the duration of the convention. Furthermore, with this position the delicate question of the theoretical parity of the Italian navy with the French navy would no longer arise. Should the Italians name a figure that equaled that of the French, the latter could assume that the level at which that parity would be realized would be too high to be obtained in the duration of a limited convention. The French put the total tonnage of the Italian navy in 1930 at 386,000. As the German navy was 144,000 tons, the potentially adverse combination was therefore 530,000 tons. The French proposed a limit of ten years for any treaty, a short enough term so that its clauses would not be affected by important changes in technology and one with an expiration date only three years before the scheduled completion on 1 January 1943 of the French *Statut Naval*.[38]

The Italian navy did not have a long-term naval statute like that of the French, and each year's annual program could vary greatly. The program of the first year after the Washington treaties, from 1 July 1922 to 30 June 1923, had only four destroyers, representing 3,740 tons. The 1923–24 program jumped to eighteen ships, representing 36,568 tons, comprising two ten-thousand-ton cruisers, six destroyers, and ten submarines. The following year, 1924–25, it fell to eight ships (8,036 tons), none larger than a destroyer, and in 1925–26 the program was even smaller, a mere three submarines (2,943 tons). From this point the Italian programs steadily increased, with twelve destroyers (19,536 tons) in 1926–27; ten ships (25,134 tons), including four light cruisers, in 1927–28; ten ships (28,064 tons), including two ten-thousand-ton cruisers, in 1928–29; and no fewer than fifteen ships (39,089 tons) in 1929–30.[39]

What did this Italian growth mean? Was this quest for parity purely a matter of prestige? The Italian naval staff in fact turned the French arguments for a stronger navy on their head. If the French maintained that they needed a stronger navy because of their two maritime frontiers, the Mediterranean and the Atlantic, the Italians claimed this was actually an advantage and not an inferiority, since it enabled the French to confine a potential foe in the Mediterranean and left the French a precious freedom of movement and supply on their Atlantic frontier. The Italians pointed out that it was precisely by way of the Atlantic that the French obtained raw materials for their war potential.[40] In addition, a maritime frontier divided by an obligatory passage through the Strait of Gibraltar was difficult to blockade. As for the argument about the French empire, the Italian naval staff not surprisingly pointed out that Italy also possessed colonies in the Mediterranean, the Red Sea, and the Indian Ocean and that the task of defending them was aggravated by the obligation to defend also the routes traversed by steamers carrying supplies for those colonies as well as the other lines of communication frequented by the Italian merchant marine. The latter was at the moment larger than that of the French and did not enjoy the support of bases and anchorages that by their very presence reduced the number of surface warships required. In addition, the Italian navy had to ensure the arrival in Italy of vital raw materials. Given that the Strait of Gibraltar and the Suez Canal were in British hands and that use of the Dardanelles and Bosphorus was limited because of the political differences between the Italian and Russian regimes, the uncertain attitude of Turkey itself, and the limited strength of Greece, the Italians could deduce that the sole means of attaining a reasonable assurance of supply was a navy that would not only arouse serious preoccupations on the part of an enemy but might also attain effective command *(padronanza)* in *Mare Nostrum*. These considerations were strengthened by the fact that supply of Italy by land through the mountain passes would not be sufficient for the needs of the nation at war. In the past, friendship with England had been a pillar of Italian policy and meant that Gibraltar and Suez would be open doors for the Italians. But in the past England had been nearly sovereign at sea, especially before the development of Germany. Now England faced a number of rivals, notably the United States, whose recent development constituted a new and formidable factor, and Russia, whose anti-imperialist activity and propaganda was directed especially at England, as were those of

Germany, which wanted to retake its lost position. The English factor for the Italians should now be given less weight.

The idea that seaborne supplies might reach Italy through the territorial waters of other states presumed a political understanding between Italy, Russia, and Greece. An agreement of this nature would be doubtful. Likewise, an understanding with Spain to establish a line Catalonia–Balearics–Sardinia–Tuscany did not give complete confidence. What was the way out? The most natural solution, and that which appeared evident, would be to possess a fleet that would be decisive. In summary, for the reasons just mentioned it did not seem possible to admit that between the Italian and French navies there could exist any difference in strength. A solution that might have an alluring appearance would be that of sustaining to the hilt the doctrine of freedom of the seas, meaning respect for neutral flags that sheltered cargoes directed toward belligerent countries not blockaded in an effective manner. The Italians in this situation might seek the tonnage of ships flying neutral flags necessary for essential raw materials to arrive at Italian ports. But, although such a principle had been periodically evoked and supported by the United States, the Italian naval staff distrusted its effective application in time of war. The abolition of the submarine might contribute to true freedom of the seas, but ominously, France had not ratified the Washington convention and was opposed to the abolition of that arm; on the contrary, it had already established a program of submarine construction. One could therefore be skeptical about the success of such an initiative. The Italian objective was therefore to obtain parity with France at a total tonnage lower than that of the French *Statut Naval* of 1924 but closely approaching what the Italians deemed indispensable for defense as a consequence of their strategic-geographical studies. By parity, the Italians meant parity in total or global tonnage and also in the individual categories into which that tonnage might be divided, or at least where one category might offset another.[41]

In another memorandum prepared before the London Conference, the Stato Maggiore again stressed that Italy was the most vulnerable of all the continental powers to attack at sea, that it was in a certain sense even more dependent than England on fuel and raw materials from abroad and on the freedom of its maritime communications. These lines of communication were forced through passages that were flanked at short distances by naval and air bases of other powers and could easily be dominated and interrupted. This situation forced the Italians to improve their strength relative to other powers, taking account of the fact that even if they reached parity they would still be in a position of precarious inferiority, since the entrances to the Mediterranean were in the hands of others and because other powers were interposed between Italy and those straits. In matters specifically related to the impending conference, the Stato Maggiore regarded the French transactional proposal as having an insidious character and as constituting a major peril, since it would preclude the Italians from reaching parity, should circumstances require it, and would sanction for the duration of the convention the existing disparity in force. This preservation of the status quo was obviously desired by the powers with larger armaments. The Italian naval staff favored the criteria of global tonnage as the most favorable to their interests and wanted the possibility of constructing at less expense a few units superior to those of the enemy—in other words, a superiority of type compensating for superiority in numbers. What the Americans and British denounced as "competitive building" was the sole means for a weaker power of imposing certain risks on a stronger adversary.[42] This Italian refusal to accept any limitation of armaments to levels that would not be exceeded by any other continental European power—in effect, insistence on parity with France—and the refusal of the French to accept that parity foredoomed any hope of Italian and French agreement at the conference.

The French delegation at the London Conference was a particularly strong one, and the relative proximity of Paris and London added to its effectiveness, even when the demands of French politics forced the premier, André Tardieu, and others in his cabinet to return to Paris for certain periods. Tardieu, a former associate of Georges Clemenceau at the 1919 peace conference and known as a modernizer who favored American style methods in industry, was destined to be frustrated in the France of the 1930s, a victim of the economic depression and the intractable problems of the Third Republic. He has been described as a man perhaps thirty years ahead of his time.[43] In London, by most accounts, he represented the French position vigorously and ably. Aristide Briand, the foreign minister, also needed little introduction to his counterparts. He had held the portfolio in many cabinets, and his name was linked with that of the American secretary of state in the Kellogg-Briand peace pact of 1928, supposedly abolishing war as an instrument of national policy. Georges Leygues was minister of marine during the preparatory stage and at the beginning of the conference. He was succeeded in March 1930 by Jacques-Louis Dumesnil, an equally (if not more) stubborn defender of French ambitions who had already served as minister of marine, from June 1924 to April 1925.[44] Much of the diplomatic load was carried by René Massigli, chief of the League of Nations Service at the Ministry of Foreign Affairs. François Pietri, then minister of colonies and a future minister of marine, was also one of the delegates. The technical advisers included the chief of naval staff, Vice Admiral Louis-Hippolyte Violette, an officer associated with the left and considered one of the "progressives" in the navy, and Leygues' former *chef du cabinet, Contre Amiral* Eugène Descottes-Genon. Possibly the most important of the technical advisers was the minister's current *chef du cabinet,* the redoubtable, clever, and industrious François Darlan, newly promoted to *contre amiral* and clearly on his way to the top of the navy.

This was a delegation that seemed at first glance to be clear in its objectives and confident of the strength of its arguments, however unpopular they might seem in a disarmament conference. Nevertheless, there was a certain tension between the diplomats and the naval technical advisers, as well as concern that Massigli and Briand, especially the latter, might bargain away too much while seeking the illusion of peace and thereby jeopardize French security.[45]

The French anticipated that their position would be unpopular. The French naval attaché in Washington reported that the Americans wanted parity with the British at the lowest possible price and that the British were restrained in their desire, however sincere, for disarmament by their idea of the necessity for a two-power standard in European waters. Since the Italians had announced that they were ready for any reduction provided they had parity with France, the fate of the conference really depended on the latter. A well known journalist had therefore remarked that the scenario was in place for France to be either the hero or the villain of the play.[46] Nevertheless, an astute observer like Darlan considered that the French were in an excellent position and appeared to be nearly masters of the game; he hoped that they would know how to use these advantages.[47] A subsequent report on the proceedings of the conference, probably the work of Darlan, would rather confidently conclude that only the French arrived in London with a clearly defined line of conduct based on their dual needs for peace and security, which furnished the axis of their policy. Their principles had been expressed publicly, and their delegation was supported by the unanimous opinion of the country.[48]

The negotiations involving the French, and indeed the work of the conference, had to be virtually suspended for a time while Tardieu sought to form a new government. The Italian delegation did not have such a problem. Italy was a one-party state and Mussolini a dictator. He was ably represented at the London Conference by his foreign minister, Dino Grandi, appointed minister of foreign affairs in September 1929, after having served as under secretary since July 1924 while Mussolini was acting as his own foreign minister. Grandi's policy has been described as the pursuit of two fundamental objectives—to end French hegemony on the continent and to create an extensive Italian empire in Africa. Italy would serve as the "determining weight" between France and Germany, notably at the League of Nations. Grandi intended to present a pacific face for Fascism, a policy that Mussolini's periodic bellicose, even outrageous, statements tended to undermine.[49] Grandi was supported at the conference at varying intervals by Augosto Rosso, head of the League of Nations office at the Foreign Ministry; the minister of marine, Ammiraglio di divisione Giuseppe Sirianni; and the capo di Stato Maggiore, Ammiraglio di squadra Ernesto Burzagli; as well by as a number of naval officers who served as technical counselors. Most of their names would be unfamiliar to historians, although men like Rosso were veterans of the disarmament negotiations at Geneva.

As for Mussolini himself, one must remember that at this moment he was still at the height of his prestige in foreign circles as a result of the Lateran Pacts of 1929. Several questions could be raised. To what extent was the demand for parity with France a matter of prestige or the result of the more rational calculations put forward by the Stato Maggiore? Was it still possible to accommodate Mussolini and Fascist Italy within the framework of the postwar settlement? How sincere were the Italians in the question of disarmament?[50] Grandi's reiteration that Italy was willing to accept limits, however low, provided they were not exceeded by the strongest continental power had the image of sweet reasonableness and, in fact, had been first proclaimed by Mussolini in June 1928.[51] However, they did not bear close examination—even the avowedly dovish Briand pointed out the apparent fallacy of the Italian argument. Given the existing ratio of tonnage between the French and Italian navies, the Italian position, "though moderate in appearance, was in reality impossible, since all Italy would agree to was the reduction of the French navy by half, i.e., to Italy's own level."[52] In slightly different words, Briand alleged toward the end of the conference that the Italian claim to parity "meant either that the Italian fleet must be doubled or the French fleet halved."[53] Moreover, Fascist claims could not be described as sweet reasonableness. Approximately a week before the conference opened, the *Official Gazette* of the Fascist Party included an article alleging that Italy claimed parity not only with the strongest naval power in Europe but also with the strongest naval power in the world. However, for financial reasons the Italian government would renounce the right to build to the level of Great Britain or the United States.[54] Needless to say, the French paid close attention to the more bellicose of Italian statements and pretensions, and they undoubtedly served to harden the stance of the French navy at the London Conference.[55]

The proposed tonnages for the fleets were subjected to close scrutiny and analysis, as well as a certain amount of tweaking at the conference. It is useful therefore to see (in table 4.1) what the 3ème Bureau of the naval staff gave as the strength of the French fleet, as well as its deployment at the beginning of 1930.

Table 4.1 Strength and Distribution of the French Fleet, 1930

Overseas divisions (*Divisions lointaines*)	89,518 tons	12%
"Flying division" (*Division volante*)	30,480 tons	4%
Schools or training	111,797 tons	15%
Metropolitan forces	310,797 tons	43%
Under construction or authorized	191,277 tons	26%
	733,869 tons	100%

The employment of the fleet in time of peace when the *Statut Naval* was fulfilled would be as shown in table 4.2. The overseas divisions represented those forces stationed throughout the French empire. The *Division volante* was to respond to unforeseen circumstances or missions in either overseas or European waters and was to be strong enough to execute all police missions and composed of a sufficient number of ships to convey an accurate impression of the power of France as well as the capabilities of French shipyards. In 1930 it was located at Brest and consisted of the first ten-thousand-ton cruisers. On completion of the *Statut Naval* it would also include four large destroyers and six high-seas submarines. The increase in tonnage of the overseas divisions throughout the French empire would come primarily from raising the numbers of cruisers from four to eleven, of destroyers from six to twelve, and of submarines of all sizes from six to twenty-two.[56]

Table 4.2 Projected Strength and Distribution of the French Fleet, 1943

Overseas divisions (*Divisions lointaines*)	173,600 tons	22%
"Flying division" (*Division volante*)	49,000 tons	6%
Schools or training	90,800 tons	11%
Metropolitan forces	491,000 tons	61%
	804,400 tons	100%

The French arrived in London prepared under certain conditions to make concessions in the approximately 800,000 tons requested by the navy. This tonnage was required to face an adverse combination of Germany plus Italy, with a question mark about Spain. The number of light ships (cruisers, destroyers, and submarines) was considered just sufficient to ensure the protection of maritime traffic. The 800,000 tons were broken down as follows:

500,000 tons to counterbalance Italian tonnage

140,000 tons to counterbalance German tonnage

60,000 tons for overseas communications

100,000 tons for special purposes, notably the transport
    of troops in the Mediterranean and Atlantic.

The last two missions might be equalized at 80,000 tons each. The Conseil Supérieur determined that French submarine tonnage might be reduced from 125,000 to 110,000 tons if the tonnage of light vessels remained fixed at 390,000 tons; conversely, if the tonnage of submarines remained fixed at 124,800 tons, the tonnage of light vessels might be brought down from 390,000 to 360,000. Battleships also offered a possibility for reduction if the conference decided to set the maximum tonnage of battleships at 18,000 tons, roughly half the Washington limit. The French might correspondingly reduce their tonnage to roughly 150,000 tons, but if the maximum tonnage remained at 22,000 they could consent to no reduction. On the whole, in rough numbers the French might therefore consent to a reduction of 50,000 tons.[57]

There was an opportunity for still larger reductions in the French naval requirements, but this would involve questions of a diplomatic and political nature, notably the creation of a Mediterranean pact providing for immediate assistance in the event of aggression. The British Mediterranean Fleet was 400,000 tons, and the French did not think it probable the British would consent to reduce it. British obligations, moreover, did not allow them to go below this figure without danger, and the French needed therefore to remain always a great power in the Mediterranean. Under these circumstances French tonnage would be:

400,000 tons in the Mediterranean

140,000 tons to counterbalance Germany

80,000 tons for colonial needs

80,000 tons for troop transport in the Mediterranean and Atlantic

700,000 tons total.

Allowing for reductions analogous to those mentioned above, French tonnage requirements would be 650,000 tons.[58]

Germany, although not part of the conference and almost three years before the arrival in power of Hitler and the Nazis transformed the situation, was nevertheless very much on the minds of the French. This was reflected in the French position on battleships. The first of the German *Ersatz Preussen* class of ostensibly ten-thousand-ton "armored cruisers" (and therefore legal within treaty limitations), armed with 28 cm guns, was laid down in February 1929 and was due to be launched in the spring of 1931. It represented a new class of warship eventually dubbed by the world press as a "pocket battleship."[59] Theoretically faster than existing battleships and more powerful than the ten-thousand-ton treaty cruisers, it represented a distinct potential threat to French lines of communication in the Atlantic. The French and the Italians had been given the right to 175,000 tons of battleships by the Washington treaties and might use it as they pleased. Consequently, French abandonment of this allowance would constitute a serious concession.

The French were disposed, for technical and financial reasons, to accept British proposals to reduce the displacement of battleships. The British had spoken of 25,000 tons, but the French could permit it to fall as low as 17,500. This would still allow them with a total of 175,000 tons within which to produce vessels individually superior to the German armored ship. It would, however, be an essential condition that the French be permitted to build eight ships to face the six new ships and two reserve ships allowed the Germans. Should the maximum individual tonnage of battleships be fixed at more than 27,000 tons, the French would insist that their total allocation be raised so they could have the eight ships. It would be only feeble compensation for the prospect of many years of supremacy for individual Anglo-Saxon battleships. The French would also find acceptable reduction of the sizes of guns, provided theirs remained superior to the 280 mm batteries of the German ships, although they would prefer 340 mm to the present 305 mm limit. However, the reduction of gun caliber would have the same advantageous result for Anglo-Saxon supremacy as the reduction in displacement and accordingly called for compensation as well. The idea of abolishing the battleship by extinction—that is, not replacing overage ships as they left service—had been sounded in the press. It would be acceptable only if all powers, and especially Germany, agreed and was therefore a subject that could be decided only at the Geneva disarmament conference. As long as Germany retained the rights accorded it by the Treaty of Versailles, the French could not give up the 175,000 tons allotted to them by the Washington treaties and ought, they felt, to insist on raising their tonnage allocation to correspond to eight ships at maximum allowable displacement.[60]

The French also continued their tradition of opposing any abolition of the submarine, arguing instead that it be brought under the same obligations of international law as to its employment as surface warships. In their eyes the submarine was essentially a defensive arm, as well as an effective means of protecting colonies from assault from the sea. French six-hundred-ton coastal submarines were employed primarily in the interdiction of close blockades, while the 1,500-ton submarines, with good speed, range, and seakeeping qualities, were especially useful for the protection of convoys, in that they would impose a certain caution on attacking warships, which would not be certain of their number, situation, or intentions. The French also intended to have a class of six very large (three-thousand-ton) submarines for use along their longest lines of communication in the South Atlantic or Indian Ocean—for example, Saigon to Madagascar.[61]

The French also appear to have had the feeling that they were in a relatively advantageous financial position. Among the great naval powers, Britain, Japan, and Italy seemed to want to maintain their acquired positions, requesting not only limitations but reductions. In contrast, the United States and France, with favorable balances of trade, accepted only theoretical or partial parities at very high levels and viewed with regret unitary reductions in tonnage and moratoriums in construction. France at this moment enjoyed a recovery of the franc, a budget surplus, full employment, and prosperous industry. This situation was not destined to last, but at the time the French navy wanted to recover lost ground and so went unenthusiastically to London. The Italians, in this French view, had reached their budgetary ceiling and were clearly losing ground, to the extent that in 1931–32 the power of the Italian fleet, with the exception of aviation, would be half that of the French fleet.[62]

The French proposals were not well received. Prime Minister Ramsay MacDonald told Tardieu that the French were converting "the present Conference into an 'Armament' and not a 'Disarmament' Conference." The Admiralty was disturbed by the French request for ten 8-inch-gun, ten-thousand-ton cruisers as against the proposed total for the Royal Navy of fifteen. This would give the French a 66 percent ratio with respect to the British, as against 33 percent under the Washington Treaty. The British allowance for French ten-thousand-ton cruisers was six, the number they had already completed (although a seventh was to be laid down in the present program). The French figure of 800,000 tons global tonnage would also give them 66 percent of British tonnage, against the Washington 33 percent.[63] Robert Craigie, who specialized in disarmament matters at the Foreign Office, made it quite clear to his French counterpart, Massigli, "that the figures presented to us were far too high" and that the French appeared to be going into the conference on the basis of a steady expansion of their naval power, while the British were looking for as deep a reduction as possible, because of the security offered by the various peace treaties and treaties of guarantee.[64] It should be obvious from this discussion that the British were doing exactly what the French so adamantly opposed—that is, seeking to extend the Washington ratios of battleships to other classes of warships.

The French claims had serious implications for the Admiralty, because in order to conserve "a proper relative European strength in 1936" the French tonnage figures for that year would require "an enormous increase" of strength over what had been proposed. They would mean laying down in each of the next four years ten-thousand-ton cruisers with 8-inch-guns, seven-thousand-ton cruisers with 6-inch guns, and proportionately large numbers of smaller vessels. The French strength would then be 45 percent of that of the British, but, ominously, the French proposals "would naturally cause a heavy building programme" in Italy.[65] This had nightmarish implications for Admiral Sir Charles Madden, the First Sea Lord. Of the British 8-inch-gun cruisers, two were "permanently locked up in Australian waters," and five were in China and probably could not be withdrawn. This left only eight for home waters and the Mediterranean; should the French have ten in any situation in which Britain and France were on opposite sides, the British "would be in a difficult situation," especially when one also considered the large tonnage of French submarines. MacDonald raised an even more alarming prospect. Should the Italians build up to parity with the French, there might be a combined total of as many as twenty-four potentially hostile 8-inch-gun cruisers in the Mediterranean (assuming the French also replaced two old 7.5-inch-gun cruisers with 8-inch cruisers) at a time when the British would have only fifteen of the class, with seven away in Australian or Chinese waters.[66]

This British dilemma was quite evident to the French delegation, especially Darlan. In his view the British had taken the initiative in calling the conference because Great Britain's financial situation no longer allowed it to maintain first place among the great naval powers, a status from which the United States might supplant it within a short time. Consequently, under the color of disarmament, the British had sought parity with the United States to avoid a disadvantageous disparity, but they also wanted a fleet superior to the combined principal European fleets. But—as always, because of their financial situation—the British wanted to obtain that superiority as economically as possible, and that is why they wanted, without lowering the figures below the minimum fixed by *British* needs, to lower the figures of other powers without considering *their* needs. Darlan also discerned that the Admiralty had found the figures set by the British government too low and that accordingly there was disagreement within British opinion, a reference no doubt to the Admiralty's desire for seventy cruisers and the government's decision to settle for fifty. The French observed similar disregard on the part of the Americans to French needs in the desire to achieve parity and economy. The Italians Darlan dismissed; their sole idea was parity with the French as a matter of prestige for Mussolini's government. This left France as the sole power having clearly stated its needs. Its situation was very strong, and the importance of its fleet had been determined taking account of not only its needs but also financial possibilities. Consequently, the French had no reason to modify naval proposals while conditions of security remained the same.[67]

The French had been willing to lower their tonnage requirements should they receive a suitable diplomatic or political guarantee. Unfortunately, there was little chance of this happening. The British cabinet was well aware of French desires, notably through Craigie's account of his conversations with the French. However, MacDonald would have nothing to do with them and harked back to the situation before the First World War. He warned against "getting into the same position in regard to France as Sir Edward Grey had got into in 1906." Rather than revert to this situation, MacDonald claimed, he would go back to the Admiralty's old program of seventy cruisers. The First Lord, A. V. Alexander, appears to have pointed out disadvantages from another aspect—that is, if a political agreement increased British political responsibility, the British themselves might want a larger program. The foreign secretary, Arthur Henderson, thought that the forthcoming incorporation of the Kellogg Pact into the Covenant of the League of Nations "really provided definite guarantees to France against aggression." Henderson had in fact said this directly to Tardieu in a meeting on 13 February.[68] The French might well counter, as Massigli subsequently did, that while the various peace pacts had a certain effect in calming world opinion, there was nothing either in the covenant of the League or the Kellogg-Briand Pact that really offered a guarantee of international protection in the event of France being subjected to a flagrant attack. The French were not likely to be convinced by British assurances that if France's policy was genuinely a pacific one, the League of Nations would never leave it to stand alone against any unprovoked aggression.[69] The United States was even less likely to assume any meaningful obligation toward France.[70]

The arguments in the conference came to resemble a circle, as Admiral Violette told his wife in early March. He doubted that any further progress could be made and felt it would take a very skillful Ariane to unravel the difficulties caused by the French demands for security, which the British would examine only if the Americans intervened—and the latter did not wish to do so. The French therefore maintained their projects, and the Italians did the same, as the British wanted to equal the two combined, while the American delegation wanted parity with the British and had told its public that this would be accomplished in 1935. But then it would be necessary to dispense enormous sums they did not have. One came back to the same starting point, Violette was convinced, but the sole possible and logical solution (the guarantee) had been pushed aside.[71] A few weeks later Violette even believed the British were afraid not only of new engagements but even of those already made and that by seeking to put a new interpretation on the Covenant of the League of Nations they would emasculate it so that it would be only an empty text. The situation was clear to the French—they had placed security as the foundation for the edifice that was to be built not only for themselves but for everyone. It had failed, they could not go any farther, and they were not the ones responsible.[72]

Not every member of the French delegation regretted the final failure of the French to obtain political guarantees. As the conference dragged on into April, Darlan wrote his wife that he hoped the latest round of negotiations would fail, for they would signify nothing and perhaps oblige the French to make concessions. When Briand's final efforts did fail, Darlan wrote: "I am delighted, because for a worthless trifle it would have been necessary to let go a certain number of tons which we would not like."[73]

One of the great difficulties in British eyes was the refusal of Grandi and the Italian delegation to name any actual figures for the Italian construction program, beyond their claim of parity with France. This made it very difficult to actually negotiate on the basis of a program up to December 1936, the term to be covered in any agreement at London.[74] MacDonald suggested as a means to get around the difficulty, and possibly reduce the "unacceptable" high French figures, that the French examine the situation on the basis of a hypothetical Italian tonnage of 400,000. What would the French figure be on this basis?[75] The French naval delegation's calculations involving classes of warships, exempt or special classes, the term of any treaty, and the rhythm of construction are too lengthy and complex to be more than summarized here:

In the Mediterranean:	Italian tonnage + 50,000
In the north (Germany)	140,000
Overseas requirements	160,000.

The minister of marine therefore considered that total French tonnage must be at least 250,000 tons superior to Italian tonnage and also that the French tonnage at the moment, 642,216, was the minimum.[76] Furthermore, in order for the French superiority over the Italian fleet to be real and not fictive the distribution of tonnage would have to be rearranged, notably by diminishing the tonnage of battleships and using the space thus liberated for battle cruisers *(croiseurs de combat)* and aircraft carriers.[77]

Massigli appeared receptive to the British proposals. He noted in a memorandum for Briand that the naval experts had unofficially indicated the possibility that based on a figure of 642,000 tons the French might reduce submarine tonnage to 90,000 tons in place of 100,000 and the number of large cruisers in 1936 from ten to nine. The conversations with British naval experts seemed to indicate that the difficulty for the British lay much less in the total French tonnage for 1936 than in the proportion of that tonnage represented by *la flotte légère*—that is, cruisers and destroyers. The British seemed to be suggesting that the French expedite the construction of aircraft carriers and battle cruisers, return to the Washington categories, and proportionately reduce the tonnage allotted to *bâtiments légers*. Massigli thought there were possibilities of negotiating on this basis but that it was not very likely an agreement could be reached with the British on the figure of 642,000 tons.

Massigli wondered if it was not worth the trouble of obtaining such an agreement by a new sacrifice of tonnage. If this did not run into insurmountable obstacles from a technical point of view, such an agreement would have certain advantages politically, although of course it would be accompanied by an escalator clause *(clause de savegarde)* in case Italian naval construction passed the determined level. If the French could harmonize their figures with the British and Americans, they could count to a large extent on Anglo-Saxon pressure to prevent the Italians from executing a program that would oblige the French to raise their ceiling *(plafond)*, which would have repercussions on the Anglo-American agreement. In the absence of such an agreement with the British, a Franco-Italian armaments race would take place; the French would conserve their lead but would set a new level that the Anglo-Saxons would take as the basis for their own programs. The French would then bear the responsibility for any growth in armaments before the next conference above the levels set at London.

An Anglo-French accord set at a French level slightly below 642,000 tons might be taken as a manifestation of French willingness not to exceed the present level of armaments. It might also be a precedent for similar accords on land and air armaments and thereby help the French preserve their present superiority. Massigli posed the questions: Did these advantages offset the additional sacrifice of tonnage? Would France's security be better ensured in 1936 by the existence of an additional 20,000 tons in its fleet or by the pursuit in years to come of Franco-British collaboration in Europe? He warned that without an accord between France and Britain, work at Geneva might be paralyzed. Also, Germany would be strongly tempted to profit from the situation to resume its liberty in land armaments if it believed that a displeased England might be inclined to let it do so, in order to give the French a warning.[78]

The possibility that French tonnage might be reduced still more was a direct challenge to the navy's position, and Darlan quickly buffered the new minister of marine, Jacques-Louis Dumesnil, with additional statistics. Darlan pointed out that the figure of 642,216 tons represented a reduction of 118,191 tons from the total regarded by the French as their absolute requirement and a reduction of 42,671 from the tonnage of the fleet in service in 1940 if an agreement was reached on the limitation of new building. The navy had always indicated that it could envisage the possibility of maintaining its tonnage at that figure up to 1940, assuming a minimum superiority over Italy of 240,000 tons, only if there was a new arrangement of total tonnage. This was because, Darlan argued, if the superiority of the French fleet over the Italian fleet was to be effective, superiority in total tonnage was not sufficient; the French had to maintain superiority in all categories. The navy, for example, needed twelve first-class cruisers. If in order to profit from an agreement with Great Britain this number were slightly diminished, the cruisers suppressed ought to be replaced by new ships in the category of capital ships *(bâtiments de ligne)* or aircraft carriers. The French were obligated to build capital ships other than battleships—presumably Darlan meant battle cruisers—because the Germans were building them. If the French kept integrally to the Washington maxima of 175,000 tons for battleships and 60,000 for aircraft carriers, there would remain only 407,000 tons for light vessels and submarines. The Italians already had six first-class cruisers, and it was consequently impossible for the French, given their needs outside the Mediterranean, to go below nine new first-class cruisers—that is 90,000 tons. There would then remain, at the maximum, 317,000 tons for light ships and submarines. If France allowed the reduced figure of 90,000 tons for sub-marines, there remained 227,000 tons for second-class cruisers, destroyers, and torpedo boats.[79]

Darlan produced elaborate calculations of possible allocations of ton-nage among various classes of warships given an increase in Italian tonnage to 400,000. The net result was his argument that below 642,000 tons it was dif-ficult for the French to possess an effective and indispensable superiority over the Italians in all categories.[80]

The French delegation also explored possible compromise on the question of submarines, on the basis of the fact that submarines of less than six hundred tons displacement had by common agreement not been subject to limitation at the conference. With a maximum tonnage of 642,216 tons, the French did not believe they could go below 90,000 tons in submarines. But, believing the destructive power of the torpedo was the same whether it was fired from a sub-marine or a surface ship, should a superiority of 240,000 tons over the Italian fleet be recognized the French would be prepared to limit their coastal-defense submarines under six hundred tons to a total of 21,000 tons. The French navy claimed 29,000 tons of coastal submarines as their absolute requirement but would accept 23,000 tons in case of a general agreement on naval construction up to December 1936.[81]

The various suggestions for compromise (including those that so alarmed Darlan) all depended on Italian acceptance of a French margin of superiority over the Italian fleet. This would not occur. Failing this, the discussions among the political leaders and diplomats, as well as the more technical arguments of the committees of experts, seemed to take on a circular appearance. The British, notably MacDonald and Henderson, both sincere champions of disarmament, as well as Craigie, the Foreign Office's expert on disarmament, all stressed that the French figures were too high and that the French were going into the confer-ence to expand their naval power while the British were committed to a reduc-tion. Furthermore, they argued, a large French building program was more likely to stir up an Italian building program than would a more moderate one. Henderson pointed out that governments had to respect public opinion. How could the British government go to Parliament and report that as a result of the conference the British were scrapping ships while the French were increasing their own? The British outlook was that at the moment "the risk of war was prac-tically nil." What, MacDonald wanted to know, dangers were the French guard-ing against? Their justifications seemed to be based on the same mentality as that upon which the British fleet had been drawn up before 1914. But now the

Locarno and Kellogg Pacts were in existence, and even Germany was a member of the League.[82] MacDonald feared that if he had to explain the large French increase to the House of Commons he would "be out of office in a week."[83]

The French answers were predictable. Premier Tardieu emphasized that the French tonnage was 450,000 tons less than in 1914, the naval budget 18 percent less, and that the need for replacement tonnage was so large because during the war French dockyards had built no ships. Furthermore, Tardieu alleged, there was now no Anglo-French agreement on the distribution of fleets as there had been in 1914 (a glaring exaggeration of the nature of British obligations to France at the time).[84] Massigli answered the argument about the Kellogg-Briand Pact by admitting that it and similar peace pacts might have had "a certain value in calming world opinion" but that nothing in them offered guarantees to a power that was a victim of a flagrant violation of the peace pact. Locarno was valuable for Germany's western frontier but left open the question of the eastern frontier; if Germany and Poland clashed, France might be forced into the conflict, whereas the guarantors of Locarno would retain their freedom of action. This necessitated France taking Germany as well as Italy into consideration and keeping a sufficient naval force in the north at Brest.[85] This aspect was succinctly expressed by Briand, for whom the Italian demand for parity "was not for real parity, but for superiority, since an equal tonnage for France and Italy would always give Italy a superiority in the Mediterranean"; if the French delegation were to envisage parity with Italy the French government "would be up-set within forty-eight hours."[86] The French desire for security in a possible Mediterranean pact also brought about considerable discussion, but it ultimately led nowhere, since neither the United States nor Great Britain were really willing to be drawn into any agreement likely to be strong enough to satisfy the French. Furthermore, other interested parties, notably Spain and Turkey, were not represented at the conference.[87]

The argument of the French that they could not accept parity with the Italians because of their obligations outside of the Mediterranean was used also by Grandi, to justify Italian claims. That is, if the French had, beyond the Mediterranean, the North Sea to defend—an obvious reference to a potential German enemy—the Italians could argue that two seas actually signified freedom for the French. It was much better for a country to have two seas to defend than to be a prisoner in one, like Italy. Grandi declared that even admitting the French had a problem in the North Sea that the Italians did not have, the Mediterranean was at least twice the problem for Italy that it was for France. If the French therefore assumed a margin of superiority because the North Sea was necessary for them, then the Italians should also have a margin of superiority for their Mediterranean needs. The sum of the two would be parity.[88] Grandi also raised the specter of Yugoslavia. It had but a tiny navy and, Grandi admitted, was in itself nothing to disturb Italy, but a Yugoslavia pushed *(poussée)* by France—a reference to the Franco-Yugoslav alliance of 1927—would be something different.[89]

Fairly early in the conference, Massigli emphasized to his British opposite number, Craigie, that "the crux of the whole situation was really Italy" and that if Italy could accept figures that were lower than the French figures, the latter could be reduced.[90] Unfortunately for hopes of success, the Italian foreign minister and delegation leader, Dino Grandi, bluntly stated a few weeks later that if Italy conceded "what had been recognized as her right at Washington"— that is, parity—Grandi "would be shot at the first station across the frontier."[91] Grandi's reports from the conference emphasized the stiff, unyielding Italian stance but constantly reiterated, with apparent sweet reasonableness, how willing Italy would be to disarm to the level of the strongest European power.

Grandi, characterized by one historian as a "mephistophelean character," was reputed to be dedicated to the reduction of French hegemony in Europe.[92] His reports to Mussolini, flagrantly sycophantic in some points, reveal that he regarded the French delegation as the primary enemy and intended that one of the results of the conference would be the "unmasking" of French designs. Another objective would be to make good propaganda for Fascism abroad. Grandi quoted approvingly Mussolini's statement that in time of peace a nation's ranking *(gerarchia)* is indicated by the power of its navy.[93] No matter how hard MacDonald or Henderson tried to find some form of compromise, such as parity of programs, with French superiority represented merely by overage ships destined to disappear, the fundamental demand of the Italians for parity and the refusal of the French to recognize it thwarted agreement. The possibility Italy might find itself isolated at the conference did not trouble Grandi; in a cable to the head of Mussolini's press office as background for the Italian press he stated that Italy's action "was independent of the action of anybody. The Fascist point of view does not need to be propped up or assisted by others; it can defend itself. Solitude does us no harm; on the contrary it is perfectly consonant with our Fascist spirit. Fascism does not stand with its hat in hand asking favors of anybody."[94]

Mussolini's attitude too was clear. The preceding month in Rome he had told Grandi that he was to inform *il duce* at the moment when the Italo-French dispute might bring about the failure of the conference; Mussolini would then decide if he wanted to alter the Italian position toward, for example, acceptance of parity of programs. On 20 March, after receiving Grandi's copious reports, he wired Grandi to "refrain from any further conciliatory proposals of any kind," repeating these instructions the following day, with orders not to swerve from the established position or, again, to make, either directly or indirectly, further conciliatory proposals of any type.[95]

Grandi repeated at the close of the conference his sentiment that it had been a triumph for the Fascist regime even as it ended in partial failure, with agreement only among the British, Americans, and Japanese. With the usual Fascist rhetoric, he reiterated how Italy had stood alone in presenting Mussolini's ideas of disarmament and that everyone had recognized the contribution made by Fascism. Moreover, he claimed that for the first time in an international conference Italy had been treated on a footing of equality with the four chief powers, a contrast to the trembling diplomacy of old liberal or papal Italy. Nevertheless, Grandi's experiences at the conference led him to recommendations for the future that would not be encouraging for the cause of disarmament. He thought the Italians had wasted at least two years after the Washington Conference in beginning to match French construction and that the past superiority in French tonnage had been used against Italian claims for parity at the conference. He now argued that Italy must, starting in 1930, lay down tonnage at least equal to that to be laid down by the French according to the program recently voted by the French parliament. Furthermore, in the future the Italians ought to be more circumspect in scrapping overage ships, since, he thought, the French made use of obsolescent tonnage to justify their superior position.[96]

Grandi was a Fascist, and Fascist rhetoric as well as flattery of Mussolini mark his reports. However, on questions of naval power more traditional Italian diplomats couched their arguments on their own experience rather than the rather crude Social Darwinian ideas about a "hierarchy of nations" employed by the Fascists. Bernardo Attolico, Italian ambassador to Brazil, spoke of the "enormous advantage France has over us, not only because she can obtain coal by way of the Channel and the Atlantic, as well as the Mediterranean, but also because of her consequent greater security and ease in making use of her ports and railways." Attolico recalled the war and what the presence of even one submarine in the Mediterranean had meant for Italian grain supplies—the reason why on the Italian side of Ventimiglia "people were eating black bread, on the other [French] side they were eating white bread."[97]

There was also a note of caution from another traditional source, the Italian naval staff. In an unsigned memorandum for Admiral Burzagli, *capo di Stato Maggiore,* a writer (or writers) on the staff warned against undertaking a vast building program in order to achieve parity with the French, or even a more advantageous position. This would pose the danger of initiating a naval armaments race with the French, a race that, based on the relative economic potentials of the two countries, would end to Italy's disadvantage. It would be preferable for the Italians to announce that, inspired by the ideal of true disarmament, they would not after the conference initiate any particular program to increase their naval armaments and in the future would regulate new construction according to the program unfolded by France. This would have the advantage, with respect to European and, especially, Anglo-American opinion, of demonstrating that it was not the Italians who were the cause of future increases in naval armaments. Moreover, the current Italian program, including ships yet to be laid down, already represented a major and homogeneous development of Italy's fleet and a far from negligible burden to its budget. However, its situation compared to France could be kept as it was at the moment; it might be easier to arrive at a future agreement.[98]

Before the end of April the Italians made a dramatic gesture. On Sunday the 27th they simultaneously launched five new warships: the ten-thousand-ton cruiser *Zara,* at La Spezia; the ten-thousand-ton cruiser *Fiume,* at Trieste; the five-thousand-ton cruiser *Alberto di Giussano,* at Sestri Ponente, near Genoa; the five-thousand-ton cruiser *Giovanni delle Bande Nere,* at Castellammare, near Naples; and the medium-size submarine *Delfino,* at Monfalcone, near Trieste. The launchings took place with great ceremony in the presence of members of the Italian royal family, the government, the armed services, and the Fascist Party.[99]

The ships themselves were not a surprise; they had, after all, been under construction for some time. But if the Italians wanted to make a point and attract attention, they certainly succeeded. The Admiralty's confidential *Monthly Intelligence Review* took note that on 30 April the Italians had also announced a new program of construction of one ten-thousand-ton cruiser, two five-thousand-ton cruisers, four destroyers, and twenty-two submarines of various dimensions—a total of about 43,000 tons to be laid down within eight months. This was higher than it had been anticipated the Italians could normally undertake; when added to ships completed, building, or projected since 1926, it was almost exactly, by Admiralty calculations, equal to the French total for the same period. The conclusion was that "the Italians are making a strong bid for parity with France in modern ships and are so far succeeding in obtaining it."[100]

The French and Italians continued to negotiate for well over a year after the London Naval Conference, but despite their own best efforts, the dogged determination of British negotiators like Craigie, and complex and clever schemes to bridge the differences, they ultimately failed to reach agreement. To use the well turned phrase of Arnold Toynbee, the negotiations were "no more readily comprehensible to the lay mind than an astronomical or a theological treatise."[101] The issue of "parity" could not be overcome, and when the building of the German *Deutschland*s eventually forced the French to respond with the *Dunkerque*-class battle cruisers, the predictable Italian response was the modernization of old battleships and the laying down of the 35,000-ton *Littorio* class. The French would eventually respond with the 35,000-ton *Richelieu* class. The French and Italian rivalry represents a notable failure of the London Naval Conference to reduce naval armaments.[102]

NOTES

1. The subject is covered at length in Mariano Gabriele, *Le convenzioni navali della Triplice* (Rome: Ufficio Storico della Marina Militare, 1969), and Paul G. Halpern, *The Mediterranean Naval Situation, 1908–1914* (Cambridge, Mass.: Harvard University Press, 1971), chap. 8.

2. [Vice-Amiral, Chef d'État-major général], *La Politique Navale Française*, n.d. [1929], 3, Vincennes, Service Historique de la Marine [hereafter cited as SHM], carton 1BB2-196.

3. See lengthy discussions in Ray Walser, *France's Search for a Battle Fleet: Naval Policy and Naval Power, 1898–1914* (New York: Garland, 1992). A summary is in Paul Halpern, "The French Navy, 1880–1914," in *Technology and Naval Combat in the Twentieth Century and Beyond*, ed. Phillips Payson O'Brien (London: Frank Cass, 2001), 36–52.

4. The French estimated their warship losses at 111,745 tons, those of the Italians 76,100 tons. *Politique Navale Française*, 5, SHM, carton 1BB2-196.

5. Ibid., 6.

6. On these subjects see A. Thomazi, *La Guerre navale dans l'Adriatique* (Paris: Payot, 1925); Thomazi, *La Guerre Navale dans la Méditerranée* (Paris: Payot, 1929); Adolphe Laurens, *Le commandement Naval en Méditerranée, 1914–1918* (Paris: Payot, 1931); Paul G. Halpern, *The Naval War in the Mediterranean,*

1914–1918 (London and Annapolis: George Allen & Unwin and Naval Institute Press, 1987); and Achille Rastelli and Alessandro Massignani, eds., *La Guerra Navale, 1914–1918: Un contributo internazionale alle operazioni in Mediterraneo* (Vicenza: Gino Rossato Editore, 2002).

7. *Politique Navale Française,* 6, SHM, carton 1BB2-196.

8. On the French and Italians at the Washington Naval Conference see Joel Blatt, "The Parity That Meant Superiority: French Naval Policy towards Italy at the Washington Conference, 1921–1922, and Interwar French Foreign Policy," *French Historical Studies* 12, no. 2 (Fall 1981), 223–48; and Brian R. Sullivan, "Italian Naval Power and the Washington Disarmament Conference of 1921–22," *Diplomacy and Statecraft* 4, no. 3 (November 1993), 220–48.

9. *Politique Navale Française,* 9–10, SHM, carton 1BB2-196. In British documents the term "auxiliary craft" is used for *"bâtiments légers."* See CP 5 (30), "London Naval Conference 1930, Memorandum respecting Proposals to be submitted by His Majesty's Government in the United Kingdom to the Conference, n.d. [1930], 17–18, ADM 116/3372, The National Archives, Kew [hereafter cited as TNA].

10. Cabinet du Ministre, "Analyse du projet de programme naval presenté par l'État-major général au Conseil Supérieur de la Marine, n.d., 2, SHM, carton 1BB8-217.

11. Vice Amiral Salaun, Rapport au Conseil Supérieur de la Marine, 30 September 1920, 1–8, SHM, carton 1BB8-41.

12. *Politique Navale Française,* 11–13, SHM, carton 1BB2-196. A convenient summary is in Philippe Masson, "La 'belle marine' de 1939," in Guy Pedroncini, ed., *Histoire Militaire de la France,* vol. 3, *De 1871 à 1940* (Paris: Presses Universitaires de France, 1992), 445–50.

13. Salvatore Minardi, *Il Disarmo Navale Italiano (1919–1936): Un confronto politico-diplomatico per il potere marittimo* (Rome: Ufficio Storico della Marina Militare, 1999), 55–56.

14. Walter Polastro, "La Marina Militare italiana nel primo dopoguerra (1918–1925)," *Il Risorgimento* 3 (1977), 128–29; Giovanni Bernardi, *Il Disarmo navale fra le due guerre mondiale (1919–1939)* (Rome: Ufficio Storico della Marina Militare, 1975), 44–48.

15. Polastro, "La Marina Militare italiana nel primo dopoguerra," 150.

16. *Politique Navale Française,* 21, SHM, carton 1BB2-196. New construction is relatively easy to account for; the problem lies in counting older ships still potentially useful. The French had six large old armored cruisers, still effective in guarding convoys, and five old second-class cruisers. The Italians had ten old cruisers.

17. Differing interpretations in *Politique Navale Française,* 15–16, SHM, carton 1BB2-196; and CP 5 (30), "London Naval Conference, 1930," 19–20, ADM 116/3372, TNA.

18. *Politique Navale Française,* 16–17, SHM, carton 1BB2-196; CP 5 (30), "London Naval Conference, 1930," 20–21, ADM 116/3372, TNA.

19. Plans Division, Admiralty, memorandum, 15 December 1927, ADM 116/2578, TNA.

20. Bernardi, *Il Disarmo navale fra le due guerre mondiale,* 205–207.

21. Conseil Supérieur de la Défence Nationale, no. 350/D.N.I., Rapport à la Commission d'Études sur la préparation de la Conférence pour la Limitation des Armements Navales qui doit se tenir à Londres en Janvier 1930 et sur la question de l'Interdependence des Armements, 4 November 1929, SHM, carton 1BB2–191; *La Politique Navale Française,* 17, SHM, carton 1BB2-196.

22. Bernardi, *Il Disarmo navale fra le due guerre mondiale,* 223–26. A fuller explanation is in Stato Maggiore della Marina, "Per quale ragione non partecipammo all conferenza tripartita, non aderimmo al compromesso navale anglo-francese, mentre oggi ci conviene aderire all'invito anglo-americano," n.d. [1929], Ministero degli Affairi Esteri, *I Documenti Diplomatici Italiani* [hereafter referred to as *DDI*], Settima Serie (Rome: Istituto Poligrafico dello Stato, 1972), vol. 8, no. 287, 303–304.

23. A summary from the British point of view is in CP 5 (30), "London Naval Conference, 1930," 23–26, ADM 116/3372, TNA.

24. Ibid., 26.

25. *La Politique Navale Française,* 17–18, SHM, carton 1BB2-196.

26. Ibid., 27; Lord Cushendun to Chilton, no. 1156, 16 August 1928, ADM 116/2579, TNA.

27. Wingfield to Lord Cushendun, 7 October 1928 enclosing Italian Note Verbale of 6 October 1928, ADM 116/2579, TNA.

28. Captain R. Bevan to C. Wingfield [Chargé d'affaires, Rome], 5 September 1928, PRO, ADM 116/2579. The lightly built, virtually unarmored and vulnerable *Condottieri* class is included in Anthony Preston, *The World's Worst Warships* (London: Conway Maritime, 2002), 123–29. Preston's comments center more on the erroneous strategic and tactical conceptions of the Italian high command and their faulty conduct of the war than the ships themselves.

29. CP 5 (30), "London Naval Conference, 1930," 27–31, ADM 116/3372, TNA.

30. Stato Maggiore, "Per quale ragione non partecipammo alla conferenza tripartita. . . ." *DDI,* Settima Serie, vol. 8, no. 287, 305–306.

31. Verbali delle riunioni del Consiglio dei Ministri cited in *DDI*, Settima Serie, vol. 8, 172, note 1. See also Bernardi, *Il Disarmo navale fra le due guerre mondiale*, 263.

32. CP 5 (30), "London Naval Conference, 1930," 33, ADM 116/3372; [État-major général], "Conférence de Londres, 1930," n.d., 30–31, and Capitaine de vaisseau De Ponteves [Naval attaché, London] to Minister of Marine, 7 November, 1929, SHM, carton 1BB2-191. The apparent Italian change on the abolition of submarines was in a memorandum for the French Foreign Minister stating that the Italian government was not in principle opposed to the abolition of submarines. See Memorandum for Briand, 21 December 1929 enclosed with Grandi to Manzoni [Italian ambassador in Paris], 18 December 1929, *DDI*, Settima Serie, vol. 8, no. 261, 275–57. For a full discussion see Minardi, *Il disarmo navale italiano*, 59–62.

33. État-major général, 3ème Section, "Parité avec l'Italie," 29 October 1929, SHM, carton 1BB2-191.

34. Ibid.

35. Georges Leygues, "Position de la Marine Française dans la question de la limitation des armements navals," 15 October 1929, SHM, carton 1BB2-191. The memorandum was enclosed in letters to the premier and minister of foreign affairs.

36. Ibid.

37. Leygues to General Serrigny [Secrétaire Général du Conseil Supérieur de la Défense Nationale], 10 November 1929, SHM, carton 1BB2-191.

38. Ibid. The French expected Italian tonnage to rise to a minimum of 500,000.

39. Programs summarized in Bernardi, *Il Disarmo navale fra le due guerre mondiale*, 720–21.

40. Stato Maggiore della Marina, "Alcuni aspetti del problema navale italo-francese," n.d. [1929], *DDI*, Settima Serie, vol. 8, no. 288, 306–307. This memorandum was one of a number prepared by the naval staff in anticipation of the London Naval Conference and placed in a volume entitled *Il problema della limitazione degli armamenti navali nei suoi aspetti tecnico-politici.*, ibid., 303, note 1.

41. Ibid., 307–309.

42. Stato Maggiore della Marina, "Conferenza Navale di Londra," 30 December 1929, extracts published in *DDI*, Settima Serie, vol. 8, nos. 288, 309, note 1.

43. Pierre Pierrard, ed., *Dictionnaire de la IIIe République* (Paris: Larousse, 1968), 235–36. See also the remarks in Stephen A. Schuker, *The End of French Predominance in Europe* (Chapel Hill: University of North Carolina Press, 1976), 81–82, and the entry in Patrick H. Hutton, ed., *Historical Dictionary of*

the Third French Republic, 1870–1940 (Westport, Conn.: Greenwood, 1986), 996.

44. *Dictionnaire des Parlementaires Français (1889–1940)* (Paris: Presses Universitaires de France, 1966), 6:1551–53.

45. See Jacques Raphaël-Leygues and François Flohic, *Darlan* (Paris: Plon, 1986), 45–46, and Hervé Coutau-Bégarie and Claude Huan, *Darlan* (Paris: Fayard, 1989), 94–97.

46. See Raphaël-Leygues and Flohic, *Darlan,* 45–46; and Coutau-Bégarie and Huan, *Darlan,* 94–97.

47. Darlan to his wife, 23 January 1930, reproduced in Raphaël-Leygues and Flohic, *Darlan,* 43.

48. "Conférence de Londres, 1930," n.d. [c. February-March, 1930], 33, SHM, carton 1BB2-191.

49. See the entry by Renzo De Felice in Philip V. Cannistraro, ed., *Historical Dictionary of Fascist Italy* (Westport, Conn.: Greenwood, 1982), 256–57. See also H. Stuart Hughes, "The Early Diplomacy of Italian Fascism: 1922–1932," in *The Diplomats, 1919–1939,* ed. Gordon A. Craig and Felix Gilbert (Princeton, N.J.: Princeton University Press, 1953), 217–19, 230–33; R. J. B. Bosworth, *Mussolini* (London: Arnold, 2002), 247; and MacGregor Knox, *Common Destiny: Dictatorship, Foreign Policy, and War in Fascist Italy and Nazi Germany* (Cambridge, U.K.: Cambridge University Press, 2000), 129–32.

50. The literature on Mussolini is enormous, but on the question of the navy and disarmament see Marco Rimanelli, *Italy between Europe and the Mediterranean: Diplomacy and Naval Strategy from Unification to NATO, 1800s–2000* (New York: Peter Lang, 1997), 528–30, 538–39; Bosworth, *Mussolini,* 250–51; Knox, *Common Destiny,* 127–31; and Denis Mack Smith, *Mussolini* (New York: Random House, 1983), 156–58.

51. Arnold J. Toynbee, *Survey of International Affairs, 1930* (London: Humphrey Milford, 1931), 33, note 1.

52. Record of a conversation between Mr. MacDonald, Mr. Alexander, M. Briand and M. Tardieu, March 16, 1930 in E. L. Woodward and Rohan Butler (eds.), *Documents on British Foreign Policy, 1919–1939* [hereafter referred to as *DBFP*] 2nd Series (London: His Majesty's Stationery Office, 1946), vol. 1, document no. 158, 254.

53. Note of a meeting of representatives of the delegations of France and the United Kingdom, April 8, 1930, *DBFP,* 2nd series, vol. 1, document no. 181, 294.

54. Toynbee, *Survey of International Affairs, 1930,* 34.

55. Although published after the conference, see for example, État-Major Général, 2e Bureau, "L'Impérialisme de l'Italie fasciste et les revendications italiennes,"

DS-C.305 Bulletin des Renseignments, Novembre 1930, 31–33, SHM, carton 1BB2–89.

56. État-Major Général, 3ème Bureau, no. 22 E.M.G.3, 9 January 1930, SHM, carton 1BB2–191.

57. Al.D [probably Darlan], "Note Relative à la discussion du tonnage de 800,000t demandé par la Marine," 15 December 1929, SHM, carton 1BB2–191.

58. Ibid.

59. The ship was named *Deutschland* (later *Lützow*) and was basically a "political ship," built to meet treaty requirements. Only three of the type were built before the Nazi government shifted to larger and more conventional warships. For details see Siegfried Breyer, *Battleships and Battle Cruisers, 1905–1970* (New York: Doubleday, 1973), 286–89.

60. "Discussion sur les diverses catégories de bâtiments," n.d., SHM, carton 1BB2–191. Similar sentiments about the necessity of an armament equaling the 280 mm of the *Ersatz Preussen* are found in A.L.D. [Darlan], "Note sur le Navire de Ligne," 31 January, 1930, ibid.

61. Delégation Navale, no. 35-Marine E, 6 February 1930, and Delégation Navale, no. 36-Marine E, "Sous-Marins," 6 February 1930, SHM, carton 1BB2–191. The planned French submarine tonnage and numbers would be broken down as:

Six large three-thousand-ton long-range submarines	18,000 tons
Fifty-two first-class submarines (1,500 tons)	78,000 tons
Forty-eight second-class submarines (600 tons)	28,800 tons
106 Submarines	124,800 tons.

62. [Probably Darlan], "Réflexions sur la Conférence de Londres," 14 January 1930, SHM.

63. Notes of a meeting of the British delegation, 12 February 1930, PRO, ADM 116/2747, TNA.

64. Note by M. Craigie of a conversation with M. Massigli, 13 February 1930, *DBFP*, 2nd Series, vol. 1, no. 144, 209–10.

65. Admiralty, "Note on the French Proposals," n.d. [c.15 February 1930], ADM 116/2747, f.73, TNA. In each of the following four years the British would be obligated to build four flotilla leaders, thirty-two destroyers, twenty large submarines, and seventeen small submarines.

66. Notes of a meeting of the United Kingdom delegation, 16 February 1930, ADM 116/2747, f.73, TNA.

67. Darlan, "Conférence de Londres–Impressions sur la conférence," 20 February 1930, SHM, carton 1BB2–191.

68. Notes of a meeting of the United Kingdom Delegation, 16 February 1930, ADM 116/2747, TNA; Notes of a meeting of the representatives of the

delegations of the United States of America, France and the United Kingdom, 13 February 1930, *DBFP*, 2nd Series, vol. 1, no. 145, 214.

69. Note by Mr. Craigie of a conversation with M. Massigli, 25 February 1930, *DBFP*, 2nd Series, vol. 1, no. 150, 236–37.

70. The almost torturous dodging of obligations can be seen in detail in the lengthy account of Anglo-American talks on the subject in Memorandum of a meeting between representatives of the delegations of the United States of America and the United Kingdom, 24 March 1930, *DBFP*, 2nd Series, vol. 1, no. 168, 266–74. See also the short contemporary account in Toynbee, *Survey of International Affairs, 1930*, 52–54, 56–58, 60.

71. Violette to his wife, 10 March 1930, Papiers Violette, SHM, Cote 5 Mi 85–86.

72. Violette to his wife, 31 March 1930, ibid.

73. Darlan to his wife 1 and 4 April, 1930, reproduced in Raphaël-Leygues and Flohic, *Darlan*, 45–46.

74. Henderson to R. Graham [British ambassador in Rome], 15 March 1930, *DFBP*, 2nd Series, vol. 1, no. 157, 251–52.

75. Record of a conversation between Mr. MacDonald, Mr. Alexander, M. Briand, and M. Tardieu, 16 March 1930, *DFBP*, 2nd Series, vol. 1, no. 158, 252–57.

76. Note pour le Président du Conseil, n.d. [24 March 1930], SHM, carton 1BB2–191. The French tonnage of 642,216 did not include 28,645 tons of "special ships" or 10,948 tons of gunboats, exempt from the treaty. There is a discrepancy in the hypothetical margin of superiority over Italy. A subsequent "Note pour le Ministre" of 1 April 1930 uses 240,000 tons, as do most of the other memoranda. Ibid.

77. Admiral Darlan's Notes, 17 March 1930, SHM, carton 1BB2–191. The term *croiseur de combat* for battle cruiser is apparently used to differentiate it from a *cuirassé*, or battleship. The term *bâtiments de ligne* presumably includes both as "capital ships." The ten-thousand-ton "treaty" cruiser with 8-inch (203 mm) guns is invariably designated a *croiseur de 1ère classe*.

78. Massigli, Note pour le Ministre, 5 April 1930, ibid.

79. Ald.D. [Darlan], "Tonnage Français," 5 April 1930, SHM, carton 1BB2–191.

80. Ibid.

81. Al.D [Darlan], Note, 6 April 1930, ibid.

82. Although the arguments appear throughout the conference, see for example: Note by Mr. Craigie of a conversation with M. Massigli, 13 February 1930, *DBFP*, 2nd Series, vol. 1, no. 144, 209–10; and notes of a meeting of representatives of the delegations of the United States of America, France, and the United Kingdom, 13 February 1930, ibid., no. 145, 213, 215.

83. Notes of a meeting of representatives of the delegations of the United States of America, France and the United Kingdom, 14 February 1930, *DBFP*, 2nd Series, vol. 1, no. 146, 223.

84. Notes of meeting, 13 February 1930, *DBFP*, 2nd Series, vol. 1, no. 145, 212. The apparent French concentration in the Mediterranean and British concentration in the North Sea in the years before the First World War were not the result of any formal agreement. See Halpern, *Mediterranean Naval Situation*, chap. 5.

85. Note by Mr. Craigie of a conversation with M. Massigli, 25 February 1930, *DBFP*, 2nd Series, vol. 1, no. 150, 236–37.

86. Record of a conversation between Mr. MacDonald, Mr. Henderson, and M. Briand, 9 March 1930, *DBFP*, 2nd Series, vol. 1, no. 152, 239.

87. For examples of the discussions see Draft of a Mediterranean Pact communicated to Mr. Craigie by M. Massigli, 26 February 1930, *DBFP*, 2nd Series, vol. 1, no. 151, 237–38; and notes of a meeting between representatives of the United States of America and the United Kingdom, 24 March 1930, ibid., no. 168, 266–74.

88. Promemoria del Ministro degli esteri Grandi sul colloquio con il Primo Ministro Francese, Tardieu, 13 February 1930, *DDI*, Settima Serie, vol. 8, no. 363, 413.

89. Conversation Grandi-Dumesnil, 7 April 1930, SHM, carton 1BB2–192.

90. Note by Mr. Craigie of a conversation with M. Massigli, 13 February 1930, *DBFP*, 2nd Series, vol. 1, no. 144, 211.

91. Extract from a conversation between Sir R. Vansittart, and Signor Grandi and Signor Bordonaro, 11 March 1930, *DBFP*, 2nd Series, vol. 1, no. 153, 241.

92. The characterization is by R. J. B. Bosworth in his review of Claudia Baldoli, *Exporting Fascism: Italian Fascists and Britain's Italians in the 1930s* (New York: Berg, 2003), in *American Historical Review* 106, no. 2 (April 2004), 604. On Grandi see Cannistraro, ed., *Historical Dictionary of Fascist Italy,* 258–59.

93. Grandi to Mussolini, 13 February 1930, *DDI*, Settima Serie, vol. 8, no. 362, 412–13.

94. Grandi to Ministry of Foreign Affairs, 28 January 1930; decrypt of Italian cable by the British in HW 12/126, TNA, "Naval Conference: Grandi on Italy's Attitude," no. NC 94, 14 February 1930. I am indebted to Professor John Ferris of the University of Calgary for calling my attention to this interesting series.

95. Mussolini to Grandi, 20 and 21 March, 1930, *DDI*, Settima Serie, vol. 8, nos. 439 and 441, 533; Grandi to Mussolini, 23 March 1930, ibid., no. 445, 539. Decrypts of these cables are also in HW 12/126, no. [illegible], 27 March 1930, TNA.

96. Grandi to Mussolini, 13 April 1930, *DDI*, Settima Serie, vol. 8, no. 489, 599–605. A short version of the argument claiming success at the conference prepared for the guidance of the Italian press is in the cable Grandi to Ministry of Foreign Affairs, 12 April 1930, decrypt in HW 12/126, "Naval Conference: A Success for the Fascist Regime," 24 April 1930, no. NC 388, TNA.

97. Attolico to Italian Delegation, Naval Conference, London, 23 January 1930, in HW 12/126, "Naval Conference: Mr. Morrow and Italy's Mediterranean Needs," no. NC 27, 25 January 1930, TNA. Attolico had learned that Dwight Murrow was with the American delegation. The two men had worked together on the question of tonnage during the war, and Attolico thought Murrow was "particularly qualified to understand the soundness of our naval thesis."

98. Promemoria per il Capo di Stato Maggiore della Marina, Burzagli, 14 April 1930, *DDI*, Settima Serie, vol. 8, no. 493, 609–10.

99. État-Major Général, 2ème Bureau, *Bulletin des Renseignements*, Mai 1930, 78. SHM, carton 1BB2–89. For added symbolism, 27 April was the date newly enrolled Fascisti took their oath and was as a result a public holiday. Foreign Office, *Italy, Annual Report 1930*, 63, FO 371/15252.

100. Naval Intelligence Division, *Monthly Intelligence Report*, M.I.R. no. 132 (15 May 1930), 16, copy in ADM 223/818, TNA. *Brassey's Naval Annual* sardonically described 27 April as "a remarkable Italian 'gesture,' in view of the success, so loudly proclaimed in Britain and the United States, of the London Naval conference as a great step towards international disarmament." Cdr. Charles N. Robinson and H. M. Ross, *Brassey's Naval and Shipping Annual, 1931* (London: William Clowes, 1931), 46.

101. Quoted in G. M. Gathorne-Hardy, *A Short History of International Affairs, 1920–1939*, 4th ed. (London: Oxford University Press, 1950), 344. Arnold J. Toynbee's account, in excruciating detail, is in his *Survey of International Affairs, 1930* (London: Oxford University Press for the Royal Institute of International Affairs, 1931), 31–82, and his *Survey of International Affairs, 1931* (London: Oxford University Press for the Royal Institute of International Affairs, 1932), 259–78.

102. John Jordan and Robert Dumas, *French Battleships, 1922–1956* (Annapolis, Md.: Naval Institute Press, 2009), 27–31, 94–99; and Erminio Bagnasco and Augusto de Toro, *The Littorio Class: Italy's Last and Largest Battleships 1937–1948* (Annapolis, Md.: Naval Institute Press, 2011), 11–22.

CHAPTER 5

Information Superiority
British Intelligence at London

John R. Ferris

Intelligence shaped naval disarmament in complex ways between 1921 and 1930. At the Washington Conference of 1921–22, the American "black chamber," led by Herbert Yardley, solved secret Japanese telegrams that outlined the lowest ratios Japan would accept in the strengths of battleships and aircraft carriers, compared to the American and British navies. This knowledge helped American negotiators force Japan to that point—a 5:5:3 ratio—down from the 5:5:3.5 level that Tokyo wanted. Sailors on both sides thought that the difference would matter in any war between the Imperial Japanese Navy (IJN) and the U.S. Navy (USN). Yet the 5:5:3 ratio might have emerged anyway, as the United States and Britain demanded it and had strong bargaining positions, while the *New York Times* guessed Japan's break point.[1] Nor was Yardley's the best code-breaking bureau working on the conference. Throughout the 1920s, the British Government Code & Cypher School (GC&CS) read in real time the major codes of most great powers, including the United States and Japan.[2] Yardley's organization, conversely, had little success against British codes during the Washington Conference, or ever. This weakness prevented the United States from exploiting its ability to intercept the telegrams exchanged between the British delegation and Whitehall, as the two debated the details of Britain's naval policy, which they had to redefine when the conference began, precisely as Japan did. Equally, the GC&CS could attack only that material it might intercept. Usually British dominance of maritime cables provided ample material, but not in this case. Britain could intercept only those telegrams that Tokyo and Washington forwarded to their embassies in Europe, whereas the United States could capture traffic sent on transcontinental and Pacific cables between Tokyo and the Japanese delegation in Washington. Since Tokyo did not inform its embassies in Europe of the instructions sent to its delegation in Washington, the GC&CS provided only secondary material on Japan. It also acquired little data on American policy, as the conference was held in the United States, allowing Washington to formulate its policy without consulting its embassies abroad. Meanwhile, United States negotiators used Yardley's intelligence on Japan in ways that suited British interests as much as their own. The success of American code breaking and the limits to that of Britain had no bearing on the major naval issues at stake in the conference involving the USN and the Royal Navy (RN).

The value of American success in intelligence and bargaining must be placed in a strategic context. Japan did better in naval matters at the Washington Conference than the United States or Britain, its real sacrifice being abandoning positions on the Asian mainland. The IJN would have slipped dramatically in strength behind the RN and USN had rivalry continued in construction. Japan achieved a better position on a 5:5:3 ratio, even though this level left it vulnerable to the United States. Through the Washington Conference, in absolute and relative terms, Japan scrapped fewer warships, built or building, than Britain or the United States—the latter sacrificing more than any other country. In private, the USN and the RN agreed that the Washington Naval Treaty left Britain stronger at sea than the United States. Soon, the American position deteriorated further, as Britain and Japan built their authorized strength in restricted classes of warships, alongside many vessels in unregulated categories, especially cruisers. Though nothing prevented the United States from doing the same, it was unwilling to spend on sea power. The USN's position declined almost to 5:4:3. This development created irritation in Washington but few warships: though its real motivation was economy, it pretended that its constraint emanated from ethics.

The danger of an arms race centering on cruisers led to a new naval conference at Geneva in 1927.[3] Before and during this conference, Yardley's organization gave nothing to American negotiators, partly because it could not intercept much relevant traffic. In contrast, the GC&CS, able to intercept American and Japanese traffic to and from Europe and reading the major systems of both, provided valuable data to Whitehall.[4] This success did not prevent a collapse of the conference, however, due to irreconcilable differences over policies. Britain offered to extend the 5:5:3 ratio to all warships, including cruisers, but at a level of tonnage no U.S. government was willing to maintain. The Americans insisted that the 5:5:3 ratio must rest on a basis that Congress would subsidize for the USN—that the RN should be cut to a level that the United States could afford, rather than kept at one wanted by Britain. Britain and the United States also differed on the number of heavy cruisers that either should be allowed to build, because their strategies and conceptions of the value of such warships were different. Japan insisted that the ratio for lighter warships must be 5:5:3.5 rather than 5:5:3.

After the collapse of the Geneva Conference, the danger of a naval arms race came to be seen as a threat to peace, during a period when hopes to establish a liberal international order were high. Meanwhile, the Washington Naval Treaty permitted the powers to begin massive and expensive programs of battleship replacement in 1931, which many politicians were reluctant to do. Thus, in 1929, when new governments took power in Washington and London, both pursued naval arms limitation, although with different aims. Herbert Hoover, the American president, married national interest to idealism, aiming to weaken British power compared to that of the United States while making a better world. In particular, Britain must cut its fleet, while the United States should build many cruisers. The prime minister, Ramsay MacDonald, leader of the Labour Party, was concerned with spurring disarmament rather than furthering narrow interests. When bargaining with Hoover over naval issues, MacDonald aimed not to maintain Britain's position against the United States but instead to change the Americans' attitudes, so as to gain their support for further moves toward liberal internationalism and disarmament in Europe. To that end, to impress Washington he accepted many of Hoover's demands, abandoning earlier British positions. In particular, he agreed to scrap many battleships and cruisers, far more than any other country, to reduce the level of tonnage in cruisers to that demanded by Washington, and to let the United States build more new warships in that class, including heavy ones, than Britain. This compromise finally created parity between the USN and the RN. Ultimately, it crippled British sea power; immediately, it weakened Britain in disputes with the United States and forced it into intricate negotiations over naval strength with all participants.[5] Nonetheless, these actions also enabled a new disarmament conference, one in which Britain held the cryptanalytical cards.

As the London Naval Conference was held in Britain's capital, the GC&CS had unmatched opportunities to intercept traffic to and from the American,

French, Italian, and Japanese delegations. It seems to have mastered all of these messages and thus the aims and means of these players. The GC&CS was a strong second to Britain's leading source, personal contacts with the other delegations. No other source mattered at all. Britain could monitor any diplomacy between other parties by cross-checking reports from several sources, including the codes of one of the participants involved, usually both. Its position was powerful and one-sided: no other state matched British cryptanalytical capacity at this conference. The United States had abolished Yardley's bureau before the conference began. Nothing suggests that Japanese code breakers provided any material from foreign powers during the conference, while those of France and Italy could not intercept most of its key traffic.

For some months, the London Naval Conference was the top priority of GC&CS, because the conference held that importance for MacDonald. Success here was intended to buy credit for the intelligence services as a whole from a Labour government that was suspicious of them. The GC&CS took the rare step of reissuing all solutions from the conference under special a numbering system, "NC" (e.g., Naval Conference 007), distinct from its usual six-figure one (e.g., 007007). The overall effort had success, but it was limited by MacDonald's attitudes. At the start of negotiations over naval disarmament, he gave American authorities unparaphrased copies of British diplomatic telegrams, which would have aided any reconstruction of Britain's codebooks, had Yardley's bureau still existed. The Foreign Office, fearing it was "quite on the cards that the U.S. Embassy have scented a useful method of trying to break our ciphers by asking No 10 for copies of F.O. telegrams," took firm measures to prevent this behavior. "This incident when explained thoroughly scared the P.M."[6] MacDonald read and acted on the GC&CS's material about the London Conference. A good Presbyterian, first he sinned and then he repented heartily; later, however, perhaps when discussing international economic issues in 1933, MacDonald warned the American diplomat William Bullitt "that every message sent or received by our [that is, the U.S.] Embassy in London is decoded at once and is on the desk of the Cabinet Minister interested the following morning."[7] This statement became common currency among American authorities. Before the 1936 London Naval Conference they would take the danger of British code breaking far more seriously than they had in 1929.

Before and during the 1930 conference, intelligence was avidly used by the Admiralty, the Foreign Office, and Labour politicians as they confronted complex political and technical issues. Whitehall and Washington hoped that everyone would reason together, but they also believed that a naval treaty could be signed even if France and Italy refused to join, as quickly became evident would be the case. That was far less true with respect to Japan, although in the worst case the British and Americans might have signed a two-power disarmament treaty, one that institutionalized rearmament against the third naval power. In technical terms, two issues were at stake, with regard to which, and with little discussion, the three powers reshaped the core of the Washington Treaty. First, they agreed to abandon the replacement of capital ships until 1936, when a new arms limitation conference would be held, and that Britain should scrap five battleships, the United States three, and Japan, the battle cruiser *Hiei*. Second, debate centered on comparative tonnage in: (a) all classes of cruisers; especially (b) heavy ones, those armed with 8-inch guns; and (c) in destroyers and submarines. The United States and Britain wanted to extend the 5:5:3 ratio to all classes of lighter warships. Japan demanded a ratio of 5:5:3.5 for them, especially for heavy cruisers, and to retain an especially large strength in submarines. Neither Britain nor the United States liked that package, though they were willing to compromise on a strict 5:5:3 ratio.

Differences also existed between Britain and the United States over their respective tonnages in light and heavy cruisers. In particular, the American delegation initially insisted on the right to build twenty-one heavy cruisers. While Britain preferred that the USN possess just fifteen of them, it was willing to agree that the United States would have eighteen, Britain fifteen, and Japan twelve. Britain also knew that if the United States insisted on more than eighteen heavy cruisers, Japan would raise its demands above twelve, forcing Britain to increase its own requirements, producing a cascade effect that might wreck the conference. This fact was one of Britain's strongest arguments to the American delegation about the number of heavy cruisers the USN should procure.

Even worse, on all of these issues MacDonald's pursuit of Washington left Britain in a weak bargaining position. It could neither block American demands that it disliked nor look as though it was manipulating Japan into opposing them. Unless these conflicts could be resolved, the conference would fail, making international relations worse than they would have been without agreement. Equally, however, compromise was possible. Britain worked for one, taking advantage of the clash between Japan and the United States to play each against the other and so reduce both of their demands, in order to further liberal internationalism and British interests.

Intelligence is about secrets. As the point of the conference was bargaining, each party had to signal its position to some degree; the Japanese, American, and British civilian delegations were open with each other, in the freemasonry of liberalism, and differed with their respective naval advisers. Yet each state had a bottom line to hide, and Britain had an edge: the British had means to discover secrets, the others did not. Before the conference, official sources, especially the Anglo-American discussions in which Hoover and MacDonald defined their policies, were Britain's main means of information. Even so, the GC&CS provided the first, though predictable, news that Japan would demand a 70 percent ratio for lighter warships. Before the conference, it revealed policy formation in Tokyo and Washington and the abortive discussions between them. The failure of these talks comforted British diplomats, who could achieve their aims only if Washington and Tokyo remained divided, feared that the United States might maneuver Japan against Britain, and yet knew they must not let Washington think "that we are using the Japanese difficulty as a lever to get the Americans even below their figure of eighteen. Any such policy on our part would be a breach of the 'Gentleman's Agreement' which at present exists between the United States and ourselves."[8] In particular, Whitehall knew that the prickly secretary of state, Henry Stimson, was searching for signs of bad British behavior. By reading the Japanese naval attaché's traffic, the GC&CS also let the Labour Party Parliamentary Under-Secretary for Foreign Affairs, Hugh Dalton, ensure that British sailors were not working with Japanese ones to thwart arms control by briefing them to take actions that might sink the conference. Although Labour overstated the danger, it was a possibility. During the conference, Japanese diplomats reported that unnamed RN officers were encouraging Japanese sailors to adopt a position that might have wrecked a treaty.[9]

When the conference began, the GC&CS did better than American code breakers had done at the Washington Conference, by reading the traffic of every delegation, instead of merely one. Its product ensured certainty, by confirming the accuracy of material acquired through official means. For instance, it confirmed that no arrangement between France and Italy could be reached— as when Benito Mussolini ordered his ambassador in London, "Refrain from making any further conciliatory proposals of any kind," ending any chance of a five-power arrangement but also indicating that Italy would not prevent a three-power pact.[10] The GC&CS also made several contributions that no other source could provide. It offered reports, sometimes the first, on debates within the Japanese and American delegations, on negotiations between them, and on their impressions of talks with Britain. Frequently, it provided both the American and Japanese accounts of their bilateral discussions. The ability to monitor all of these issues at the same time, in real time, illuminated Japanese and American perspectives and policies. In particular, the GC&CS broke all the reports of the Japanese delegation, including material that, during the middle stage of the conference, its naval and civilian sides hid from each other, as well as their back-channel communications with different superiors in Tokyo, conducted on separate cryptographic systems.

Whereas the British easily read these diplomatic codes, the naval traffic, some protected by the first Japanese use of a cipher machine, was a tougher nut.[11] Nonetheless, for several weeks Britain understood the divisions and the strategies of the two factions within the Japanese delegation better than either of them did themselves. Ironically, these factions focused more on hiding their traffic from each other than against foreigners—IJN code breakers in Tokyo were reading messages sent by Japanese diplomats![12] The Japanese civilian delegation's greatest enemies were in Tokyo, not Washington. Against this, the Japanese civilians did not hide the fact of these splits, which improved their bargaining position vis-à-vis other countries—thus, to some degree code breaking reinforced Britain's will to compromise.

In fact, communications intelligence reinforced Britain's basic approach toward negotiations. The GC&CS showed that IJN leaders suspected secret Anglo-American "collusion" and were embittered by British "obstructionist tactics," while Japanese diplomats saw signs of "a delicate position of some kind or other" between London and Washington. Meanwhile, when talking to Japanese diplomats, the American delegation criticized Britain for having "no concrete proposals" and stated they themselves would take the initiative.[13] This material shaped British willingness to let the American team lead negotiations with Japan, while still talking with both sides. That approach reduced Japanese suspicions of Anglo-American collusion (which, in fact, had happened) while leaving the Japanese to blame Washington rather than Whitehall for challenging their case, which suited Britain and irritated Stimson (though he had caused the situation).

The GC&CS also revealed the realities behind diplomacy—what could not openly be said by participants. Thus, on 14 February the American ambassador to Tokyo, William Castle, told the Japanese foreign minister, Shidehara Kijuro, that the United States was concerned "primarily" with Britain, Japan being "of no more than 'secondary importance.'" Nonetheless, he confided, some Americans feared that Japan wanted a 70 percent ratio in order to attack the Philippine Islands. Could Japan do anything to convince Americans "from the technical point of view of the necessity of a 70% ratio[?] It was of course possible that in the same way as no reasons could be given technically for American parity with Great Britain so too it might be impossible to explain technically Japan's claim for a 70% ratio." Shidehara replied that such discussions risked turning the conference into a "miniature field of battle," but then,

> speaking frankly between ourselves, I said, Japanese military and naval men were under an impression that with a ratio under 70% Japan could not possibly win should the United States attack her, but that with a ratio of 70% she would, while of course unable to attack the United States, have some slight "chance" of victory were she herself attacked by the latter. The Government therefore was not going to advocate as right and fair an arrangement that held out no hope whatever of victory. To place the Navy in a position in which it had no prospect of winning must result in a lowering of the morale of the fighting forces, and no condition of affairs could be more productive of apprehension than this. Considering the question next from a point of view other than the technical, the Japanese public did not understand the reason why the United States was opposed to the claim for a 70% ratio, and they regarded American fears of the capture of the Philippine Islands by Japan as ridiculous and groundless. Supposing, for instance, that Japan did succeed in seizing these Islands by force of arms, that would be but the beginning of the war between the two countries; it would not be the end. The Japanese public wondered therefore why the United States, the possessor of superior strength on the sea, should be so apprehensive of Japan's seizing the Philippine Islands.[14]

During the first two months of the conference, a tense and inconclusive period, the GC&CS provided comfort by showing that an acceptable deal could be reached with Japan. Politicians in Tokyo told their civilian delegation that when they had made the best settlement they could, the government would sell that settlement at home and make the admirals accept it.[15] This knowledge reduced the nervousness that had strengthened Japan's bargaining position. The GC&CS also provided some sense of what arrangement the civilian and naval delegations would accept, even though, following a familiar pattern, the Japanese bargaining strategy was not to define explicitly its own position but rather to have other powers make offers, which they then would try to raise. Thus, on 30 January the delegation reported home about discussions with Britain: "As it was the wish of the Japanese naval experts that the production of figures by the Japanese side should as far as possible be avoided, Mr. Saito let Mr. Craigie produce them, contenting himself with asking questions and offering comments as necessity arose."[16] Japanese reports of such conversations illuminated what arrangements they thought were acceptable. The GC&CS also revealed a key issue for Britain—the conflict between Japanese and American policies, including details that both sides kept from Britain, though it also demonstrated that what they did report to British delegates was truthful and fairly comprehensive. The GC&CS also penetrated the position of the Japanese Admiralty (the Kaigunsho) and the Japanese naval delegation, a position that was the hidden dimension of these negotiations. In particular, the GC&CS revealed that Japanese naval authorities would oppose any sort of agreement that Britain or the United States could accept thus hampering the freedom of their civilian colleagues and the chances for success at the conference.

By 13 March 1930, after a month of secret talks, the British, American, and Japanese civilian delegations accepted a complex deal that let all claim victory—the Reed-Matsudaira agreement, named after its negotiators, Senator David Reed and Ambassador Matsudaira Tsuneo. The United States and Britain offered Japan 100 percent parity in the tonnage of submarines, though this level fell beneath the IJN's demands. The United States agreed to settle for eighteen heavy cruisers. While the GC&CS was irrelevant to that decision, it shaped another one, the American offer not to lay down three of these cruisers until the end of the period covered by the treaty. In practice, though not in theory, this offer would give Japan almost a 70 percent ratio to the USN both in heavy cruisers and in the aggregate tonnage of all classes of lighter warships during the tenure of the treaty, and for some years after, while also containing construction on both sides, nicely suiting Britain.

Britain's chief negotiator, Robert Craigie, had originated this alchemy, secretly suggesting that the Japanese delegation fall back on it in case of deadlock. Craigie, a shrewd bargainer with a powerful grasp of the technical issues at stake, was the GC&CS's main consumer during the conference. His actions stemmed from knowledge of the issues and intelligence on them. Press reports, statements by American and Japanese delegates, and decryptions of their traffic showed the details of their discussions, the internal politics of their policy, and their governments' desire for a deal. Acting on this knowledge and able to monitor the reaction of his targets to his pressure by reading their body language and their reports, Craigie pressed the other sides to negotiate, fed them a solution that met both their bottom lines (while pushing their programs down as Whitehall wanted), and rejected any alternatives that Britain disliked. Even more, he achieved these ends without the Americans suspecting his role or even breaking the "gentleman's agreement"—he believed his proposals were the only way to crack the deadlock, and probably he was right. Craigie, that is, used communications intelligence on Japan so as to guide its policy in a direction that furthered Japanese (and British, and probably even American) interests. Ironically, the GC&CS's decryptions of Japanese messages provide a better picture of Craigie's conversations with that delegation than do the accounts he placed in the official record. This triumph of policy and intelligence overcame Britain's bargaining weakness and allowed it to meet its aims with respect to cruisers and disarmament. It was the GC&CS's greatest contribution to British policy during the conference. Craigie might have been able to achieve these ends without its support, because his approach was an obvious solution to the problem, but the task would have been harder.

Precisely as a provisional agreement emerged, so did a crisis, as the Japanese naval delegation, and through them the Kaigunsho, learned what their civilian counterparts had been doing. Throughout this crisis, intelligence kept British decision makers better informed than either Japanese faction. The GC&CS read all the communications sent on their respective back channels, including one message that the civilian chief of the delegation, Wakatsuki Reijiro, asked Shidehara and the prime minister, Hamaguchi Osachi, to "commit to the flames after perusal."[17] The GC&CS showed that the civilian delegates advocated the offer as the best possible and acceptable. The only other option, they argued, was to wreck the conference, creating British and American hostility, and possibly naval construction against Japan. The GC&CS also demonstrated that Shidehara and Hamaguchi were willing to accept that deal. Before they would present it to the Japanese cabinet, however, they wanted the civilian delegates to convince the heads of the naval delegation, the minister of marine, Admiral Takarabe Takeshi, and the technical chief, Admiral Abo Kiyokazu, to support that offer.

Meanwhile, a united front of all other members of the naval delegation, led by Admiral Yamamoto Isoroku, was preventing Takarabe from accepting the offer, on the grounds that Japan could get a better deal by holding out, especially if working with France. Even worse, the GC&CS indicated that such an unholy alliance might be at hand, when it finally broke a month-old message from the Kaigunsho. Had this message been solved when sent, on 8 February, Whitehall would have been concerned and might have changed its actions. This message (like some others read between 13 and 18 March) showed that the Kaigunsho absolutely demanded a real 70 percent ratio in lighter warships. Rather than accept anything less, it wished to wreck the conference, by exploiting the stalemate between the five powers; this implied that it would work with another party. Whitehall feared that France might take the same view. The GC&CS closely followed all French and Japanese reports of their discussions during the conference, reports that showed they had some common ground. In particular, the French chargé d'affaires in Tokyo, M.

Doubler, was pressing Japan toward positions on submarines that might sink the conference—indeed, seemed to have precisely that intent in mind. British and American statesmen, suspicious of France, took this possibility seriously. These circumstances threatened catastrophe. Stimson and MacDonald agreed privately that if Japan rejected the compromise of 13 March, Britain and the United States should sign a two-power arrangement that maintained the battleship replacement program of the Washington Naval Treaty.[18] Thus, a naval disarmament conference would produce a naval arms race.

At this stage, British statesmen began to work closely with the American authorities in London, especially Stimson, informing them of matters that Whitehall knew through code breaking, though without revealing the source. Ironically, Stimson had closed Yardley's "Black Chamber" several months before on the grounds, he later recalled, that "gentlemen should not read each other's mail."[19] Now he was acting on the reading of gentlemen's mail, at second hand, without knowing it, and British code breakers were helping to further his policy.

The British and Americans directly queried the French and Japanese foreign ministers about Doubler's proposals, aiming to destroy any intrigue by showing it was known. In hindsight, Doubler's actions and the possibility of cooperation between the French navy and the Kaigunsho posed little danger, because they were unauthorized by Paris and rejected by Shidehara, who was too shrewd to be manipulated, especially by a diplomat whom he held in contempt and thought was acting without instructions.[20] However, these facts were unknowable at the time. The British and Americans ended the problem by bringing it into the open. Dealing with another issue, and intelligence on it, however, was harder to handle. The Kaigunsho's opposition to the proposed agreement became public knowledge four days after the GC&CS first detected it, when naval officers started a press campaign in Japan against the Reed-Matsudaira compromise. Meanwhile, for several weeks the Japanese government made no decision on the issue. The Foreign Office saw "a strong possibility of the naval element in the Japanese delegation overwhelming their political colleagues and preventing an agreement," while "a most determined effort is being made by Japanese naval authorities to reject this compromise and nothing should be left undone to prevent such a disaster occurring."[21] In hindsight, this assessment was alarmist; in practice, little could be done. As Britain opposed further concessions to Japan, it could neither appease sailors nor strengthen civilians. It did have modes of leverage, but each was problematical.

That Japan suffered from financial weakness was known, but the GC&CS demonstrated that its government was extremely sensitive on the issue. The latter twice warned its delegation to avoid any discussions that might invoke the matter, especially because Tokyo was renegotiating major loans precisely as it was doing so with sea power. Indeed, the GC&CS showed that the civilian delegates and Shidehara were reluctant to start the battleship replacement program, fearing the cost would cripple the economy.[22] If communications intelligence showed any Japanese vulnerability to exploit, this was it. However, British and American decision makers were careful in playing this card, for two reasons. First, Japan's financial embarrassment existed in part because it was preparing to join the gold standard, which was a major priority for the British and American treasuries, the Bank of England, and the Federal Reserve Bank. This fact prevented pressure on the issue. Had they been consulted, as would have been necessary, British and American financial authorities probably would have refused to place such pressure on Japan, because it would endanger aims they cared about. Even more, to raise this issue too openly would seem a threat and antagonize the Japanese government. Hence, in private discussions with Japanese civilians British and American decision makers referred to Japan's financial weakness—but carefully, in polite terms. Craigie, for example, warned one Japanese diplomat that if the conference failed, "it was as clear as daylight that the nerves of the American people would be affected and that they would carry our construction on a large scale." Then American financial and naval strength would overwhelm Britain and Japan. (Craigie overstated British weakness so as to sweeten his comments for the third naval power.) Failure to agree about lighter warships would prevent any revision of the replacement schedule for capital ships, forcing Japan into a construction race. Japanese civilians understood these risks and emphasized them in their reports to Tokyo. So too, without benefit of communications intelligence, Castle told Shidehara that if "an agreement could be reached with Japan, this would have a particularly good repercussion upon public opinion, whereas, if an agreement confined to the United States and Great Britain should emerge, really deplorable consequences upon relations with Japan were to be apprehended."[23]

The second form of leverage was to act elsewhere. Britain and the United States could gain nothing by working on the Japanese delegation; useful action could be taken only at Tokyo. The Foreign Office thought the Kaigunsho had little power in the government or with the public. It believed public opposition to arms limitation was artificial, an impression no doubt reinforced by decryptions indicating that the Kaigunsho was manipulating opinion against the 13 March compromise.[24] The Foreign Office also believed the Japanese cabinet was strong and wise enough to accept the compromise and not subvert the conference. Still, the Foreign Office immediately reported the facts (though, again, not the source) to American authorities, including Stimson, and to its own ambassador in Tokyo, John Tilley. The latter was to "keep in close touch" with Shidehara and "use all your influence with the Japanese Government in favour of a reasonable settlement of this particular question at the earliest possible moment." Tilley should act with Castle, while avoiding anything that looked like "joint or concerted pressure." Stimson sent equivalent instructions to Castle. Notably, the men who decided how to act on these instructions did not know at first hand the intelligence that had inspired them. Meanwhile, the GC&CS monitored American and Japanese reports of their discussions on these topics, thereby outlining what Tilley and Castle were doing—thus Japanese telegrams revealed actions by Tilley that he did not tell his own superiors at the time. The GC&CS also showed how the Japanese were reacting to this ambassadorial pressure. In particular, it revealed that Shidehara said precisely the same to Wakatsuki as he had to Castle and Tilley—that he was delaying any action on the treaty until he could finesse the political support needed to pass it easily through the cabinet, by working behind the scenes in Tokyo and having the civilian delegation convince Takarabe to support the proposal.[25]

Tilley chose to work "almost entirely" through Shidehara, refusing to contact Hamaguchi, who "not only does not speak English but abstains in the most marked way from any communication with foreigners. Conversation with him would be very difficult, would be most unlikely to elicit any statement of opinion and would attract great and probably unfavourable notice in the press." Further, "any attempt to influence the Press would have been exceedingly dangerous." Nor would he use the naval attaché to contact the Kaigunsho, as "the real problem is a political one." The position of Shidehara, "who was disposed to defend the compromise even at the risk of having to resign, might be weakened if it were known, or believed, that a violent Anglo-American campaign was in progress and because alternately his own sympathy might be diminished if he learned that we were working by other means than through himself."[26] The GC&CS almost immediately broke a telegram in which Castle expressed identical views to Stimson. Tilley carefully avoided "too much trace of concerted action" with Castle, but they had similar views, compared notes, and moved in parallel. Castle thought any effort to contact Hamaguchi could backfire and would be pointless: "The Prime Minister is a silent man, but in spite of the general belief that does not prove that he is a strong man. And could anyone be stronger than Shidehara has proved himself to be?" Tilley, Castle noted, "feels also that Shidehara himself is our best bet and that we cannot afford to alienate him. Sir John is a pretty wise old boy in the ways of diplomacy."

Both diplomats sounded circles linked to the emperor's political adviser, the *genro* Saionji Kimmochi, and discovered that he favored the Reed-Matsudaira proposal. However, Castle's effort to have a subordinate send Saionji a message through a dinner conversation with his political secretary, Baron Harada, failed, as "the good Baron got tight so that he would not have appreciated any message." For an uncertain reason, and to no effect, Tilley "arranged for confidential communication with the Chief of the Naval General Staff," Kato Kanji, a great opponent of the deal. Both diplomats pressed Shidehara and asked him to deliver messages to Hamaguchi from MacDonald and Stimson in praise of the 13 March compromise. Neither told the full story to his superior, though in each case the GC&CS generally followed the course of these diplomatic efforts. According to Japanese records, once he realized Shidehara's resolve Tilley told him to "just pigeon-hole the message." Castle records in his diary that he left Shidehara the message to do with as he chose, after first using scissors to remove from the text his name as sender and Hamaguchi's as the recipient![27]

These diplomats discarded what their superiors intended to be trump cards, so as to show Shidehara how much they trusted him. He picked these cards up and played them in a game of his own: he publicized that situation among leading liberals in Japan, to show how he mastered problems with *gaijin* and Japanese. Nothing more could be done, though the situation frustrated British and American leaders, who looked for "some method of hurrying up the Japanese." Castle wrote, "It is rather maddening to sit around when there ought to be so much to do to help on the Conference, but there are times, of which this is emphatically one, when any obvious efforts to push things along would probably end in disaster." This situation also frustrated the Japanese civilian delegates. Wakatsuki warned Shidehara, "I must be prepared in so negotiating to face unconcerned a breakdown of the Conference. If you should require a person unfamiliar with diplomacy like myself to embark upon negotiations of this kind, you must make up your mind in advance to the probability of the Conference being wrecked. To the unhappy consequences of such a breakdown upon Japan you are yourself fully alive." Ultimately, however, despite their inability to gain support from Takarabe in London, Shidehara, Hamaguchi, and their allies in Tokyo convinced the cabinet to accept the Reed-Matsudaira proposals as a basis for negotiations. In the last stage of the conference, the Japanese gained further concessions, in part because British and American negotiators realized their difficulties.

The GC&CS's intelligence on the Kaigunsho's position affected British actions but not events in Japan. Britain and the United States would have done much the same without it—indeed, when Britain first pressed Stimson on the need for "stirring . . . up" Japanese civil authorities, he retorted that he already had done so: "British should now do their share. . . . [I]t was now up to them because we had done all we could and . . . they should send a telegram."[28] Although this information affected the form and the timing of British and American approaches to Shidehara and Saionji, the latter would have acted as they did anyway. These efforts did nothing except to irritate precisely the Japanese with whom they were working. Reading comments to that effect from Tilley, Castle, and Japanese authorities seems to have led Whitehall to abandon its pressure in Tokyo. Stimson, lacking that evidence and dubious of Shidehara's character, remained more insistent, but Castle contained such pressure. MacDonald apologized to Wakatsuki for these actions, perhaps after reading a telegram in which the latter had said they "savour of coercion" and had "stiffened perceptibly" the "antagonism" of his naval delegation. Wakatsuki replied that "some members of his Delegation had been indignant at what they considered an exertion of pressure. He himself had thought it an indifferent plan but he was more concerned with a general settlement than with such a question of procedure." The Japanese press, moreover, soon detected and reported on this pressure and on an independent attempt by an American ex–military attaché who was attached to the U.S. delegation in London. Castle thought this publicity "was dynamite pure and simple."[29] That reportage could have had counterproductive consequences had it occurred before the cabinet reached its decisions, and it probably did shape subsequent hostility in Japan toward the London Naval Treaty.

For British decision makers at the London Conference, communications intelligence provided situational awareness. They knew they were not missing an obvious opportunity to take a trick or respond to a threat to their own position, that they understood their environment and were behaving appropriately. Communications intelligence confirmed the accuracy of material in other sources (primarily by comparing what one's diplomats heard and foreign ones said). It revealed the real positions of rivals, the accuracy of their statements, and thus their sincerity, which in this case increased confidence in the value of their promises and of an agreement with them. Communications intelligence steadied nerves when things seemed to be going nowhere or wrong. It increased knowledge of a rival's position and how to manipulate it. Communications intelligence was a tool and a balm and an insurance policy. It let one know when one might try gambits, what they might be, how they were working, and when one should amend or abandon them because they were having no effect or perverse ones.

In particular, the GC&CS revealed four opportunities for Britain to exercise diplomatic leverage and means by which to do so. Of these, the first, playing off Japan against the United States over heavy cruisers, was obvious but still a delicate task eased by precise knowledge. The second, referring to Japan's financial weakness so as to move its government, could be used only with caution and when unavoidable, though little pressure was needed to make the point; precise knowledge enabled effective work. The GC&CS illuminated in a way no other source could have done the third instance, the problem posed by the Kaigunsho in Tokyo, yet attempts to act on that information did not work as intended and in fact caused more trouble than they solved. Finally, knowledge of Doubler's actions caused more alarm than was warranted, though it also sparked actions that easily removed the problem. Britain might have achieved its ends at the London Conference anyway, but in the world as it was, communications intelligence was fundamental to that success.

A complete assessment of how intelligence affects any act of diplomacy requires consideration of its strategic consequences—in this case, of who won and lost at the London Conference, how, and why. Here, one is assessing what did happen in the context of what might have happened. Had the stable environment of the later 1920s endured, the policies pursued at this conference might have had different outcomes. Hoover and MacDonald might have recast the world around liberal internationalist principles, underwritten by armed liberalism. In the world as it was, the story is unpleasant and ironic. In material terms, the great loser at the London Naval Conference was Britain, which sacrificed more warships than its partners and gained less new construction than the United States, so crippling its shipbuilding industry. This outcome, however, was guaranteed before the conference began. In the negotiations at London, Britain used intelligence well, overcoming the weaknesses in its bargaining position and achieving its immediate objectives.

Ironically, the process of liberal diplomacy allowed Japan, the weakest of the great naval powers, to do best among the parties at London, just as at the Washington Conference. The Reed-Matsudaira agreement was generous to Japan, which later budged it further still, because Whitehall and Washington realized they must work to sell the deal to Tokyo. These facts, clear from official sources but doubly so through cryptanalysis, reinforced Britain's willingness to let Japan make gains on the Reed-Matsudaira agreement during the final stage of the conference, although the American delegation too actually made compromises on its behalf. In particular, they let Japan turn *Hiei* into a gunnery training ship, by removing most of its turrets and armor, rather than scrapping it entirely, enabling that vessel later to be rebuilt as a battleship. *Hiei* was to play an active role in the Pacific War until sunk off Guadalcanal on 13/14 November 1942. Neither Britain nor the United States recommissioned any capital ship they scrapped after the London Conference. Thus, at London, the RN and the USN together sacrificed almost as many capital ships as the IJN possessed, while Japan really lost none at all. Even more, unbeknownst to Britain, the United States, or to Japanese civilians, the tonnage of Japan's heavy cruisers was 33 percent heavier than the IJN acknowledged—by 35,000 tons, because of cheating or inexperience when Japan created these warships, the first they had built without foreign assistance. The IJN actually matched the RN in the tonnage (though not the numbers) of heavy cruisers and had a 5:5:3.8 ratio in the weight of lighter warships as a whole. Thus, the negotiations about tonnage that dominated the London Conference seem unreal, as often occurs when one examines any negotiation in hindsight.

The London Naval Treaty left Japan master of the western Pacific and the strongest power in East Asia, which could not have happened had it confronted serious naval construction against Britain and the United States. These countries accepted that position because they regarded Japan as a liberal, aligned, power. As Stimson told a Japanese diplomat, "Japan stood in the Far East in the position of the interpreter of Western civilisation to Orientals and that for this reason not merely was her position of predominance in those regions not a cause of uneasiness to America but on the contrary it was rather regarded by the latter as being to America's advantage."[30] British and American leaders also hoped that the London Conference would boost the power of liberal internationalist rules in the world. Instead, it began the process by which Japan became a revisionist power, attacked liberal internationalism, and broke the armed liberalism that underlay international stability.

Ironically, that process was propelled in part by the past successes of Anglo-American code breaking. During 1930–31, the role of code breaking at the Washington Conference and of Anglo-American pressure on Tokyo during the London Conference became public knowledge. That publicity delegitimized these agreements and the Japanese liberals who had made them. The London Naval Treaty lit the fuse for a political explosion that blew Japan down the road to the Pacific War. Ironically, the best outcome for Britain, the United States, and for Japan would have been for the Kaigunsho to wreck the

London Conference, so forcing a bilateral Anglo-American treaty and maintaining the battleship replacement schedule of the Washington Naval Treaty. That arrangement would have driven Japan far below a 5:5:3 ratio and thereby given its leaders a better sense of the limits to their power, while bolstering British warship-building capacity. In statesmanship and intelligence, wisdom is to information as three is to one. For Britain at the London Conference, excellence in diplomatic intelligence was harnessed to mediocrity in policy and disaster in outcome.

NOTES

1. David Kahn, *The Reader of Gentlemen's Mail: The Story of Herbert O. Yardley* (New Haven, Conn.: Yale University Press, 2004). A useful study of the conference itself is *The Washington Conference, 1921–22: Naval Rivalry, East Asian Stability and the Road to Pearl Harbor*, ed. Erik Goldstein and John Maurer (London: Frank Cass, 1994), for its naval consequences, see John R. Ferris, "'It Is Our Business in the Navy to Command the Seas': The Last Decade of British Maritime Supremacy, 1919–1929," in *Far Flung Lines*, ed. Keith Neilson and Greg Kennedy (London: Frank Cass, 1996).

2. See John Ferris, "The Road to Bletchley Park: The British Experience with Signals Intelligence, 1890–1945," *Intelligence and National Security* 16, no 1 (Spring 2002), 53–84.

3. Tadashi Kurumatsu, "The Geneva Naval Disarmament Conference of 1927: The British Preparation for the Conference, December 1926 to June 1927," *Journal of Strategic Studies* 19, no. 1 (March 1996), 101–26; Richard W. Fanning, *Peace and Disarmament: Naval Rivalry and Arms Control 1922–1933* (Lexington: University Press of Kentucky, 1995); Sadao Asada, "From Washington to London: The Imperial Japanese Navy and the Politics of Naval Limitation, 1921–1930," *Diplomacy & Statecraft* 4, no. 3 (November 1993), 147–91.

4. Cf. Kurumatsu, "Geneva Naval Disarmament Conference of 1927," and the HW 12 series, for 1926–27, The National Archives, Kew [hereafter cited as TNA].

5. See Ferris, "'It Is Our Business in the Navy to Command the Seas.'"

6. Colesworth, Minutes, 7 September 1929, 11 September 1929, *passim*, FO 371/13523, A 6037, TNA.

7. Orville H. Bullitt, ed., *For the President, Personal and Secret: Correspondence between Franklin D. Roosevelt and William C. Bullitt* (London: Andre Deutsch, 1973), 249.

8. Craigie, minute, 22 November 1929, FO 371/13526, A 126, TNA.

9. Ben Pimlott, ed., *The Political Diary of Hugh Dalton, 1918–40, 1945–60* (London: Jonathan Cape, 1986), 69–72, 80–81; NC 278, 27 March 1930, HW 12/126.

10. NC 275, 27 March 1930, HW 12/126, TNA.

11. NC 3, 23 January 1930, HW 12/126, TNA.

12. Sadao Asada, "From Washington to London: Imperial Japanese Navy and the Politics of Naval Limitation, 1921-30," in *Washington Conference, 1921-22, ed. Goldstein and Maurer*, 177.

13. NC 11, 24 January 1930; NC 16, 25 January 1930; NC 23, 27 January 1930; NC 47, 30 January 1930; NC 97, 14 February 1930; all HW 12/126, TNA.

14. NC 116, 14 February 1930; NC 121, 14 February 1930; 20 February 1930; all HW 12/126, TNA.

15. NC 135, 25 February 1930, HW 12/126, TNA.

16. NC 51, 1 February 1930, HW 12/126, TNA; Michael Blaker, Paul Giarra, and Ezra Vogel, *Case Studies in Japanese Negotiating Behaviour* (Washington, D.C.: United States Institute of Peace, 2002).

17. NC 124, 21 February 1930, HW 12/126, TNA.

18. NC 215, 18 March 1930, HW 12/126, TNA.

19. Kahn, *Reader of Gentlemen's Mail.*

20. NC 123, 21 February 1930, HW 12/126, TNA.

21. Thompson, minute, 25 April 1930, and Tokyo embassy to Foreign Office, despatch no. 145, 25 March 1930, A 2796, FO 371/14263, in *Documents on British Foreign Policy, 1919–1939*, ed. E. L. Woodward and Rohan Butler, second series (London: HMSO, 1946) [hereafter *DBFP*], 1:249–66.

22. NC 132, 24 February 1930, HW 12/126, TNA.

23. NC 193, 12 March 1930; NC 222, 19 March 1930; both HW 12/126, TNA.

24. NC 183, 11 March 1930, HW 12/126, TNA.

25. NC 276, 27.3.30, HW 12/126, TNA.

26. Thompson, minute, 25 April 1930, and Tokyo embassy to Foreign Office, despatch no. 145, 25 March 1930, FO 371/14263 A 2796, in *DBFP*, 1:249–66; *FRUS, 1930*, 1:66–79; William Castle Diary, MF89/2687, Herbert Hoover Presidential Library, West Branch, Iowa, entries 21 March 1930, 24 March 1930, 28 March 1930; Henry Stimson diary, reel 2, vol. 2, entry 25 March 1930); Thomas Francis Mayer-Oakes, *Fragile Victory: Prince Saionji and the 1930 London Treaty Issue* (Detroit, Mich.: Wayne State University Press, 1968), 100. For these events as a whole, cf. ibid.; Asada, "Washington to London"; Ian Gow, *Military Intervention in Prewar Japanese Politics: Admiral Kato Kanji and the "Washington System"* (London: Routledge, 2004); James William Morley,

ed., *Japan Erupts: The London Naval Conference and the Manchurian Incident, 1928–1932* (New York: Columbia University Press, 1984).

27. Castle diary, entries 21 March 1930, 24 March 1930, 28 March 1930.

28. Stimson diary, 19 March 1930, "Very Confidential Memorandum of Conversations March 19–20, 1930."

29. Castle diary, 3 April 1930.

30. NC 224, HW 12/126, TNA.

CHAPTER 6

Naval Strategy and Force Structure

Norman Friedman

T he position of the United States at the 1930 London Naval Conference can best be explained by the outcome of the previous naval arms control conference at Geneva in 1927 and also by the rather different outlooks and objectives of the three main players on the American side: the Herbert Hoover administration, the U.S. Navy, and Congress, particularly the Senate, which had to approve the resulting treaty. Congress was a surrogate for the public, and a good deal of what was done at the administration or navy level was patently designed for public consumption. That was much less the case in Great Britain, where individual members of Parliament enjoyed far less independence and power, the entire administration being answerable at general elections. Therefore the British administration, as represented by the prime minister and the cabinet, could conduct much more of their business unaffected by the public mood on a day-to-day basis. In both countries in the 1920s and well into the 1930s, the public believed government claims that arms control provided increased security and therefore rejected rearmament. The British system made it possible for a government aware of increased danger (before that was obvious to the public) to begin rearmament earlier, albeit on a basis limited by public opinion.

The usual narrative of treaty making fails to distinguish national political systems and thus avoids taking into account the consequences of their differences. For example, in the British system administration and Parliament were effectively unified, so it was possible to describe a two-way negotiation between the Admiralty and the prime minister. Thus it was possible for the Admiralty to negotiate with the prime minister without disclosing publicly the basis for its concerns, although even so the Admiralty avoided disclosing a great deal. For example, several times the Admiralty felt compelled to explain to different prime ministers the need for seventy cruisers. One such paper was marked to show what could *not* be shown to the prime minister, in particular the fact that the seventy-cruiser goal was connected to the demands of a Far Eastern war.[1] In U.S. policy, given the need to appeal to American public opinion (and the advantage of doing so), an important but subtle factor was the momentum enjoyed by ideas that had been introduced into public debate for quite different purposes, particularly that U.S. naval strength was justified by a British naval threat or rivalry.

The stated U.S. objective at London was to extend the tonnage ratios agreed at Washington in 1921 to smaller classes of warships: cruisers, destroyers, and submarines, without compromising some key U.S. requirements for Pacific warfare, such as the size of individual cruisers. For the U.S. government the outcome also had to reduce overall fleet sizes, so it was unacceptable for the U.S. Navy simply to be granted the right to build up to the size of the considerably larger British cruiser force in order to extend equality in capital ships to equality in cruisers. Because the two navies had radically different cruiser needs, the ideal solution to this problem was to create a cruiser "yardstick" making some sort of compromise possible. Accounts of the U.S. role at London generally focus on the creation of this yardstick, the assumption being that a failure to agree on one had doomed the previous attempt at Geneva to extend the treaty ratios.

Widespread anti-British sentiment was a particularly important factor in promoting U.S. naval programs. The big U.S. 1916 program had been predicated on the need to ensure "freedom of the seas" in the face of the British, who had the world's largest navy. American history had begun with a revolution against supposed British tyranny, and Americans were taught that the War of 1812 had been a struggle to protect American seamen from impressment by the Royal Navy. Many Americans were probably aware that Britain came close to intervening in the Civil War. In the 1920s an increasing number of Americans were led to believe that U.S. entry into World War I had been engineered by the Allies, led by the crafty British. Given all of these factors, naval rivalry against the British was by far the easiest explanation the U.S. Navy of the 1920s could muster for its desired programs of capital-ship modernization and new cruiser construction.

It is only fair to note that U.S. naval developments often figured in British internal documents of the interwar period. That made sense. Information on Japanese developments was difficult to obtain, even before the wave of militarism transformed that country after 1931. The British used the U.S. Navy as a surrogate for the Japanese, on the theory that the U.S. Navy represented the sort of modern technical practice that the Japanese might adopt. For example, about 1930 the British found it relatively easy to discover that the U.S. Navy planned to fight at much longer ranges than it could achieve itself (except for the two *Nelson*-class battleships), but its annual gunnery and tactical publications contain nothing so specific about the Japanese.[2]

An important factor in accounts of the treaty negotiations seems to have been the mutual *un*intelligibility of the U.S. and British political systems. Too, neither American nor British negotiators nor home authorities seem to have appreciated how different the Japanese system, which formed the other main element in negotiations, was. That system offered the military far more power than was true in either the United States or Great Britain. Particularly after 1930, Japanese nationalism seems to have been much underestimated by the American and the British governments, although both were well aware of the strong current in Japanese politics advocating their ejection from the Far East in favor of Japan. That was, after all, why both the U.S. Navy and the Royal Navy spent most of the interwar period working through the problems presented by war in the Far East against Japan.

The 1927 and 1930 conferences were called to fill gaps in the agreements reached at Washington in 1921. The 1921 treaty limited battleship construction for a decade, and it also set tonnage ratios between the powers.[3] From a U.S. point of view, the great achievement at Washington was surely that the greatest naval power, the United Kingdom, felt compelled to accept parity with the United States. A modern reader might see this much as the Soviets saw the SALT I (Strategic Arms Limitation Treaty) of 1972, as the acceptance of parity by what had until then been the dominant power, the United States. In both cases the driving factor was industrial strength. The British were well aware that the United States could, if it chose to, outbuild them. They presumably greatly underestimated American reluctance to keep building, but they also tended to see little point in Anglo-American rivalry. Aside from the industrial strength of the United States, its geography and relative industrial autarky made naval warfare against it difficult at best: the United States was unique among indus-trial powers in that it could largely shrug off any maritime blockade.[4]

The agreement reached in 1921 imposed both individual limits and total tonnage limits on capital ships, including the new category of aircraft carriers. Attempts at Washington to limit the numbers of lesser warships failed, although it did prove possible to impose a tonnage and gun-caliber limit on individual cruisers.[5] That was necessary because without such a limit any signatory might have built cruisers so large that they could serve as capital ships. As it was, with the number of capital ships so severely limited, large cruisers often served in effect as capital ships during World War II. British records suggest that in 1921 an explosion in cruiser size seemed likely and that the ten-thousand-ton limit set at Washington was a successful British attempt to cap probable growth in this category.[6] Subsequent British treaty proposals were intended to force the size of cruisers farther down to make them affordable.

The Washington Treaty also banned fortification of American posses-sions in the Pacific west of Hawaii, as part of a wider agreement that it was hoped would defuse hostility in that ocean. U.S. naval officers much disliked this agreement but reluctantly accepted it, at least partly because they had no hope whatever that Congress would pay for such fortification. The ban pro-foundly affected U.S. naval thinking, which after 1919 concentrated on the likely demands of a war against Japan. For example, the U.S. Navy had to develop a fleet train that could be convoyed across the Pacific to create a for-ward base from which the fleet could operate. In a war against Japan the end-game would be a blockade (by 1929 a bomber offensive had been added, to be mounted in the event the Japanese refused to see sense as they ran out of cru-cial imported material).[7] The blockade, in turn, could be mounted only if the U.S. Navy secured domination of the western Pacific, presumably by defeating the Imperial Japanese Navy in a decisive battle. Thus U.S. naval war planners contemplated a voyage by the U.S. battle fleet across the Pacific to a battle near the Philippines. The fleet would have to pass through chains of islands, such as the Marshalls, mandated to Japan at Versailles in 1919. Those advocating the nonfortification clause at Washington clearly hoped that it would prevent the Japanese from fortifying those islands.[8]

From the point of governments anxious to use arms control to reduce naval spending, the hope in 1927 and in 1930 was to impose limits on the total tonnage of cruisers, destroyers, and submarines, which the various treaty powers were then building. In addition, qualitative (tonnage and gun-caliber) limits could be imposed on destroyers and submarines. The British said that they hoped to ban submarines altogether, although that was unrealistic. The Admiralty hoped to use its massive destroyer force as a bargaining chip, offering to cut destroyer numbers dramatically if submarines, nominally the justification for the size of that force, could be eliminated. To the Admiralty's great displeasure, in 1930 the British government chose to offer the destroyer cut without the submarine quid pro quo, and the Admiralty found itself scrambling to produce substitute anti-submarine ships over the next decade.[9]

Governments also hoped to avoid the expense of restarting capital-ship construction when the battleship-building "holiday" expired at the end of 1931. By 1928 designers in the United States and the United Kingdom were beginning work on new capital ships. During the run-up to the London negotiations the British hoped that any new treaty would reduce the size of new battleships, hence their cost. They wanted a maximum displacement of 25,000 rather than 35,000 tons and a maximum gun caliber of twelve rather than sixteen inches. The U.S. Navy was unwilling to accept smaller capital ships, on the ground that although gun caliber might be reduced, many other weapons the ships would face, such as bombs and torpedoes, could not be limited. Only sheer size made it possible to protect a ship against these unlimited weapons.[10] The 1930 treaty embodied the U.S. proposal to extend the battleship-building holiday to 1936— that is, for another half-decade. Both the U.S. Navy and the British agreed to eliminate a few existing overage battleships, while retaining the 5:5:3 tonnage ratio. The U.S. Navy scrapped the battleship *Florida* and converted her sister *Utah* into a radio-controlled target. Of the next oldest class, *Wyoming* was demilitarized into a training ship. These were by far the oldest and weakest U.S. battleships and arguably they would not have been effective alongside the remaining ships. The British gave up the four *Iron Dukes* (*Iron Duke* herself was demilitarized) and the battle cruiser *Tiger* (some of these ships compensated for the completion of the two modern *Nelsons*). Japan demilitarized the battle cruiser *Hiei,* which was to be the only one of the demilitarized ships converted back into first-line service. These reductions in capital ship strength seem not to have been particularly contentious.[11]

For the U.S. Navy, limitations on neither destroyers nor submarines presented great problems. The United States had a large fleet of new destroyers built during and just after World War I to support the Allied antisubmarine program. The numbers were greatly in excess of what was needed to support the fleet directly, and the U.S. Navy did not envisage another large antisubmarine campaign. The British similarly had a large destroyer fleet, although in their case they considered numerous older destroyers key to a future antisubmarine campaign. Similarly, in submarines the U.S. Navy had sufficient numbers that it found some sort of parity acceptable.

An important factor in the thinking of the time, at least in the United States, was the perceived unlikelihood that any country would repeat the German World War I submarine campaign against merchant ships.[12] The experience of World War I showed that such a campaign would tend to outrage neutrals with large numbers of merchant ships, many of which would inevitably be sunk. The German campaign had, at the least, sensitized the United States to the point where it did not take much (in this case, the Zimmerman Telegram) to tip it over the edge into combatant status. For example, American naval officers, well aware that Japan was vulnerable to a submarine campaign, argued that any such policy on the U.S. part would outrage the largest maritime power in the world, the United Kingdom, and thus possibly bring it into a war on the Japanese side. Those making this argument were apparently entirely ignorant that the focus of British naval policy was a potential war against Japan and that few in the United Kingdom could imagine fighting alongside the Japanese. From a treaty point of view, what mattered was that the U.S. Navy could accept having a limited submarine fleet, because it did not envisage a massive underwater campaign as part of an "Orange" war against Japan. Conversely, if there was no great point in unrestricted submarine warfare, it was unlikely that the Japanese would mount mass attacks against American merchant ships—which in any case were a minor factor in U.S. economics.

U.S. naval officer delegates to the 1927 Geneva Conference successfully disrupted it, to the disgust of the Calvin Coolidge administration, which had called the conference in the first place.[13] In effect, the successor Hoover administration had its revenge on the U.S. Navy in 1929, as it managed the public narrative of the failed past conference and also of what it planned as the future successful one. The usual narrative of the 1930 conference concentrates on the dissipation of the Anglo-American hostility that had been displayed at Geneva in 1927; in 1929, the two sides were at pains to reach an agreement on the thorny but clearly technical cruiser question. That they succeeded in doing so made the treaty possible.

The reality was different and also subtler. Between the two world wars both the Royal Navy and the U.S. Navy concentrated their planning on the war they both expected against a Japanese attempt to eject the Western powers from the Far East. The British requirement for seventy cruisers was designed to meet the demands of a Far Eastern war. The U.S. Navy's General Board, which was responsible for the basic requirements for the designs of new ships, always asked at its hearings, "How does this work in the Orange war?" For all the public talk of a possible war between the United States and the United Kingdom, which was often the basis of demands for new construction, such a war never seems to have figured in General Board discussions. To be sure, each navy did formulate a war plan against the other, but these were exercises rather than serious studies. One pointer to American concentration on Orange was the fact that the student exercises conducted at the Naval War College generally involved parts of the Orange war plan.

Particularly for the U.S. Navy, the problem was that it had to look decades ahead, to a time of probable Pacific crisis, which the American public, which ultimately controlled its budget, did not envisage. It was far easier for the navy to exploit the widespread sense of hostility against the British.[14] The post-1921 British cruiser building program could be used to justify the U.S. Navy's desired cruiser-building program. The factor of momentum entered because once this sort of justification had been accepted by the American public (and by Congress), it was difficult or impossible to abandon or reverse.

Another factor in American planning was that given the vastness of the Pacific and the absence of fortified bases (thanks to the Washington Treaty of 1921), the U.S. Navy needed a considerable margin of strength over the Imperial Japanese Navy. Yet the public might well feel that parity with Japan would suffice. It was much easier to demand parity with the much larger Royal Navy, which itself was designed to have a sufficient edge over the Japanese. There is no documentary proof that this was the case, but it seems obvious that this view was taken, in view of exclusive U.S. concentration on the demands of a war against Japan rather than the United Kingdom.

Ironically, it seems that neither the American nor British navy was aware that the other had the same ultimate enemy in mind.[15] Neither talked publicly about what a Pacific war would entail. Neither government was very much interested in such warfare during the 1920s. For example, as chancellor of the exchequer in the late 1920s, Winston Churchill cut the Royal Navy's budget by using the Foreign Office to undercut the navy's reliance on a future Japanese war to justify its strength.[16] This view was reversed as the Japanese demonstrated their aggressiveness in China after 1931. Although China was hardly part of the formal British Empire, much of it was very much part of the British informal or economic empire, and Japanese treatment of British subjects showed that the important British investment in China was very much at risk. Japan was not, of course, the sole country the British tried to match (the situation vis-à-vis the United States was different). Despite their alliance with France during World

War I, the British felt a need to be able to counter the French navy, and that in turn made their attempt at stability through arms control hostage to some extent to the competition between France and Italy. However, the primacy of Japan as a threat explains why the British (and the Americans) were willing, in the end, to accept a tripartite treaty, and also why the Japanese withdrawal from the treaty structure (in 1934) effectively killed the naval arms control enterprise.

Until 1914, the U.S. Navy had calculated in terms of a possible war against Germany, the main scenario for which was a German attack in the New World to overturn the Monroe Doctrine. U.S. war planners concentrated on the need to develop an extemporized Caribbean base for a fleet moving into position to deal with the expected German attack. (In one exercise, a Naval War College student pointed out that in many parts of the Caribbean the Germans might be considerably more welcome than the Americans.) To some extent the U.S. intervention in Mexico in 1914 represented part of this scenario. U.S. naval expansion in World War I, particularly the massive 1916 program, was justified in part by the fear that whichever side won, the war might turn on the United States. The U.S. Navy had to be "second to none."[17] The fear was not unreasonable: in 1870 Germany had extracted enormous sums from France after defeating it, and there was later speculation that the German government had borrowed money in the expectation that it could pay its peacetime debts with the fruits of wartime victory. With the end of the war, such problems clearly no longer mattered, and the U.S. Navy transferred most of its strength to the Pacific. Potential differences with Japan had already surfaced before 1914. The voyage of the U.S. Great White Fleet (1907–1909) was designed specifically to demonstrate that the U.S. Navy could execute a Far East war plan (in contrast to the failed 1904–1905 voyage of the Russian Baltic Fleet to defeat at Tsushima). However, it was generally accepted, outside the U.S. Navy, that the Washington Treaty and the accompanying Nine-Power Security Treaty for the Pacific had effectively ended any threat of a Pacific war.

The successive Coolidge and Hoover administrations both sought deep cuts in naval spending, on the theory that defense spending was a brake on the economy. President Coolidge called the 1927 Geneva Conference specifically to expand the provisions of the Washington Treaty to cover smaller warships, such as cruisers and destroyers. The U.S. naval delegates in effect aborted the conference. In the United States, the public narrative of the run-up to the 1930 conference blamed the 1927 disaster on "big-navy men" aided and abetted (and perhaps motivated) by representatives of U.S. shipbuilders. The Hoover administration benefited from newspaper articles implying that any pressure to preserve the U.S. naval program was little better than self-serving.[18] It did not have to argue that the existing U.S. fleet could or could not execute the existing naval war plan for the western Pacific. It seems fair to see in the administration's efforts the effective beginning of the argument, made frequently in the 1930s, that U.S. entry into World War I had been the work of arms merchants and bankers and had been in no way related to U.S. national interests. The end result was isolationist legislation limiting the ability of the French and the British to obtain U.S. munitions in 1939–40, with serious consequences.

That U.S. administrations wanted naval arms control to succeed did not mean that the U.S. Navy in any way shared their view. The situation is familiar to anyone who experienced arms control in the 1970s. Presidents in those years saw arms in symbolic terms and hoped that cuts would somehow lead to peace. In retrospect, this seems a very naive view. However, no one who had lived through World War I welcomed the prospect of a repeat performance. Against that background ideas like outlawing war in favor of international mediation (the Kellogg-Briand Pact) were not nearly as insanely naive as they now seem. They even seem to parallel the view in the 1970s that nuclear weapons were unusable, hence largely symbolic. Unfortunately, the most significant potential aggressor (from a naval point of view) was Japan, which had not experienced the western front in World War I. Japanese memories of the Russo-Japanese War did not turn Japanese society away from the possibilities that war could create. In the 1920s, however, it appeared that the Japanese government, at least, shared the Western horror of war.

It also seems not yet to have been appreciated that in another World War I combatant, Germany, much effort had been made to convince the population that it had simply been cheated of victory—that if there were only a next time, all would be different. In 1930 Germany was not a factor in naval arms control, but in the aftermath of the London Treaty the Germans consistently demanded equality in arms, equality that the major Western powers rejected. This demand broke up the League of Nations disarmament negotiations in Geneva in the early 1930s. The announcement in 1929 of the "pocket battleship" *Deutschland* certainly complicated British naval thinking, although it did not reverse the British attempt, supported by the Admiralty, to slash cruiser size, hence cost, through arms negotiation. The French did take the new kind of commerce raider seriously at the time, and they became more interested in resuming battleship construction. To some extent the French reaction (ultimately the *Dunkerque* class) to the German ship was the spark that ignited renewed battleship building in the 1930s, but to blame that on the emergence of a particular ship would be misleading. The renewed battleship competition was part of a more general slide toward World War II.

In Britain and in the United States, the military had a darker—in retrospect, more realistic—long-term view that the tensions leading to war were the causes of arms programs, not the other way around. Unless the underlying issues could be resolved, no treaty agreement would be worthwhile. It would only cut naval strength, strength that would be vital once reality reasserted itself. In the United States, this view usually meant general hostility to any form of naval arms control. It also meant that both the Royal Navy and the U.S. Navy focused on what they would need to fight the future war against Japan. In the 1920s that included exactly the categories of warships left unlimited by the Washington Treaty, most prominently cruisers. To complicate matters, however, the two navies saw cruiser roles and requirements very differently, which made it difficult or impossible for them to agree on anything like a common limit for such ships. In retrospect, battleship limitation at Washington in 1921 was far easier, because both navies had seen the role of the battleship more or less identically.

In this view of the role of the battleship, the conflict of battle fleets would ultimately determine the outcome of a naval war, because the winning battle fleet could wipe out lesser warships and back up a blockade, which it was assumed would be decisive in the case of Japan—a nation dependent on imports by sea. The dominant battle fleet would have other vital, if indirect, effects. For example, during World War I the Allies had been able to maintain successful antisubmarine convoys using minor warships only because these same ships did not have to face the threat of German battleships and cruisers—which the British Grand Fleet had bottled up on the other side of the North Sea. Without British battle-fleet supremacy, the German surface fleet could have wiped out vital Allied shipping; relatively fast surface ships were potentially far more efficient commerce killers than slow submarines. Until aircraft carriers became much more effective, a battle-fleet-on-battle-fleet contest would ultimately be determined mainly by battleships. A navy inferior in battle-line strength had to look to equalizers, mainly in the form of torpedo craft, to change the balance of numbers prior to any decisive battle. The effect of the Washington Treaty was to place Japan permanently in the weaker position and hence to give it an incentive to try to wear down the enemy battle fleet before any decisive battle. In this context, cruisers were vital auxiliaries for the U.S. Navy—scouts for the battle fleet to enable it to get into position as the enemy fleet approached, and also counters to enemy light (torpedo) craft attempting to get at the battleships.

However, cruisers had other roles as well. For example, they might be needed to deal with enemy surface raiders preying on merchant ships. How many and what kind of cruisers a navy needed depended on how the various cruiser roles were evaluated.

For both the U.S. Navy and the Royal Navy, the central problem was that it was impossible (for logistical reasons) to maintain a battle fleet in the Far East in peacetime. The British could at least envisage basing, in wartime, a fleet at Singapore, apparently beyond Japanese reach. Singapore was imagined as analogous to the World War I fleet base at Scapa Flow. The obvious U.S. war base, Cavite, in the Philippines, was very much within Japanese reach, to the extent that the 1935 version of the U.S. Orange war plan accepted its loss (and that of the Philippines) early in a war. Given the provisions of the Washington Treaty, neither it nor a possible auxiliary base on Guam could be fortified and hence held against determined attack. (Singapore was outside the area in which fortification was prohibited.) In both cases, it would take time for the battle fleet to get into position to threaten, and then to fight, the Japanese fleet.

In the late 1920s the U.S. Navy's war plan against Japan was what Edward Miller, the historian of the U.S. Navy's planning against Japan, calls the "through ticket to Manila."[19] The concentrated U.S. fleet would steam west to the Philippines, where it would defeat the Japanese in a decisive naval battle. The "through ticket" required the fleet to cross the Central Pacific, steaming through the island groups mandated to Japan by the League of Nations. The fleet steaming west had to be aware of the movements of the Japanese fleet, because it would have to form up for battle before the Japanese came upon it. Its normal steaming formation included convoyed base ships that would help form the fleet's forward operating base; they had to be separated from the main body of the fleet before battle. The mandated islands provided the Japanese with potential seaplane bases, from which aircraft could fly to detect and track the approaching U.S. fleet. The U.S. fleet would enjoy no such long-range support, because it had no fixed bases near the Japanese (except those in the Philippines), and its organic aviation (carrier aircraft and surface-ship floatplanes) had limited range. For the U.S. Navy, large cruisers could solve the problem, because they could survive in the forward areas through which the Japanese fleet would have to come, and because they could form a scouting screen hundreds of miles ahead of the main U.S. fleet.

The U.S. Navy considered alternatives to large cruisers; it was also interested in long-range submarines and even in large rigid airships. However, neither was a viable alternative in 1929–30, when policy for the London Conference was formulated and implemented. Big cruisers would be essential.

The cruisers the U.S. Navy required were utterly unlike those standard in various navies at the time.[20] They were large, fast, and armed with the most powerful possible guns. In effect, they were scaled-down equivalents of the battle cruisers of the U.S. 1916 program. Their unusual characteristics occasioned a bitter fight within the U.S. Navy immediately after World War I. At that time war planning and ship characteristics were the province of the General Board, an advisory body reporting to the civilian secretary of the Navy. The Office of the Chief of Naval Operations (OpNav) was responsible for day-to-day operations. OpNav grew enormously, both in numbers and in responsibility, during World War I. Its foreign arm was the U.S. naval planning and operational staff in London. When that staff came home, its members felt that they were far better suited than the homebound General Board to understand truly modern naval warfare, as experienced in the North Sea in 1914–18. In 1918, for example, the London staff had sent home a proposed naval building plan that mirrored current British ships, including what amounted to a more powerful equivalent to HMS *Hood,* at that time the most advanced capital ship in the world. The returning London staff favored the same relatively small ships (comparable to the British E class) preferred by the Admiralty.[21]

The General Board naturally was unwilling to die. The fight was reflected in competing proposals for postwar cruisers. The General Board justified much larger cruisers, armed with more powerful (8-inch) guns, on the basis of Pacific strategy. It won. The extent to which the General Board had had to think through the need for a particular kind of cruiser to fight the expected Pacific war surely affected its later advice as to what the U.S. Navy needed and made it unlikely that the navy would embrace the British argument for smaller, cheaper ships.

The cruiser issue was critical in 1919 because the U.S. Navy had no modern cruisers at all at the time. Through the run-up to World War I, Congress, providing an average of two new battleships each year, had rejected repeated navy requests for cruisers for fleet scouting. The U.S. Navy was not even able formally to propose the ideal heavy fleet scouts, battle cruisers, although it certainly evaluated them favorably. Finally, in 1916 it did receive approval for six huge battle cruisers—the only type of ship that, it seemed, could press home reconnaissance in the face of serious opposition—and ten smaller cruisers. In theory the battle cruisers would form a scouting force well ahead of the advancing U.S. fleet, just as Admiral Beatty's Battle Cruiser Fleet had operated independently of the main body of the wartime British Grand Fleet. They were expected not only to find the enemy fleet but also to report its speed, course, and formation, all of which would be essential to a U.S. fleet commander trying to deploy his own force.

The smaller cruisers might form a close-in scouting line, but more likely they would be used within the battle fleet to beat off enemy torpedo attacks, as the British were then using their own small cruisers. The Washington Treaty killed the U.S. battle-cruiser program, leaving only the small cruisers (the *Omaha* class) authorized in 1916, which were ill suited to distant scouting. To make matters worse, the Japanese had four battle cruisers of their own, the *Kongo* class. The *Kongo*s could drive off any small U.S. cruisers trying to penetrate to observe the Japanese battleships. The U.S. Navy did convert two incomplete battle cruisers of its own into the huge carriers *Lexington* and *Saratoga,* but they were unlikely to help solve the long-range scouting problem. For that the U.S. Navy needed ships that could operate independently in forward areas on an extended basis. Big scouting submarines might have helped, but in the 1920s attempts to design such ships were not particularly successful, partly because the U.S. Navy lacked an entirely satisfactory diesel to power them.

The U.S. Navy did have a variety of older cruisers, but they were clearly obsolete. Their main significance from a public-relations or treaty-making point of view was that they made the U.S. cruiser force seem considerably larger than its effective core (ten 7,500-ton *Omaha*s) and so helped conceal from casual observers the gross disparity with respect to the British cruiser force.

At this time the British had the most numerous and newest cruiser force in the world, but in their own view it was obsolete and inadequate. Nearly all the cruisers built from 1912 onward were designed specifically for North Sea warfare, as the antidestroyer element of the battle fleet. They lacked the endurance for Far Eastern operations (as did the destroyers built in large numbers during the war). Only the two E-class cruisers and the five *Hawkins*-class cruisers seemed even barely adequate for the new postwar situation. Thus, in the British view, new cruisers were an important postwar priority. However, to the U.S. Navy the British already had what it wanted, a large, modern cruiser force. Even if U.S. naval officers understood what had happened, the American public did not. From a British perspective, the need for massive cruiser construction in the face of very limited resources demanded not only that British cruisers be of limited size but also that every effort should be made to limit the sizes of foreign cruisers they might face. This objective was so important that the Admiralty was willing to see naval arms control as a means to that end, in marked contrast to the U.S. naval view of such agreements.

Successive British governments accepted the Admiralty's view that, uniquely, the British Empire needed cruisers like those of every other navy for its battle fleet, plus (in effect) an entirely separate cruiser force for trade protection. It made sense to limit the first along the same lines as battleships were limited, because in theory a fleet cruiser force should be proportional to the battle force.[22] However, it made no sense to accept similar limits on the trade-protection force. Not surprisingly, a U.S. public looking at overall force ratios was unwilling to accept an argument that granted the British any kind of numerical superiority. The U.S. Navy helped by claiming that American overseas trade routes roughly matched those of the British, as though cruiser numbers should be apportioned according to the lengths of the routes being protected (which made sense only to nonnaval minds). Although Americans preferred not to admit as much, the United States had little or no vital overseas commerce that had to be protected against commerce raiders. The main U.S. convoy role in wartime, as it was understood in 1930, would have been to protect troopships and supplies headed for the western Pacific.

The U.S. cruiser problem explains what happened at Geneva in 1927 and also what happened at London in 1930. Prior to the Geneva Conference, Congress approved eight ten-thousand-ton cruisers, the first of the much larger force the U.S. Navy wanted. It must have been obvious that any cruiser agreement struck in 1927 would preclude further authorizations, and that it might well preclude actual construction of the ships already authorized. With the collapse of the 1927 conference, a bill was introduced in Congress calling for further cruiser construction, ostensibly to force the British (who in the U.S. narrative had killed the conference) back to the bargaining table. This further cruiser construction bill was passed in 1929. It called for fifteen more ships. There was still a real question as to whether ships would actually be ordered, but it seems clear that passage of this additional cruiser bill made it possible for President Hoover to hope that the navy would not sabotage the next conference.[23] Blaming the collapse of the 1927 conference on irrational "big-navy men" working for the shipbuilding industry presumably helped deter any navy revolt against the treaty that emerged in 1930.

That left the issue that has received the publicity, the need to reconcile U.S. and British cruiser needs. That was impossible, given the dramatic difference between cruiser roles in the two navies. Even the fleet support roles differed, because in 1930 the British had four battle cruisers of their own (one of which,

HMS *Tiger,* they would have to discard). Like the U.S. Navy, the Royal Navy needed strategic scouts, but it did not have to reckon with the same distances as the U.S. Navy. The British thought that large submarines based in Hong Kong, lying off Japanese bases, would suffice. They had used exactly that approach to North Sea strategic scouting during World War I.

Thus none of the key British cruiser roles quite matched what the U.S. Navy had in mind. The British needed numbers above all. During the run-up to the treaty, much was made of the length of British trade routes (as a measure of numbers needed to patrol them), but really effective patrolling would have entailed numbers the British could never have afforded. Instead, they wanted enough cruisers to form squadrons within reach of critical areas. In wartime they expected to use their global radio system to detect and track raiders, partly by having merchant ships radio special signals when they fell victim. The cruisers (supplemented by armed merchant ships) would be vectored to deal with the raiders. The British also wanted large cruisers in the Far East to tie down the Japanese early in a war by threatening their own trade routes. The overall British plan for protecting trade was surely far too sensitive to discuss either publicly or in the course of treaty negotiations. All the British could do was say that they were willing to agree to a limit on cruisers intended to work with the fleet but that they had to be accorded a large allowance for trade protection, which other naval powers did not need.

That could not satisfy the U.S. Navy, which needed a large cruiser force for the strategic scouting the British were not doing and also needed to make up for the lack of battle cruisers (treaty rules accepted in 1921 lumped battle cruisers and battleships together as capital ships, but that appears naive in retrospect). Moreover, the U.S. Navy had excited American nationalist sentiment against the British when it sold the 1929 cruiser program. It could not suddenly step back and accept what uninformed voters would interpret as a vast superiority in British cruiser numbers. Nor was simple parity possible. The conference had been advertised as an opportunity to reduce the cost of navies. Accepting parity with the British fleet, as it was in 1929, would demand increased naval construction on the part of the United States. To President Hoover, and to the Senate to which he had to sell the resulting treaty, that would be a swindle. From a political point of view, then, the treaty had to impose deep cuts on the Royal Navy.

The British proposed specific limitations on cruisers armed with 8-inch guns: fifteen for themselves, eighteen for the United States (the U.S. Navy's General Board consistently argued for more such ships), and twelve for Japan. In the British view, the great objective of any new treaty was to cap construction of these large, expensive ships. The 1929 meetings culminated in what would now be termed a summit between President Hoover and Prime Minister Ramsay MacDonald in October 1929. MacDonald pressed the British proposal to reduce battleship size and main battery armament, while deferring replacement by increasing the age before replacement from twenty to twenty-six years. Hoover was clearly aware that the U.S. Navy would reject the small battleship, but presumably in his view the issue was irrelevant for the present, because the battleship-building holiday would be extended. Cruisers were what mattered, and MacDonald left the United States with the crucial agreement on large cruisers in hand. For his part, he offered a greatly reduced British cruiser force. He told Hoover that the Royal Navy needed at least forty-five cruisers to protect British trade.[24] Hoover presented the summit as a triumph for himself and for arms reduction in the face of the "big-navy" lobby.

MacDonald could not completely control information. The governments invited to London for the 1930 conference included those of the British Dominions (who were of course vitally interested in whether the Royal Navy and the Dominion navies, subject together to limitation, could defend their trade). New Zealand sent its governor-general, Admiral of the Fleet Lord Jellicoe, who had helped create the British Far Eastern strategy in 1919. He announced that the empire required seventy cruisers for its protection—that the proposals already accepted by MacDonald at the 1929 summit (which cut the underage British cruiser force to fifty) were, in effect, suicidal. Jellicoe did not explain the origin of the seventy-cruiser requirement. The First Sea Lord felt compelled to tell the Dominion governments that whatever cuts were accepted in 1930 could only be considered temporary. No one on the British side pointed out that unless the construction rate was much accelerated, the British could not have more than the allowed fifty underage cruisers at the end of the treaty period (1936) no matter how the treaty read.

The British already had enough large cruisers to execute their strategy of tying down the Japanese during the first months of a war. They needed numbers of smaller cruisers, and in 1929 they thought that a seven-thousand-tonner armed with 6-inch guns would suffice. To make it viable, they had to stop foreign construction of cruisers with the much more powerful (8-inch) guns permitted under the previous (Washington) treaty. The two-inch difference in gun caliber translated into more than double the shell weight; no cruiser designed to withstand 6-inch fire would survive 8-inch. The British imagined that no navy would want large cruisers armed with 6-inch guns. They therefore pressed for the new gun limit but not for a new ship-tonnage limit. They were aware that the U.S. Navy favored the 8-inch gun, and they accepted a deal in which the United States was permitted to build a total of eighteen 8-inch gun cruisers, as against fifteen for the British Empire (and twelve for Japan).[25]

However, the U.S. Navy wanted strategic scouts, and survival in the western Pacific, far from any U.S. base, required sheer size. The U.S. Navy might favor large cruisers with 8-inch guns, but if it could not get them it would accept large cruisers armed with the permitted 6-inch guns (the *Brooklyn*s). The Japanese took the same view, with the added incentive that they planned eventually to replace 6.1-inch turrets with 8-inch turrets in their *Mogami*s. The effect of both choices was to overturn a British policy aimed at gaining numbers at an affordable cost. Within a few years the British felt compelled to build their own large cruisers, the *Southampton*s, also armed with 6-inch guns (twelve, compared to the fifteen in the U.S. and Japanese ships). At that point they found the agreed overall limit on cruiser tonnage a distinct problem, and before it was lifted (at the next conference) the Royal Navy found itself looking for ways to build "semi-cruisers" without infringing on cruiser tonnage. The big Tribal-class destroyers resulted.

The U.S. Navy's technical expert at London was Rear Admiral William Veazie Pratt, who had been at Washington in 1921.[26] In 1929, Pratt was CINCUS—Commander in Chief, U.S. Fleet. In November 1928 he met President-elect Hoover when the latter visited the Battle Fleet (which Pratt then commanded). There is no indication of what, if anything, they discussed, and Pratt's biographer suggests that he was unaware of Hoover's determination to avoid the cost of new warships. In his 1929 annual report, Pratt noted fleet deficiencies in cruisers and aircraft carriers. If Hoover was unaware of the issue when he took office, in May 1929 he received a memorandum from his director of the budget laying out the cost of bringing the fleet to treaty strength over the next twelve years.[27] Pratt himself published an article on naval disarmament in the September 1929 issue of the *Proceedings* of the U.S. Naval Institute. He argued that naval limitation on a treaty basis (but emphatically not by example) would preserve the balance of power on an affordable basis.[28]

On 15 September 1929 Pratt was invited to Washington to see President Hoover. Pratt wrote his wife that he had succeeded well as an advocate of moderation, and that the 5:5:3 ratio he had championed was finally coming into its own; clearly, he expected to be involved in the coming arms control conference. Pratt later wrote that he found the British offer quite reasonable, as "we would never go to war with England . . . and an agreement with England was far more important than to haggle over what seemed rather unessential details." Pratt was selected to head the technical staff the United States would send to the conference. The General Board still much disliked any attempt to cut the force of heavy cruisers, and there was a successful campaign to have another admiral, Hilary P. Jones, taken from retirement and sent to London. Although there was considerable discussion of various proposals among the technical staff, the eighteen-cruiser agreement had already been made by the president and the prime minister; it did not really matter what the technical group thought. Jones in particular thought that in backing the president Pratt was selling out the navy. Pratt also seems to have been instrumental in proposing modified treaty terms to convince the Japanese to sign.[29]

After the conference, Pratt told the General Board that he had gained some important victories, in the form of clauses encouraging or at least permitting construction of "flight-deck cruisers" and cruiser-gunboats. The U.S. Navy was the most air-minded of the interwar navies, and it supported a large naval air force. By 1930 it was beginning to feel the limits imposed at Washington in 1921, which at the time must have seemed quite generous. How could aircraft be integrated with scouting forces when the navy operated only a few carriers? One answer was to build hybrid warships called flight-deck cruisers, with guns forward and viable flight deck aft. The terms of the new treaty were written so that such ships could be counted as cruisers and not as carriers, hence not subject to the total carrier tonnage limitation. A quarter of cruiser tonnage could be devoted to flight-deck cruisers.

From 1927 on, discussions of a new treaty had envisaged an unlimited class of gunboats or sloops, restricted in speed and firepower so that they could not substitute for cruisers. The imperial powers could use them in place of cruisers for police work, thus reducing the pressure to maintain large peacetime cruiser forces. The U.S. contribution seems to have been to set their maximum gun caliber at 6.1 inches, like that of a cruiser. A gunboat armed with such guns could, it seemed, be an effective convoy escort against surface raiders, which would probably be armed with similar guns. This argument was irrelevant to the Royal Navy, which envisaged a very different means of protecting trade against surface ships—cruisers vectored by a global intelligence system based on radio intercepts.

Neither of Pratt's victories turned out to amount to much. Contract plans for a flight-deck cruiser were drawn, but analysis suggested that the sacrifice in gun armament was not balanced by sufficient offensive power gained with aircraft. That was presumably somewhat short-sighted, as airplanes were evolving rather rapidly, but the U.S. Navy abandoned the idea. (A flight-deck cruiser was, however, proposed for construction as late as 1940.) Two cruiser-gunboats were built (*Erie* and *Charleston*), but they were never repeated, being apparently seen mainly as a drain on scarce resources. It turned out that the surface raider threat had been much overrated, and when the treaties lapsed the U.S. Navy preferred to build large numbers of entirely conventional cruisers.

As Admiral Pratt returned from London in the spring of 1930, the fall command arrangements were announced: Pratt would become Chief of Naval Operations in October. His promotion to that post had been predicted the previous September, when he had been selected by President Hoover to head the technical delegation. Upon his return Pratt found himself defending the treaty terms when the Senate was asked to ratify it. Pratt justified the treaty partly on the basis of a need for 6-inch cruisers for "fleet work," which meant beating off enemy destroyer attacks, rather than strategic scouting or running down surface raiders (a role the General Board espoused). Pratt also argued that the treaty helped the U.S. Navy by setting out a cruiser program that could be fulfilled on a steady basis. Pratt seems to have believed that he had a contract, in effect, with President Hoover—in return for Pratt's help getting the treaty passed, Hoover would support enough naval construction to create a treaty navy. Without substantial new construction, aggressive Japanese building programs might well change the actual ratio of forces from the barely acceptable 10:7 ratio of the treaty to something in Japan's favor.

According to Rear Admiral Frank H. Schofield, prospective Battle Fleet commander, 70 to 80 percent of U.S. Navy officers disagreed.[30] The General Board testified against the treaty. However, the Senate ratified it. The administration's attack on the "big-navy" men undoubtedly helped negate professional naval testimony against the treaty, and its supporters drew considerable comfort from Pratt's advocacy. It is difficult to see Pratt's selection as Chief of Naval Operations as anything but a generous reward for having helped the administration do what it badly wanted to accomplish.

The negotiations in London came just after the October 1929 stock market crash, at the onset of the world economic depression. In 1929–30 it must still have seemed that U.S. shipbuilding resources were vast. Once the Depression set in, however, it became difficult for the U.S. Navy even to build some of the ships Congress had authorized, let alone seek more. Work on ships already on slips was slowed. President Hoover called for further naval arms limitation (a League of Nations conference was due to open at Geneva in 1932), and he seemed to like an Italian proposal for a moratorium on construction. There was no longer much point in using the Royal Navy as a bogey. Moreover, in 1931 the

Japanese dramatized the Far East problem when they seized Manchuria. Asked to react, the U.S. Navy pointed out that the recent Japanese maneuvers showed that Japan was entirely capable of beating off the planned U.S. "through ticket to Manila" strategy and that something very different was needed.

For the U.S. Navy, the lasting effect of the London Naval Treaty came with the passage in 1934 of its first rearmament bill. The Vinson-Trammell Act abandoned the annual authorization process in favor of a policy of maintaining a modern treaty navy—that is, it used the London Treaty as a target for new construction. Pratt had predicted that the London Treaty would help the navy in exactly this way, by setting targets that could be met, rather than by leaving requirements vague. The key word turned out to be "modern," because the various treaties included sections that set the allowable minimum ages of ships before they could be discarded and replaced. By the end of 1936 there was no longer any requirement to discard overage ships, but the Vinson-Trammell Act made it possible to build new ships in addition to older ones. On this basis, for example, the United States could begin to build new battleships without discarding existing overage ones. The act in effect camouflaged U.S. naval rearmament as nothing more aggressive than maintaining the naval strength the treaty allowed.

However, the way in which the Vinson-Trammell Act and its 1938 successor were worded had an unanticipated effect. By 1934 aircraft carriers were far more important than they had been in 1921, when their total tonnage was set in the Washington Treaty. An act that authorized full treaty tonnage for the United States could not provide for more carrier tonnage, and there were no overage carriers. The 1938 act was an across-the-board percentage increase over the treaty navy authorized in 1934, so the proportion allocated to carriers could not increase. It took specific acts to authorize the new carrier tonnage the U.S. Navy would use to fight the Pacific War.

The expiration of the battleship-building holiday, as extended by the 1930 treaty, engendered one final conference, at London in 1935. President Roosevelt's instructions to the U.S. delegates read as though he agreed with the Coolidge and Hoover administrations, that peace could be maintained by limiting arms. However, he was also aware that the Japanese had renounced the Washington Treaty in March 1934 and that Hitler in particular seemed bent on a new war. Roosevelt was shrewd enough to have announced his policy in the certainty that it would fail; after that failure his domestic critics, who were far more convinced of the virtues of arms control, would be unable to criticize him for the necessary buildup of the U.S. Navy. Given the withdrawal of the Japanese from the treaty structure, it was pointless for either of the two navies expecting to fight them to accept further limits on their size. They did draw up further qualitative limits—the British, for example, still wanted to hold down the cost of individual cruisers.[31] The 1936 London Naval Treaty was designed to provide the Japanese with an incentive to accept these limits, even if it rejected any sort of limit on its overall size. The treaty included "escalator clauses" that would be activated if a nonsignatory—obviously Japan—refused to abide by the limits. The battleship clauses in particular were activated in 1937–38, although parallel cruiser clauses were not, though it now appears that about January 1938 the British seriously considered activating them.

NOTES

General comments on U.S. cruiser and submarine policy were derived from the author's research on U.S. warships and their design, as published by the Naval Institute Press in the series of U.S. warship Illustrated Design Histories, particularly *U.S. Cruisers: An Illustrated Design History* (1984) and *U.S. Submarines through 1945* (1995). For British cruiser policy, see the author's *British Cruisers: Two World Wars and After* (Annapolis, Md.: Naval Institute Press, 2011).

1. Naval Staff memorandum, "Cruiser Replacement Programme," ADM 1/8672/228, The National Archives, Kew [hereafter cited as TNA]. The various explanations given differed enough that none is likely to be valid. The seventy-cruiser number can, however, be rationalized on the basis of five-cruiser squadrons operating both with the fleet (two in a scouting line and two to repel or support destroyer torpedo attacks), plus groups on various stations to run down surface raiders, with the 25 percent reserve some papers mention (to make up for ships refitting on the outbreak of war). The fleet cruiser numbers are justified by internal Admiralty papers describing the appropriate fleet force.

2. It may be significant that before 1930 the United States led the foreign section of the classified British gunnery and tactics annuals, but afterward first place was taken by the Japanese.

3. The key ratio was the 5:5:3 capital-ship tonnage ratio between Britain, the United States, and Japan.

4. Blockade required a base or bases from which cruisers and lesser ships could interdict trade going to the blockaded state. That base also had to be far enough offshore to be reasonably safe from seizure—as Singapore was seen as being far enough from Japan to be reasonably safe. The British had numerous potential bases in the Caribbean, off the U.S. coast (Bermuda), and in

Canada, but none of them could be considered beyond U.S. reach. When the Admiralty advocated new capital-ship construction to match new U.S. construction after World War I, the argument was that obvious U.S. superiority would encourage the U.S. government to press for peacetime advantages—for example, in trade, which would be difficult to withhold.

5. The limits were 8-inch guns and ten thousand tons. Limits on new cruiser construction were impossible to impose, because several countries, such as France, badly wanted to replace obsolete cruiser forces.

6. ADM 1/8653/266, TNA, contains a lengthy analysis of the cruiser sizes favored by various naval powers and urges attempts to cap cruiser size. This paper was written prior to the Washington Conference. It and the minutes of the British delegation to the conference make clear that the ten-thousand-ton limit adopted at Washington was an attempt to forestall further cruiser growth rather than a reference to the existing British *Hawkins* class. As in the case of HMS *Hood,* an exception to the treaty limit could have been made for an existing ship. The papers in the docket cited seem to have been the basis for the initial British cruiser-building program, which produced the ten-thousand-ton County class.

7. The combination of blockade and bombing is evident in the 1929 version of the Orange war plan, preserved as a microfilm at the Naval Historical and Heritage Command (Operational Archives), Washington, D.C. According to this plan, actual invasion of Japan was ruled out, on the theory that the United States could not raise a large enough army. Blockade in particular was expected to require seizure of bases near Japan for the numerous small surface craft required. Note that the plan did not contemplate a submarine blockade.

8. There were periodic unsuccessful attempts to find out whether the Japanese were violating the treaty by fortifying the islands. The subject was raised again after the end of World War II. It seems that little or nothing had been done prewar, but the time scale of World War II operations gave the Japanese plenty of time to fortify the islands the United States eventually had to seize. On the other hand, the Japanese did create a large fleet base at Rabaul, in the Mandates.

9. See the author's *British Destroyers and Frigates: The Second World War and After* (London: Chatham, 2006). Given the limit on destroyer building, the Admiralty opted to build sloops (which the treaty did not limit) with antisubmarine capability; previously such ships had been designed mainly for wartime minesweeping.

10. It took space to absorb a torpedo explosion, in the form of increased beam. Beam and displacement provided the stability necessary for deck armor against bombing. The same deck armor was wanted, at least by the U.S. Navy, to improve protection against long-range (plunging) shell fire; since 1918 the

U.S. Navy had been working hard to increase gunnery range, using measures such as improved fire control computers and air spotting. The Royal Navy was much less interested in greater range, and in the mid-1930s it tended to associate deck armor exclusively with better protection against bombing (which it took very seriously). It is not clear whether British sketch designs of 25,000-ton battleships offered the sort of underwater and deck protection the U.S. Navy wanted, but it seems unlikely that they could accommodate it.

11. The classified British treaty memoranda in ADM 116/2746, TNA, give the British position and the expected U.S. position. The British wanted to reduce battleship size and gun caliber and to extend battleship lifetime to twenty-six years, with a proviso that the United States and Britain could lay down only one ship per year, with Japan building on a pro rata basis. The objective of the proviso was to maintain existing industrial infrastructure. The United States proposed extending the building holiday to 31 December 1936 and rejected the reduction in size and firepower. The official U.S. justification was that by 1936 battleships might no longer be so useful, so their construction could be abandoned altogether. President Hoover said as much on several occasions, but he was considered naive. The Washington Treaty had set final strengths for the three major sea powers as, respectively, fifteen, fifteen, and nine ships of 35,000 tons. The scrapping after the 1930 treaty reduced the fleets to those numbers of ships, albeit of lesser tonnage (except for HMS *Hood*). The theory seems to have been that this was necessary because once replacement began, ships would be replaced on a one-for-one basis. In 1930, the United Kingdom had twenty capital ships, the United States eighteen, and Japan ten. The Admiralty file cited includes a paper by Chief of Naval Staff (First Sea Lord) Admiral of the Fleet Sir Charles Madden, arguing that Britain needed at least fifteen capital ships if it was to retain a viable force in European waters while sending a fleet to the Far East. Madden argued that he would want to send eleven ships east to face the nine Japanese capital ships while maintaining a bare minimum force of four in European waters. Moreover, reducing the British force below fifteen would almost inevitably raise a Japanese demand to increase their 5:3 ratio, since no smaller whole number of Japanese battleships would represent the allowed 60 percent strength. The British file includes the tentative U.S. plan, dated 15 February 1930. It seems noteworthy that the first part of the plan is devoted to cruisers. The battleship section includes the extension of the building "holiday," immediate scrapping of old ships down to the 15:15:9 figure, and retention of up to two old ships by each signatory for training purposes, provided they were demilitarized. To make up for the advantage the Royal Navy enjoyed in the form of the *Nelson*-class battleships, the United States wanted the authority to lay down one new battleship in 1933; on her completion, the battleship *Wyoming* would be scrapped. If the United States exercised this option, Japan would be allowed a similar option. In this

version, the battleship *Arkansas* was to have been scrapped or demilitarized instead of *Wyoming*. Finally, the U.S. delegation wanted the right to increase gun elevation during battleship modernization (which the United States was already exercising) explicitly recognized. The call for new construction was presumably a bargaining chip, and the British rejected it. It did not survive into the final treaty, but the other U.S. provisions did. From a U.S. perspective, the three ships scrapped were disproportionately weak compared to the ones retained, because they had the weakest guns among the three main powers (12-inch, with 12-inch, 50-caliber guns on board *Wyoming* and *Arkansas*). All other U.S. battleships had either 14- or 16-inch guns, as did all the Japanese ships. The British ships being discarded had 13.5-inch guns comparable to other navies' 14-inch; those retained all had 15- or 16-inch guns.

12. This point was raised explicitly in 1920, when the future of the U.S. submarine force was being discussed. Capt. Thomas Hart, the senior U.S. submariner, advocated what amounted to unrestricted submarine warfare against Japan, but he was argued down. In 1941 Hart commanded the U.S. Asiatic Fleet.

13. See, for example, Stephen Roskill, *Naval Policy between the Wars* (London: Collins, 1968), vol. 1, chap. 14, 506–16. Roskill cites Gerald E. Wheeler's statement in *The Road to Pearl Harbor* (Columbia: University of Missouri, 1963), that the British were merely used as the excuse for the General Board's attempt to retain big cruisers to fight Japan, but he rejects it in favor of the U.S. Navy's "second to none" dogma. Wheeler's interpretation is obviously the correct explanation for what happened at Geneva. The key would seem to be that only eight such cruisers had as yet been authorized.

14. A noncruiser example was the fight over supposed British modifications to their battleships to increase gun range, which was used in congressional and other debates to justify similar modifications to U.S. battleships. In fact the British did not increase their ships' gun ranges, and eventually the U.S. Navy felt free to do so (and did so without incurring British protests). The annual interwar editions of the Admiralty publication *Progress in Tactics* shows that the Royal Navy spent considerable time on the problem of closing to within effective range of an enemy fleet that enjoyed superior gunnery range. This publication is held by the Royal Navy Historical Branch, Portsmouth.

15. ADM 1/27401, TNA, is a British file, dated 1921–25, on "Choosing of Allies in Event of War with Japan: Points of advantage and disadvantage in alliances with various powers (China, Russia, USA, Holland, and France)." It concluded that the United States offered the greatest advantages but could not be relied upon as a probable wartime ally.

16. Roskill, *Naval Policy between the Wars*, 1:464–66, describes Churchill's 1926 objection to "our measuring our naval strength against this fancied danger" from Japan. He reiterated this theme in connection with an attempt to cut the

1928–29 estimates. See Christopher M. Bell, "Winston Churchill and the Ten Year Rule," *Journal of Military History* 74, no. 4 (October 2010).

17. See, for example, General Board 420-2 (naval policy papers) of 30 July 1915, explaining the need for a more powerful fleet, p. 7. Other justifications included likely Japanese expansionism, with the comment that Japanese agreements with Russia and with the United Kingdom had freed the Japanese of concerns about their rear. It also seemed that the agreements the British had made to convince Japan to enter the war would allow Japan to work freely against U.S. interests in the Far East.

18. ADM 116/2686, "USA and British Naval Policy," TNA, is largely a file of U.S. news reports connected with the run-up to the 1930 conference, including the Hoover administration's claims that the conference and the Kellogg-Briand treaty were parts of the same policy looking toward peace and arms control, and also the articles revealing the alliance between the "big navy" men and the shipbuilders, particularly Bethlehem Steel, in derailing the 1927 conference.

19. Only in 1930, after the London Conference, did U.S. signals analysts discover that the Japanese were well aware of the U.S. war plan and that they had developed adequate measures to defeat it. That was why the U.S. Navy switched in the early 1930s to a step-by-step offensive through the mandated islands, acquiring temporary bases from which the fleet might gain essential support. The step-by-step advance, however, would take so much time that the Japanese would surely have conquered much or all of the Philippines before the fleet could arrive. A step-by-step advance reduced the need for detailed knowledge of the early movements of the Japanese fleet, because, given the temporary bases, the U.S. fleet would always have land-based aircraft (seaplanes) to probe the relatively short distance to the next base. The step-by-step strategy explains the great U.S. Navy interest, particularly in the 1930s, in setting up a mobile fleet base in the western Pacific—as was successfully done at Ulithi in 1944. NARA II Record Group 457, SRH-355, is an internally produced history of the U.S. Navy's Naval Security Group (i.e., code breakers) before 1941. The U.S. success against the Japanese in their 1930 maneuvers was surely the most striking achievement of pre-1941 U.S. naval code breaking.

20. The only near equivalents were the British *Hawkins* class, intended for operations in distant waters.

21. The difference was probably that the British did not envisage strategic scouting by individual cruisers; they had enough battle cruisers for that role. They wanted cruisers mainly for scouting near their fleet and for dealing with commerce raiders, which would probably not be armed by anything more powerful than 6-inch guns (the largest guns that could be loaded by hand). The General Board envisaged cruisers operating individually in the western Pacific. When the Royal Navy built its *County*-class, its characteristics

were justified by the needs of individual operation in the Far East, but that requirement was not evident in 1919.

22. This was almost certainly fallacious in practice. The Royal Navy grouped its cruisers in five-ship squadrons. In the 1920s a British fleet commander wanted four such squadrons with his force: two to form a scouting line ahead of it and two to beat off enemy destroyer attacks (plus one or two individual ships to lead the fleet's own destroyer force). This calculation made no direct reference to the number of British capital ships in the fleet, although it might have been argued that a far more numerous battle fleet would have needed more cruisers attached to them to deal with enemy destroyers.

23. At this time, U.S. practice was for Congress first to authorize ships and only later to appropriate the funds to build them; thus in a few cases ships were authorized but never built at all. The fifteen-cruiser bill was authorization, not appropriation. In British practice the two steps were combined in estimates approved by Parliament.

24. Roskill, *Naval Policy between the Wars*, 2:45–48. The U.S. Navy also pushed for a reduction in the total carrier tonnage and in unit size, but this proposal seems to have been dropped. The battleship proposal was to cut tonnage to 25,000 tons and gun size to twelve inches; U.S. files include sketch designs of such ships that showed how weak they were. The battleship-size-reduction idea was revived for the 1935 London Conference, with similar results.

25. Surviving British files reveal no attempt to work out the characteristics of a 6-inch-gun cruiser of ten thousand tons. Most likely the British imagined that their own practice of using twin turrets was best, in which case the ideal 6-inch cruiser would have four twin 6-inch turrets—and would thus resemble the seven-thousand-ton *Leander*. There had been studies of 8-inch cruisers with triple turrets, as in the U.S. Navy, and it is not clear why there was no awareness that a ship with four (or more) triple 6-inch turrets might be attractive. British documents uniformly suggest that the big U.S. *Brooklyn*s and Japanese *Mogami*s were a terrible surprise, since the British felt compelled by them to build their own large 6-inch cruisers (*Southampton*s), badly upsetting their attempt to build sufficient numbers of ships. However, note that Roskill mentions a British offer, early in preconference negotiations, to allow the U.S. Navy to build ten large 6-inch cruisers.

26. The standard biography is Gerald E. Wheeler, *Admiral William Veazie Pratt, U.S. Navy: A Sailor's Life* (Washington, D.C.: Navy History Division, 1974). Pratt's papers are held in the Naval Historical Collection at the Naval War College, in Newport, R.I., and include his notes on the Washington Conference. At this time, he was a member of the General Board. Wheeler, 182, quotes Pratt's justification for the ratios chosen at the Washington Conference: they would maintain Anglo-Saxon naval dominance, "which

assures the Anglo-Saxon peoples that the rule of constitutional government and its ideals during years of peace or of war shall be the law of land and of the sea . . . control of the seas . . . shall be obtained and maintained by agreement and not through unlimited competition." Wheeler points out that this certainly was *not* a view generally held throughout the U.S. Navy. Pratt also expressed the view, which was probably quite widespread at the time outside the services, that preparation for war (i.e., arms races) "does almost inevitably and in time lead to war, while limitation, even with all its very apparent weaknesses, does tend to waken a peaceful spirit, and to keep it alive for longer periods." Pratt published four articles in 1922–23 explaining and defending the Washington Treaty to both civilian and naval audiences. Wheeler credits Pratt's public statements with helping enormously to convince the Senate to pass the treaty. He notes that Pratt misjudged badly in imagining that the treaty ratios would be used by Congress as a guide to further U.S. naval development—something that did not happen until the Vinson Act of 1934. During the run-up to the 1927 Geneva Conference, Pratt was president of the Naval War College and hence an ex officio member of the General Board, involved in drafting policy statements. If American officers at Geneva were in effect assigned to disrupt the conference, his own warm support for further arms control cannot have been popular. Wheeler, 249, cites limited evidence that Pratt's continued support for arms control under the existing ratios was disliked by officers senior to him.

27. Ibid., 285. The list included the cost of building the fifteen cruisers and one carrier authorized on 13 February 1929 (in the "Fifteen-Cruiser Act"), plus the cost of four carriers (which could be built within the U.S. treaty allowance), nine destroyer leaders, thirty-two submarines, nineteen destroyers, and attendant tenders, plus fifteen replacement battleships. Wheeler sees the memorandum as Hoover's incentive to push for naval arms control, but surely his contact with his predecessor and the widely known failure of the 1927 conference would have been enough.

28. Unfortunately, Wheeler does not give the date on which the article was submitted; given Pratt's seniority, it would quickly have been accepted for publication. That suggests submission about July or earlier, which would be not long after Hoover received his budget memo. According to Wheeler, *Admiral William Veazie Pratt, U.S. Navy,* 292, Pratt wrote the article while at sea in June 1928, intending it for a conference on international relations at the University of Washington in July 1928. It seems arguable that publishing the article in *Proceedings* greatly increased its impact and helped justify Hoover's campaign for naval arms control to the navy.

29. Wheeler, *Admiral William Veazie Pratt, U.S. Navy,* 304. The Japanese demanded a 70 rather than 60 percent ratio, and the treaty offered them that in light cruisers and destroyers. The United States also agreed not to lay

down the last three 8-inch cruisers until 1933, 1934, and 1935. Assuming that construction would take three years, none of these ships would be completed during the life of the treaty (ending in 1936), in effect providing Japan with its desired 70 percent ratio in heavy cruisers. Pratt argued that this limit was merely acceptance of the fact that Congress was unlikely to appropriate for these ships before the dates agreed.

30. Ibid., 308.

31. The new cruiser limit was eight thousand tons. Only Britain and France were much affected, and the seven Covers on the designs concerning the British eight-thousand-ton cruiser (*Fiji* class) demonstrate that the tonnage limit was a brutal burden.

CHAPTER 7

The London Conference
A Strategic Reassessment

John H. Maurer

Introduction

The London Conference of 1930 represents a watershed, a turning point in the history of the interwar period. At London, leaders espousing a liberal world order marked by the fashioning of solemn treaty obligations achieved their goal of curtailing the international competition in warships and promoting mutual security among the great powers. This agreement was widely lauded at the time as a major step toward constructing a framework for peace, using arms control to reduce spending on weaponry, increase international transparency, and thereby build confidence among world leaders. The London agreement fit the temper of the times, when in the aftermath of the hideous experience of the Great War the leaders of the major powers concluded that "a frank renunciation of war as an instrument of national policy should be made."[1] Statesmen at London believed they were avoiding the mistakes of the recent past by seeking to arrest the rivalries in armaments that had contributed to making war between the great powers seem inevitable.

What was accomplished at London, of course, did not prove lasting; nor did it lead to additional meaningful arms control or prevent future wars. Instead, London proved a dead end in the evolution of interwar international relations. The London Treaty marked the high point of interwar arms control. When measured against the magnitude of the international catastrophe that would unfold over the next decade, this achievement in arms control now appears practically meaningless at best and dangerous at worst. Critics of interwar arms control argue that by weakening American and British naval power, as well as stirring up the radicalization of Japanese internal politics, the London agreement represents a case study in political folly, contributing to the awful events that were to follow. The policy commentator Walter Lippmann would ridicule the efforts at arms control:

> [The] idealistic theory of disarmament was that if everyone had less capacity to wage war, there would be a smaller likelihood of war. Big warships meant big wars. Smaller warships meant smaller wars. No warships might eventually mean no wars. . . .
>
> The overall effect has been to impair radically the Anglo-American control of the sea communications of the world. That was not the intention, of course.[2]

The story of the negotiations and the resulting agreement at London is thus overshadowed by the arms race and war that followed. London did not put an end to the international competition in armaments. Instead of setting up the conditions for a lasting peace, the London Conference, by contributing to the disarmament of Britain and the United States, champions of an open, liberal international world order, helped to bring on the clash of arms. In the rough-and-tumble world of international rivalry and the armed search for security, the preservation of the peace required strong navies in the hands of American and British statesmen, determined to use these instruments of power to deter aggressive regimes. London 1930 raises profound, harsh, and troubling questions about whether statesmen are to be judged by the results of their handiwork or by their intentions.

How then to assess the strategic effects of the London Conference? Which is it—a successful attempt at arms control, dampening international rivalries if only for a short while, or a dangerous illusion that contributed to coming troubles? My aim is to consider these questions, assessing the strategic consequences of the conference. This aim requires an examination of the role played by the London Conference in helping resolve the naval rivalry between Britain and the United States that was a signal feature of the international political and strategic landscape between the world wars. In addition, an examination of the strategic aftermath of the London Conference calls for an assessment of the special challenge posed for Britain and the United States by the rise of Japan's power. The negotiations at London sought to untangle the knotty problems generated by the dynamic, triangular relationship intertwining Britain, Japan, and the United States. Finally, an assessment of the London Conference must take into account how the larger international environment changed in ways that undermined the effectiveness of arms control as a method for dampening the security dilemmas of the great powers. Only by examination of these inter-related problems can a strategic assessment of London emerge.

Appeasing America

The first half of the twentieth century can be viewed as the "rise of the rest"— that is, the emergence of rival great powers to challenge Britain's leading position on the international stage—and the creation of a post-British world.[3] At the beginning of the twentieth century Britain stood as the world's lone super-power. Britain was a global imperial power, controlling a quarter of the world's population and landmass. One of the mainstays of Britain's leading position in world politics was its navy. With the rise of industrial competitors, how-ever, Britain's strategic position began to erode.[4] Industry provided the sinews of power to build navies competitive with that of Britain. Germany harnessed its industrial strength before the First World War to challenge Britain's com-mand of the maritime commons. The victory over Germany in the Great War put an end (at least for a time) to the naval challenge from that quarter. Still, other rising great powers—most importantly the United States and Japan— were building navies that threatened Britain's lead at sea. The fact that both the United States and Japan are situated far from the British homeland made them more difficult to blockade and defeat by economic strangulation. Coming to terms with these challenges tested all the skills of British decision makers, who wanted to avoid the kind of bloody end to these rivalries that had occurred with the challenge from Germany. At the same time, British leaders refused to concede their country's leading role as a naval and maritime power. Arms con-trol emerged as the preferred course of action for British leaders, who believed that they could obtain their strategic objectives without recourse to expensive naval competition.

The late 1920s marked the nadir of Anglo-American relations in the twenti-eth century. The naval rivalry proved a critical element in the deterioration that took place in the relationship. In particular, during the summer of 1927 the fail-ure of arms control talks at Geneva provided a useful object lesson in how not to conduct a negotiation. At the beginning of the Geneva talks, American and British leaders held high expectations for reaching an agreement. Preliminary talks between American and British naval officers and diplomats seemed to indicate that a new round of naval arms control talks, building on the achievements of the Washington Conference, would prove a success. Admiral Hilary P. Jones, the U.S. Navy's representative on the American delegation involved in the work of the Preparatory Commission to the Disarmament Conference in Geneva, held discussions in London with British naval leaders about the prospects for a three-power arms control conference involving Britain, Japan, and the United States. Admiral David Beatty, Britain's First Sea Lord, assured Jones in a conversation that Britain "would bring up no question as to our equality in naval armaments." American naval leaders had thought that Britain would object to any attempt by the United States to make a bid for parity in all classes of warships. With Beatty's pronouncement, however, the main stumbling block to an Anglo-American agreement thus appeared to disappear as an obstacle. According to Jones' account of their meeting, Beatty expressed more concern about reaching an agreement with Japan over relative strength in cruisers: Beatty told Jones that the Admiralty "could not accept" a five-to-three ratio in cruiser strength with regard to Japan. Another concern held by Beatty was that Britain would want any future agreement to include France and Italy, whereas neither of these countries—in particular, the French—was likely to join the negotiations. These concerns would not prohibit Britain and the United States from reaching an agreement. Jones, wanting to make sure that he grasped correctly the Admiralty's position, pointedly asked Beatty, "'Now, let us understand each other perfectly so that there can be no doubts as far as the United States is concerned: Great Britain accepts equality in all categories [of warships]. In any conference we would establish a level of armaments in all categories in which each nation would have equality.' He [that is, Beatty] agreed to that unequivocally."[5] This discussion between Beatty and Jones appeared to indicate that the top American and British naval leaders had settled in principle the most contentious issue standing in the way of an arms control agreement between the two countries.

Secretary of State Frank Kellogg also did not see any insurmountable problems in the way of agreement. In a very revealing personal letter to Alanson B. Houghton, the American ambassador in Britain, Kellogg explained why negotiations would prove successful: "Great Britain and Japan seem very anxious to enter into an agreement and, as you know, we have had every assurance from Great Britain that she is willing to use the 5–5 basis so far as the United States is concerned." In other words, Britain had already agreed to parity in overall naval strength with the United States in preliminary discussions: "I do not think she [that is, Britain] will insist on anything that will make an agreement impossible."⁶ American leaders believed that a settlement with Britain was readily at hand.

This optimism on the American side was misplaced. British decision makers had reached no consensus among themselves about the meaning of parity between the American and British navies. Beatty's statements to Jones proved particularly misleading, giving American leaders a false optimism about the chances for success in future negotiations. Jones too failed as a negotiator, in that he did not push Beatty nearly far enough, did not ask precisely what an agreement about parity might entail for each major category of warship. Consequently, Jones did not discover that Beatty had no real intention of supporting an agreement that did not permit Britain to build up a much larger force of cruisers than what the United States considered necessary. The admirals did not discuss whether parity would occur at the relatively low number of cruisers favored by the United States or at the much higher force levels wanted by the British naval leaders. At the beginning of the Geneva Conference, Britain's presentation of its cruiser demands, which seemed to run counter to the statements made earlier by Beatty to Jones, thus came as an unpleasant surprise to the American side. By encouraging a false set of expectations about the ease with which Britain and the United States could reach an agreement, Beatty and Jones deserve some considerable blame for the breakdown in negotiations that occurred in Geneva. These discussions showed that the admirals were out of their depth as negotiators. The difficult obstacles in the way of an agreement were not identified as they ought to have been before the negotiations began.

The American demand for naval parity across the board in all types of warships perplexed and infuriated some British decision makers. It was axiomatic to Britain's leaders that their country required naval superiority, because of its unique position as a global superpower and trading state. No other great power, in their view, relied so heavily on access across the maritime commons. Britain depended on access to overseas resources of all kinds, from food supplies for the population of the home islands to raw materials for industry. This heavy dependence on imports represented a strategic vulnerability. Britain's enemies could by severing these transoceanic lines of supply exploit this vulnerability to gain victory in wartime. The German campaign against British and neutral shipping during the First World War had showed the seriousness of the danger that Britain faced on the seas. Protecting critical sea-lanes was for Britain a matter of survival. British statesman and naval leaders quite naturally sought to maintain a navy that possessed the strength to secure these sea-lanes.⁷

In a future war, British naval planners maintained, Britain would require in particular a large force of cruisers to protect these global sea lines of communication. The Admiralty aimed at the opening of the Washington Conference at a two-to-one superiority in cruisers over the United States.[8] In the aftermath of the Washington Conference, British naval planners came up with a requirement for no fewer than seventy cruisers to protect Britain's oceanic sea-lanes and to carry out its strategy for a maritime war. In negotiations with the leaders of other countries, British leaders were not bashful about asserting Britain's requirements for a stronger navy. At the end of the First World War, Prime Minister David Lloyd George had told Col. Edward House, President Woodrow Wilson's representative, "Great Britain would spend her last guinea to keep her Navy superior to that of the United States or any other powers, and that no cabinet officer could continue in the Government in England who took a different position."[9]

That Americans did not agree with this point of view shocked and dismayed British leaders. The American secretary of the Navy, Josephus Daniels, for example, stunned David Lloyd George when during negotiations at the Paris Peace Conference he produced for the British prime minister maps that purported to show how the United States actually needed to defend a longer set of sea-lanes than those Britain sought to secure. These maps showed that in the estimation of American naval planners, the defense of the Western Hemisphere and the requirement to be able to deploy a powerful fleet to East Asia created a need for the United States to possess a navy as large as the one maintained by Britain. When showed these maps, Lloyd George exploded: "That is preposterous!"[10] Sir William Bridgeman, Britain's First Lord of the Admiralty during the Conservative government of the late 1920s, complained about American demands for cruisers when he led the British negotiating team at the Geneva Conference of 1927. At Geneva Bridgeman wanted to find some way to regulate the cruiser strengths of the major naval powers. Working with the Americans, however, taxed his patience. The Americans, in Bridgeman's view, showed an "obstinate reluctance . . . to consider anybody's proposals or needs except their own." Bridgeman thought the Americans "not only very conceited, but very stupid, and their form of intelligence is more slimness than anything else." The Japanese negotiators, on the other hand, came across to Bridgeman as "very pleasant, real gentlemen."[11] Given Bridgeman's views, it is hardly surprising that the British delegation could not overcome the differences separating them from the Americans negotiating at Geneva. Diplomacy, in the view of those who espoused British dominance at sea, was simply a means to uphold Britain's naval superiority at the negotiating table.

The negotiations at Geneva provoked British leaders to dig in their heels against American demands for parity. Lord Birkenhead asserted that parity in cruiser strength between the two countries would reduce Britain to the status of "vassals of the United States. . . . In my opinion the moment has quite definitely come when we must stand up to them."[12] Prime Minister Stanley Baldwin made clear the British government's position in negotiations, instructing the British delegation at Geneva:

> We certainly do not mean to quarrel with America if she chooses to build up to any [naval] strength which she deems necessary. But we cannot admit by treaty that in regard to small cruisers the case of the British Empire resembles other Powers; or that parity of number means parity of strength. We cannot consent therefore to the insertion in a great international instrument of any provision which could be interpreted as meaning that we had bound ourselves to any arrangement which placed us in a position of permanent naval inferiority.[13]

At Geneva Britain did stand up to the United States, with the result that negotiations broke down amid the glare of considerable publicity. This very public breakdown in talks infuriated Baldwin. In conversations with the Canadian prime minister, William L. Mackenzie King, Baldwin "spoke very strongly & bitterly of the American press starting & circulating lies which could not be overtaken." While Mackenzie King agreed that the American press posed "a great menace," the Canadian premier "tried to lessen B[aldwin]'s bitterness against the U.S."[14] What was self-evident to Baldwin about Britain's special requirements for naval defense did not appear so obvious to U.S. political and naval leaders and the American public.

Nor was Baldwin alone among Britain's political leadership in holding that appeasing the United States on the cruiser issue would jeopardize British security. Winston Churchill, the chancellor of the exchequer, argued forcefully against trying to placate the United States by accepting the American position on arms control. In a paper prepared for the cabinet, Churchill argued, "No doubt it is quite right in the interests of peace to go on talking about war with the United States being 'unthinkable.' Everyone knows that this is not true. . . . [T]onnage parity means that Britain can be starved into obedience to any American decree. I would neither trust America to command, nor England to submit. Evidently on the basis of American Naval superiority speciously disguised as parity immense dangers overhang the future of the world."[15] In another assessment presented to the cabinet, he wrote about American naval ambitions in a way reminiscent of a famous speech that he had given in 1912, when he called the German navy a "luxury fleet." Churchill maintained: "there can be no parity between a power whose navy is its life and a power whose navy is only for prestige. . . . It always seems to be assumed that it is our duty to humour the United States and minister to their vanity. They do nothing for us in return, but exact their last pound of flesh."[16]

Meanwhile, another leading member of the government, Neville Chamberlain, considered a steady program of warship construction as essential to keep Britain from falling behind the United States in naval strength: "Unless such a programme [of warship construction] existed it would be impossible to keep the dockyards efficient and the skilled men would drift off elsewhere. He [that is, Neville Chamberlain] was not satisfied that the United States of America did not intend to build a large fleet; if so, there would be a big demand for skilled craftsmen in America, and our best dockyard hands would migrate there and would not return. If this happened our boasted supremacy would have vanished for good."[17] The three dominant political figures in the Conservative government—Baldwin, Churchill, and Neville Chamberlain— thus agreed on the need to keep Britain in the forefront, ahead of the United States, in the ranks of the world's leading naval powers.

The negotiations in Geneva, then, broke down because Britain's political leaders were not willing to seek a compromise on the matter of cruisers. To be sure, as Brian McKercher has pointed out, both President Calvin Coolidge and Kellogg were unwilling to overrule the American negotiating team in Geneva and seek a compromise by setting limitations that provided for greater strength in cruisers, as demanded by the British government.[18] In that regard they resembled Baldwin and Austen Chamberlain (Neville's half-brother), who failed to understand the difficulties ahead in the negotiations. When these difficulties became clear, they too became unwilling to seek a compromise with the Americans. Baldwin was out of touch, having set off for a tour of Canada with the Prince of Wales. In any event, Baldwin's style of leadership, one of delegating authority to colleagues, meant that he had not mastered the matter of naval arms control to the extent needed to set a clear lead for the government. Chamberlain, who was left to manage the crisis, lacked the political clout, detailed knowledge about naval arms control, and vision to find a way out of the impasse. Instead, the conference was allowed to break down. This breakdown would lead, to the embarrassment of Baldwin and Chamberlain, to the resignation of Lord Robert Cecil, who had disagreed with the stance taken by the British government during the negotiations of not finding a compromise on the cruiser question. The leadership failures of Baldwin and Chamberlain put them on a self-defeating course, hurting them on the domestic political front as well as antagonizing the United States. The perceptive William Castle noted the interaction between the Anglo-American relations and the domestic political problem facing the Baldwin government: "Great Britain is helping us build a good navy and we are helping to put in a Liberal Government in England."[19] The impasse at Geneva did certainly call into question the competence of the Conservative government in crafting a coherent foreign policy and arms program.

The hard-line stance taken by the British government at Geneva might have made more sense had the government been willing to build up a force of seventy cruisers. Then at least a rational argument could have been adduced for why Britain could not compromise with the Americans on cruiser strength. In abjuring parity with the United States with regard to cruisers, Britain would match rhetoric about dominating the maritime domain with deeds, in the form of a robust shipbuilding program. In Britain, however, the political will to build a force of seventy cruisers did not exist during the late 1920s. Outside the Admiralty, not even Churchill wanted to build such a large force of cruisers. Further, neither in Britain nor in the United States could those who favored a buildup in warships expect to garner a strong political consensus to stay in place, a position that would sustain a competition in naval armaments against the other country. A backlash would almost certainly emerge to derail any attempt by either to rival the other in the building of expensive cruisers. Both in Britain and the United States, determined opposition existed to any repetition of the naval rivalry that had existed before the First World War; the view had taken hold in both countries that arms races provided a trigger for war. In addition, within both governments stood powerful actors who wanted to hold down spending on the armed forces. Any government that tried to carry out a naval buildup would provoke a divisive political debate and galvanize considerable opposition. The government initiating a major naval buildup might find itself out of office before it could carry through to completion the construction of warships. The domestic political environments in both Britain and the United States practically ruled out a full-fledged competition in naval forces between the two countries.

Churchill, perhaps the political figure most outspoken against further naval arms control, decried the views of the Labour and Liberal parties on naval security as "reckless" and as leading to "a Navy definitely inferior to that of other Great Powers." If that occurred, Churchill feared, "the food supplies on which we live, the trade by which we get our living, and the whole physical cohesion of the British Empire, [which] all depend upon the British Navy, would be held only on sufferance and at the good will . . . of the stronger Naval Power." Churchill did not want to see any restrictions on the British armed forces that would "render them incapable of affording the minimum security which the life of our island and its empire requires."[20] Britain's heavy dependence on controlling sea-lanes for its security and well-being, Churchill maintained, put it in the position of requiring a navy superior to that of competitors. If the United States persisted in constructing cruisers, then Churchill as chancellor of the exchequer intended to find the money needed to finance a dramatic buildup of Britain's naval strength. Britain, in Churchill's estimation, would show greater determination and stamina in a naval competition than would the United States, thus staying ahead. While the United States might possess four times the industrial plant of Britain, translating that economic strength into a superior navy would prove a difficult proposition. In a grim twelve-page memorandum, Churchill outlined Britain's prospects for maintaining its superiority at sea during "the twenty or thirty years lying before us":

> We ought not too readily to accept the suggestion that all naval competition with the United States is hopeless. Although their wealth is greater, our needs for a navy are so much more real than theirs that we should probably make far greater sacrifices for sea-power over a long period of time. The addition of 20 or even 30 millions a year, which we could easily afford if we had to, would soon carry our fleet to dimensions which the United States could not surpass without encountering the gravest problems.

Rather than maintain the challenge, the American government, faced by escalating costs, would tire of the competition and give up the attempt.[21] This assessment by Churchill paralleled the views of the new president, Herbert Hoover, who had reached much the same conclusion: "We cannot get parity by naval building: the UK . . . will continue to build as long as we do."[22]

In the aftermath of the Geneva debacle, Baldwin, stung by this failure and fearful of the consequences both in the domestic political and international arenas if Britain and the United States could not find a compromise on naval arms control, came to realize his error. Baldwin understood that the British government needed to take the initiative in managing the critical issue of naval rivalry with the United States. Once the general election that needed to occur in

1929 was behind him, presumably with the Conservatives remaining in office, Baldwin intended to reconstruct the government by making important changes in personnel. One change Baldwin considered was bringing the elder statesman Lord Grey of Falloden into the government as foreign secretary. Baldwin even wrote Grey, offering him the position if the Conservatives won the election. Domestic political considerations played a big part in the prime minister's offer to Grey. (Baldwin assiduously tried to damage the electoral standing of the Liberals by recruiting some of its prominent leaders into the Conservative Party's fold, twice asking Reginald McKenna to serve as chancellor of the exchequer and, most famously, taking on Winston Churchill.) Nonetheless, international considerations—in particular, the need to reach an arrangement with the United States about warship construction—must also have prompted Baldwin to approach Grey, who was well known for his pro-American views. With Grey as foreign secretary, Baldwin would have definitely committed the government and signaled its intention to heal the rift in Anglo-American relations.[23] This meant too that Churchill, who had taken a determined stance against arms limitation, would not go to the Foreign Office to replace Chamberlain.[24] Regardless of the election outcome, then, Britain's political leaders intended to move decisively to reach an accommodation with the United States.

One way, of course, to get around this problem was to drop the idea of looking at the United States as an enemy. If British leaders could categorically rule out war between the two countries, Britain would not need to go to the expense of arming against the United States. Even before the First World War, some British leaders had wanted to exclude the United States from any list of countries against which Britain needed to build warships. Lord Grey, for example, had maintained that Britain should simply rule out the United States as a prospective adversary. When asked by Lloyd George to lead a special diplomatic mission to the United States in 1919, Grey would take the appointment only on the condition that the British government accepted his view that Britain did not look upon the United States as a naval rival. Lloyd George and Lord Curzon, then serving as British foreign secretary, agreed to Grey's demand. By conceding parity in naval strength to the United States on that occasion, Britain did successfully appease American ambitions. Appeasement worked to remove the naval issue as a controversy in Anglo-American relations. While arms control enabled British leaders to manage the rise of American power, however, it did not lead to a coalition between Britain and the United States to preserve the peace. Arms control helped to turn Britain and the United States from viewing each other as adversaries; it did not make them into allies.

The naval balance codified at the London Conference, then, reflected an underlying political reality that existed in both Britain and the United States. The political mainstreams in both countries steadfastly wanted to avoid the expense of a naval rivalry. It seems simply implausible to imagine that a British government headed up by Ramsay MacDonald or an American administration led by Herbert Hoover would ever spend large sums of money on building warships in a contest for naval supremacy. In imperial Germany before the First World War, Kaiser Wilhelm II was devoted to a major naval buildup, spurning efforts to moderate the competition at sea. Wilhelm surrounded himself in his government with those who agreed with him about the necessity of building a fleet to challenge that of Britain; those who questioned the fleet program were marginalized or removed. No such domestic political situation existed in Britain or the United States during the late 1920s. Neither the American nor the British government had the stomach for pursuing a naval rivalry against the other.

Both governments looked to curtail expenditures by cutting naval construction. Hoover explained to MacDonald that he wanted a continuation of the holiday in the building of battleships, because if both countries continued to delay new construction, these warships might become obsolete. When, on the eve of the London Conference, British Treasury officials estimated that Britain might save over £14 million in naval spending if the major powers could reach an agreement to abolish capital ships and submarines, this assessment impressed MacDonald, even if this outcome was to prove too difficult to achieve in practice.[25] President Hoover predicted a reduction in spending as one of the important results of the London Conference: "The saving on the present basis [is] $1,000,000,000 in the next six years." Furthermore, Hoover praised the "whole agreement as a great step in world peace and an assurance of American parity in naval strength." Hoover and MacDonald thus did not shrink from contemplating even deeper cuts in armed forces that already suffered from the effects of stringent budgets. In addition, as Brian McKercher has emphasized in his work, even if the Conservatives had won the 1929 election, Baldwin intended to break the deadlock in Anglo-American relations caused by the rivalry in cruisers.[26] Baldwin and MacDonald were like Tweedledum and Tweedledee when it came to arms control and Anglo-American relations. The impulse of these leaders was to work diligently against a competition in naval armaments. The risks of a full-throttled competition in naval armaments between Britain and the United States outweighed the danger of appeasing American ambitions by conceding parity at sea.

Rising Threats in Asia

Arms control does not take place in an international political and strategic vacuum. Nowhere is this truism better illustrated than the changes taking place in the balance of power on the Asian mainland, changes that provided another current that stoked Japanese nationalism and called into question the continued viability of the whole enterprise of naval arms control. Japan's dominance of the region, won at heavy cost in previous wars against China and Russia, now stood challenged as both countries recovered from defeat and revolution.

The growth of Soviet military power in Northeast Asia, as Stalin's armaments buildup began to tell, made Japanese military leaders apprehensive about the empire's future. Stalin's ruthless economic policies and police-state rule were building a military superpower. This adverse trend in the military balance meant that Japan would face increasingly stiff competition in trying to hold on to its positions on the Asian mainland against the Red Army. A replay of the Russo-Japanese War might result in a Soviet victory on land once the Red Army's buildup matured.

The reemergence of a militarily powerful China too boded ill for Japan. The apparent success of the Nationalists in unifying China under their banner undermined yet further Japan's security on the continent. Japan, then, faced the grim prospect that Soviet Russia and Nationalist China might use their growing military power to overturn the earlier victories achieved on the battlefield by Japanese arms. In June 1927, when Prime Minister Tanaka Giichi called together Japan's civilian and military leaders at the Eastern Regions Conference, the Japanese government deliberated on the shift taking place in the balance of power on the Asian mainland. Japan's leadership agreed: "If disturbances should spread to Manchuria and Mongolia and menace Japan's special position and interests in these regions, the Imperial government must be prepared to combat this menace, regardless of where the danger may originate."[27] Standing up to the increased threats from both Soviet Russia and Nationalist China meant that Japan could not afford to make further cuts in the strength of its army, as it had in 1924. Instead, Japan would need to undertake a greater military effort just to keep what it already possessed.

Faced by the revival of Soviet Russia and China as serious military powers in Asia, Japan's leaders should have seen the strategic sense of maintaining the closest possible security cooperation with Britain and the United States. By cooperating with the West they could attempt to gain international support in case Japan faced confrontation with rivals on the Asian mainland. Japan, earlier in the twentieth century, during the Russo-Japanese War, had derived considerable strategic benefit from its alignment with Britain and the United States; now it needed to work with Britain and the United States in seeking to manage the power transition taking place on the Asian mainland. To be sure, this task for Japanese diplomacy would not prove easy, because neither Britain nor the United States saw eye to eye with Japan's rulers about the rise of Nationalist China.

The path actually pursued by Japanese nationalist extremists—setting a course to antagonize Britain and the United States by building warships against them—was strategic folly. Not content with the prospect of having to defend against the growing threat from Nationalist China and Soviet Russia, Japan added to its enemies by making itself a pariah in the view of both Britain and the United States. The recklessness of Japanese nationalist extremists, who sought hegemony in East Asia, meant that Japan's policy was almost bound to lead to disaster. Whether or not Britain and the United States accorded parity in naval forces to Japan thus ultimately mattered little in determining Japanese behavior. The larger forces at play during the 1930s—the economic downturn, the emergence of serious military rivals on the Asian mainland, and the growing assertiveness of the Japanese armed forces in the country's domestic politics—helped shape to a far greater extent Japan's actions. That Japan would ultimately face a powerful coalition made up of a resurgent Nationalist China, the Soviet Union, the British Empire, and the United States is striking testimony to the political and strategic recklessness of Japanese leaders.

The Washington Conference and the subsequent agreement at London conferred on Japan naval hegemony in East Asia. While some Japanese extremists bitterly resented the inferior ratio in naval strength accorded to their country in these arms control treaties, Japan actually acquired a very strong strategic position thereby in the western Pacific. American and British forward fortified bases in the region were prohibited. Surprise and major offensive operations at a war's outset by the American and British navies were thus ruled out as strategies. Japan stood secure from assault at the outset of a conflict, holding the strategic initiative during the initial stages of a war with Britain or the United States.

Japan's naval leaders viewed the West as seeking to impose on Japan an inferior status, refusing to accept it as an equal within the international system. Yet the ratio accorded Japan in naval forces gave it the ability to deter Britain or the United States from pushing a confrontation to the point of war. Defeating Japan would require naval superiority in the western Pacific, which in turn would entail a major naval buildup and the development of forward bases. A war with Japan would thus prove costly and protracted. There was little stomach for such a contest in Britain or the United States.

Japan, however, squandered this strong defensive advantage by acting in an aggressive way. If Japan had not decided to strike out against the West, Britain and the United States would have been unlikely to provoke war themselves, because the costs would far exceed any advantage that they could win by fighting. Imposing a peace on Japan, as the Pacific War would show, would prove extremely costly. By acting aggressively to seize hegemony in East Asia, Japan gave Britain and the United States little choice. Attacking Britain and the United States changed the stakes at risk in their relationship with Japan, converting the two Western nations from deterred rivals into determined adversaries. Western leaders came to view Japan's international behavior as reckless to the point of madness.

Churchill provides a good example of this point of view. As chancellor of the exchequer, Churchill consistently downplayed the possibility of the British and Japanese empires going to war with one another. He would later maintain, however, that the decision for "war by Japan could not be reconciled with reason. . . . But governments and peoples do not always take rational decisions. Sometimes they take mad decisions."[28] Two historians have argued that Japan's actions represent "the turning of a collective back on Western values, a return to one's own historic values and history, and a recourse to armed struggle alongside a belief in force as a means of forging a distinctive national identity and ensuring national liberation. Thus, war was the means whereby discipline could be imposed upon society, and, in a self-fulfilling manner, this discipline was the basis of a moral advantage that would ensure victory."[29] Japan's aggressive behavior instead provoked the resolve in the United States and Britain to fight for the aim of unconditional surrender—the destruction of the Japanese empire, the military occupation of its homeland, the punishment of its wartime leaders, its demilitarization, and the imposition of a government acceptable to the West.

Japanese naval leaders contributed to Japan's disastrous confrontation with Britain and the United States. Critics of arms control within Japan viewed Britain and the United States as forming an "iron ring" to contain Japanese expansion. The work of Sadao Asada has underscored the critical role played by Admiral Kato Kanji in radicalizing the Imperial Japanese Navy's leadership. In turn, Kato sought greater independence for the navy from the control of the government. Kato had nothing but contempt for Western liberalism and democracy. He railed against what he called Japan's "Judaized society" and "the Jewish enemy in our hearts." The extremist thug Sagoya Tomeo who shot Prime Minister Hamaguchi at Tokyo Station did so because he was angered by the government's overruling the views of the Navy General Staff and supporting the London Treaty.[30] This violence, the first of the political assassinations of the 1930s and triggered by the navy's dissatisfaction with the negotiations at London, would help to overturn Japan's foreign policy during the 1920s of cooperation with Britain and the United States in the international arena.

Japan embarked on a new program of naval construction not long after the end of the London Conference. In November 1930, the Japanese cabinet approved a plan submitted by the Navy Ministry to build thirty-nine new warships. The construction of four cruisers of the *Mogami* class constituted the centerpiece of this program. These formidable cruisers mounted no fewer than fifteen 6-inch guns and were armored to fight opponents armed with 8-inch guns. Britain and the United States, faced by Japan's naval buildup, responded with their own heavily armed 6-inch-gun cruisers, the *Southampton* and *Brooklyn* classes, respectively. The London Treaty, then, did not stop the competition in cruisers that formed such a prominent part of interwar naval rivalries and arms control efforts. In addition, arms control did not prevent the expansion in strength of Japanese naval aviation, which also became more proficient in this period. David Evans and Mark Peattie have noted that "the new limitations imposed on warship construction by the London Naval Treaty caused the Navy General Staff to view naval aviation as a new and important means to make up for the deficiencies in the navy's surface forces."[31] These advances in naval aviation during the early 1930s would contribute to the stunning Japanese victories, spearheaded by the navy's air forces, both carrier-borne and land-based squadrons, over the American and British navies during the initial campaigns of the Pacific War.

Meanwhile, and throughout the interwar period, Japanese warship construction provided American and British admirals with the best justification for their own naval efforts. In the minds of some British naval leaders, Japan's naval buildup resembled the very recent memories of Germany's naval challenge before the First World War. Japan, like Germany before it, seemed to them a militarized monarchy bent on building up a powerful navy as a way to obtain regional hegemony. In the eyes of both British and American naval planners, the goal of Japanese warship construction was to drive the influence of the West out of East Asia. Admiral Sir Roger Keyes, one of the Royal Navy's most distinguished officers in the era of the two world wars, argued that "unless she [that is, Japan] knows we are in a position to resist her by force, she will gradually but remorselessly push forward her policy of expansion and domination in the Pacific, and always at the cost of the European races." Keyes feared that by not responding in a timely way to Japan's actions Britain would encourage Japanese leaders "to further activity in the direction of ousting us—say in a generation— from the Pacific altogether."[32] In order to prevent Japan from achieving hege- mony in East Asia, Britain and the United States needed to acquire the ability to project naval power into the region. That ability would require more than ships but also include fortified bases and fuel supplies, to permit powerful, forward- deployed fleets to contest with Japan control of the seas in the western Pacific. Unfortunately for naval planners in both Britain and the United States, how- ever, the price tag for this kind of naval and military effort was far more than what the people and their elected representatives in either country would con- sider paying.

Conceding parity to Japan would not have sated Japanese ambitions in East Asia. Larger international and domestic currents were to pull Japan away from cooperation with Britain and the United States during the 1930s. The onset of the Great Depression contributed to the collapse of the international econ- omy, contributing to the rise of nationalist extremism within Japan. The break- down of international economic cooperation gave impetus to Japan's drive to take unilateral measures to ensure access to resources and markets. Conquest, instead of commerce, became the chosen path to national greatness. Faced by the rise of Chinese and Soviet power, Japan's rulers failed signally in not using arms control, in collaboration with Britain and the United States, as a way to improve their strategic position.

Farewell to Arms Control

In any assessment of the London Conference, it is important to highlight the cooperation between Britain and the United States in settling differences that arose about relative naval strength. This outcome should not be under- rated. That Britain and the United States could settle the naval rivalry between them without conflict is a considerable achievement, one that flies in the face of much realist thinking about the determinants of international politics. As the late Samuel Huntington noted, Britain and the United States did not fight a hegemonic war to determine which of the two countries would emerge as the dominant power in the international system. "Within Greek civilization," Huntington writes, "the increasing power of Athens, as Thucydides argued, led to the Peloponnesian War. Similarly the history of Western civilization is one of 'hegemonic wars' between rising and falling powers.... The missing hegemonic war in Western history is that between Great Britain and the United States, and presumably the peaceful shift from the Pax Britannica to the Pax Americana was in large part due to the close cultural kinship of the two societies."[33] It is not necessary to subscribe to Huntington's cultural explanation to marvel at how an underlying change within the international order occurred without the accompanying violence that might have been expected. The dynamics of domestic politics in both countries, in which moderate liberal opinions triumphed in policy debates over advocates of naval strength, along with the dangers that the two nations faced in common on the international scene, played roles at least as big as any cultural explanation in determining the outcome.

The London Conference, along with the earlier conclave at Washington, defused one of the most important problems that can lead to conflict between great powers—namely, that of security. Decision makers in Britain and the United States saw strong navies as essential to their countries' security and welfare. At a basic level of threat assessment, leaders in Britain and the United States concluded that they could have security at sea by refusing to see each other as adversaries. The primacy of domestic political considerations pushed leaders on both sides of the Atlantic away from a naval competition. Even though responsible naval leaders in Britain and the United States continued to think about the strategic contours of an Anglo-American hegemonic war, that impulse to rivalry was muted by larger domestic political forces at play in both countries. The triumph of prudent statecraft over narrow operational concerns mitigated mutual fears about security.

In Japan, however, that was not to prove the case. More extreme Japanese naval leaders proved able to exploit the breakdown of Japan's political system and press for a naval rivalry with Britain and the United States. The slow starts made by Britain and the United States in building up their navies offered Japanese naval leaders the tempting possibility of building a navy to rival the American and British fleets. By appearing at first unwilling and then progressing to rearmament only slowly, Britain and the United States showed little appetite for a competition with Japan. Also, the failure of Britain and the United States to offer more assistance to Nationalist China once it became involved in a major life-and-death struggle with Japan indicated a lack of resolve on the part of the Western powers to stand against aggression. Meanwhile, inside Japan, no effective brake on the ambitions of the admirals came from the politicians, as occurred in Britain and the United States. Consequently, the Japanese navy received the resources to develop and build weapons that rivaled and in some cases surpassed those in the hands of American and British navies. Japan's superbattleships, night-fighting equipment, torpedoes, submarines, and aircraft, along with realistic programs of training, produced a formidable fighting force by the war's outset, capable of inflicting stunning defeats on its enemies. The Imperial Japanese Navy demonstrated its fighting prowess by inflicting severe defeats on the Royal Navy—destroying Force Z off Malaya and negating the ability of the British fleet to offer effective resistance when the main Japanese carrier force conducted a raid into the Indian Ocean during April 1942—during the opening stages of the Pacific War.[34]

The London Treaty did not satisfy naval leaders in any of the three countries. In Britain and the United States, the opposition of distinguished naval leaders made barely a ripple politically. In Japan, however, the opposition of Japanese admirals produced considerable political fallout. Japanese admirals, most notably the navy's chief of staff, Kato Kanji, insisted that the treaty would jeopardize Japan's security. Some historians agree with them that the agreement reached at London "compromised the principle of Japanese naval hegemony in Japan's own waters."[35] The claim that Japan's ability to defend itself was severely compromised by the London Treaty is of course outlandish, The actual difficulties facing the United States in projecting naval power across the Pacific were daunting. Before a successful offensive could take place, the United States would need to build a much larger force than the ratios spelled out by the London agreement. These ratios, which naval planners spent so much time analyzing, bore little relationship to the actual strategic and operational problems that the American, British, and Japanese, navies would face during the Pacific War.

Here is a good example of misplaced theory taking on reality in the minds of planners and decision makers. The hard fact was that only the United States had the strength to launch a successful offensive into Japan's home waters. Further, the power to launch that offensive drive would require an intense national determination. This awakening of American resolve—required to build a gigantic navy, to withstand the privation of protracted war, and to endure heavy casualties—depended on Japan acting out a nationalist extremist fantasy of trying to impose a stern imperial rule on the rest of East Asia. Japan's security in Northeast Asia was hardly endangered by Britain or the United States. Self-defeating Japanese policies of expansion were required before the United States would make the gigantic effort required to carry out a successful offensive into Japanese home waters.

Even Yamamoto, who appears as a moderate in comparison to Kato Kanji in most narratives of the interwar Japanese navy, exhibited an aggressive instinct that would contribute to Japan's encirclement and defeat. In a letter written in November 1934, when he served on Japan's negotiating team a second naval limitation conference in London, Yamamoto outlined his views about the negotiations with the Americans and British, as well as a sketch for Japanese grand strategy:

> One thing that has surprised me . . . is the willingness—however irksome they may privately find it—of the three British ministers, the American ambassador, and the chiefs of Naval Operations and the Naval Staff to listen politely, at least on the surface, to the foolish views being put forward by a youngster like myself; it shows what an immeasurable difference there is in Japan's strength now compared with the time of the Washington Conference, and I feel keenly that the time has come for this mighty empire rising in the east to devote itself, with all due circumspection, to advancing its own fortunes.
>
> The example afforded before the Great War by Germany—which, if only it had exercised forbearance for another five or ten years, would by now be unrivaled in Europe—suggests that the task facing us now is to build up our strength calmly and with circumspection. Even though the present conference may not be successful, I sense that the day may not be so distant when we shall have Britain and the United States kowtowing to us.
>
> For the navy, the most urgent task of all is to make rapid strides in the field of aviation.[36]

In this note Yamamoto puts forward contradictory views. To be sure, he understood that Japan might find itself encircled and defeated like imperial Germany if it pursued too aggressive a stance in foreign policy and naval armaments. The lesson was for Japan to show prudence—Yamamoto's word is "circumspection"—in its actions. Yet he failed to draw the conclusion that if Japan wanted to avoid Germany's fate it was essential to follow a genuinely cooperative approach with Britain and the United States. Instead, Yamamoto looked forward to a time when Japan could humble them. To Yamamoto, the naval officer, it seemed that Japan needed to develop new, more powerful weapons to gain the edge required to prevail. In spurning compromise in arms control and wanting to build up Japan's naval strength by acquiring cutting-edge weaponry, Yamamoto resembles Admiral Alfred von Tirpitz, the architect of imperial Germany's failed strategy to challenge Britain.[37] Without the guidance and restraint of statecraft, the admiral not surprisingly wanted to maximize naval capability to fight. Under this formulation, weaponry becomes equated with security. For Japan, as for imperial Germany, that calculation led to self-defeating strategic behavior.

In August 1934, a month before Yamamoto set sail to hold arms control talks, the Japanese Navy General Staff had secretly resolved on a warship construction program to build four superbattleships. The two superbattleships that resulted from this decision, the *Yamato* and *Musashi* (a third was completed as an aircraft carrier), outclassed in fighting power the battleships contemplated and built at the same time by Britain and the United States. The leadership of the Japanese navy had convinced themselves that without the constraints of arms control Japan could provide for its own security in the western Pacific.[38] This confidence in Japan's ability to stay ahead in a naval arms race with the economically more powerful Britain and United States smacks of hubris. Still, given the tardy response by the American and British governments to the breakdown of naval arms control during the late 1930s, as well as to the rising power and threat posed by Nazi Germany to Britain, the strategy adopted by the Japanese naval leadership is not outlandish.

Ramsay MacDonald showed no inclination to attempt to work with Japan against the United States on the naval issue. He harbored no nostalgia for the Anglo-Japanese alliance, as did some Conservative political leaders—quite the reverse. MacDonald was devoid of the anti-American bias held by some colleagues; all of his instincts were to forge a close relationship with the United States. The success achieved at the London Conference in limiting the naval competition was due in considerable measure to the actions of the British prime minister. MacDonald possessed vision: nothing ranked higher on his policy agenda than striking an arms control agreement with the United States and avoiding conflict with that country. His personal diplomacy, which conciliated his American interlocutors, demonstrated his talents as a statesman on the world stage. Meanwhile, in the domestic political realm he forged a consensus among British decision makers about how to proceed in reaching an agreement. MacDonald skillfully played off against each other the competing players involved in the making of Britain's foreign and naval policies. Consequently, the British Labour government did not fall into disarray during the negotiations in London, as had the Conservatives during the Geneva Conference. MacDonald showed a kind of leadership that Baldwin had proved unable to muster.

The political leaders of Britain, Japan, and the United States imposed a top-down decision on the negotiation of a settlement at London. The direction from the top was clear. The challenge to the political leadership was how to prevent opponents of the treaty from upsetting it. In the United States, President

Hoover obtained bipartisan political support in the Senate for the treaty. Senator David Reed played a key role in crafting a settlement with Japan. Senate ratification received impetus also from the part played by Secretary of State Henry Stimson, who possessed a forceful personality as well as a reputation for integrity. In addition, neither the Chief of Naval Operations or Britain's First Sea Lord saw the treaty as requiring him to resign in protest. While important voices spoke out against the treaty in both Britain and the United States, their political strength was minimized by the consensus that had emerged in both countries to curtail the international rivalry in shipbuilding. The opponents of the treaty were pushed to the political margins. In the absence of a settlement, it is difficult to imagine a major burst in warship construction by its signatories, given the domestic political realities in Britain and the United States.

The London Conference thus ratified an underlying political reality. Governments led by Osachi Hamaguchi, Herbert Hoover, and Ramsay MacDonald had no intention of spending large sums on navies. They, and the people they represented and who had put them in power, did not see how a competition in warship construction would enhance their countries' security. Quite the reverse, they found appalling the prospect that such a competition might take place. A naval competition, in their view, would undermine security, not promote it. In a world where Hamaguchi, Hoover, and MacDonald were the dominant leaders, their views shaped the international reality. The London Conference was a triumph for the leadership of the three men. They showed determination in pursuit of their goal of naval arms control. Nor was it easy for them to reach agreement at London—they faced considerable domestic opposition from political opponents and within the navies. All three were attacked as weak in their concern for the defense of their countries. (Of course, in the case of Hamaguchi, who would die from wounds suffered in an assassination attempt, the attack was quite literal.) That their shared vision of an international order marked by the strict limitation of arms would not long survive does not detract from the resolve that they showed in pursuit of their goals. Whether wise or strategically shortsighted, Hamaguchi, Hoover, and MacDonald fought with all the skill that they possessed as political operators to reach a settlement at London.

Even in the late 1930s, when the danger at sea to the security of Britain and the United States grew dramatically, neither country's leaders moved as decisively as they ought to have to carry out naval rearmament. Neville Chamberlain, as chancellor of the exchequer during much of the 1930s, sought to prevent a British naval buildup whose main purpose was to prepare for a conflict with Japan. Rather than arm against Japan Chamberlain stubbornly sought to reach an accommodation with it, even if that harmed cooperation with the United States. The Franklin D. Roosevelt administration too proved slow in building up naval power in the wake of Japan's refusal to remain linked to arms control. When Japan walked away from the international arms control regime at the Second London Conference, the United States did not move decisively to rearm. The dangerous deterioration in the international environment dragged the leaders of both countries into rearmament only later and much against their will. The consequences of this tardiness to rearm proved disastrous, in that it undermined the ability of the West to deter Japan from attacking: Japanese naval planners in the autumn of 1941 possessed an incentive to strike before Britain and the United States could make up the ground they had lost.[39]

The leaders of Britain, Japan, and the United States could not insulate arms control from larger forces already emerging that would lead to another great war. The struggle for mastery in Asia remained, despite their efforts to regulate the three-way naval competition involving their countries. Dramatic changes in the international environment and deeper currents in domestic politics would soon wash away the barriers to competition that Hamaguchi, Hoover, and MacDonald sought so ardently to erect at London. An arms-limitation regime cannot long survive if important members of the international system make a determined effort to overthrow it in favor of building up their military capabilities. That arms control reflects the larger international environment more than it shapes that environment is one of the hard lessons that this important episode teaches.

The London Conference was the culmination of the attempts made by statesmen during the 1920s to limit arms. The conference, however, was not a good guide to the troubled decade of the 1930s that would follow. Major actors on the international stage were already showing determination to break restraints that hindered the buildup of military power. Even before the London Conference Stalin's Russia had started an arms buildup—creating a command economy under the first of a series of five-year plans designed to solidify communist rule and build up an industrial base to produce large quantities of weapons—that pointed to a great-power war. The Soviet Union's militarization, its arms and industrial buildup, would as a matter of course push other countries to undertake their own armaments programs. The Depression, contributing to the radicalization of politics in Germany and Japan, and the emergence of extremist leaders intent of waging war of expansion meant the end of meaningful arms control. Even before Hitler came to power, the Weimar Republic began German rearmament. In the late 1920s, the German navy started construction of the so-called pocket battleships, warships of an innovative design meant to disrupt the sea lines of communication of the stronger maritime powers. The Nazi seizure of power in Germany gave a greater shove to accelerated rearmament. With Hitler at its head, only a coup or preventive war would have derailed a buildup of Germany's military power. Japanese army leaders, planning for an eventual showdown with China and the Soviet Union, also adopted a more aggressive stance. Confronted by this deteriorating international situation, in which Stalin, Hitler, and Japanese nationalist extremists exerted dominant roles in shaping the international system, self-imposed arms limitation by the Western democracies was folly. Within less than three years the London system of arms limitation would be no longer viable. The leaders of Britain and the United States, having lacked political will and been unprepared to take preventive military action, now needed to undertake a massive rearmament, actively engage in an arms race, and forge a coalition in peacetime like the Atlantic Alliance of the Cold War era if they were to have any hope of deterring a war or fighting effectively in the initial stages if the peace broke down. The vision and leadership of Hoover and MacDonald did not fit the international environment of the 1930s. Churchill's alternative narrative of increased efforts to rearm and secure alliances provided the West with its best chance of success in preparing for the impending tempests generated by the storm centers in Germany, Japan, and Russia.

NOTES

1. The Kellogg-Briand Pact of 1928. The text of the Pact can be accessed at http://www.yale.edu/lawweb/avalon/imt/kbpact.htm#art1.

2. Walter Lippmann, *U.S. Foreign Policy: Shield of the Republic* (Boston: Little Brown, 1943), 54, 57.

3. On "the rise of the rest," see Fareed Zakaria, *The Post-American World* (New York: Norton, 2008), 2.

4. The classic formulation of these shifts in international power balances is provided by Paul Kennedy in *The Rise and Fall of the Great Powers: Economic Change and Military Conflict from 1500 to 2000* (New York: Random House, 1987), 194–343, and Kennedy, *The Rise and Fall of British Naval Mastery* (London: Ashfield, 1983), 205–98.

5. "Memorandum," 10 November 1926, Hilary P. Jones Papers, carton 4, Manuscript Division, Library of Congress.

6. Kellogg to Alanson B. Houghton, 2 May 1927, roll 25, Frank B. Kellogg Papers [hereafter cited as Kellogg Papers].

7. For an insightful analysis of Britain's dependence on overseas imports at the beginning of the twentieth century, see Avner Offer, *The First World War: An Agrarian Interpretation* (Oxford, U.K.: Clarendon, 1991).

8. Hankey to Lloyd George, 29 December 1921, Lloyd George Papers F/62/1/12, Parliamentary Archives.

9. Quoted in Josephus Daniels, *The Wilson Era: Years of War and After, 1917–1923* (Chapel Hill: University of North Carolina Press, 1946), 381.

10. See ibid., 376–80. The maps used by Daniels in his discussions with Lloyd George are printed on p. 379.

11. Philip Williamson, ed., *The Modernisation of Conservative Politics: The Diaries and Letters of William Bridgeman, 1904–1935* (London: Historians' Press, 1988), 205.

12. Birkenhead memorandum, "Naval Conference," 21 July 1927, CP 210 (27), CAB 24/188. National Archives, Kew [hereafter TNA].

13. Prime Minister for Bridgeman, 15 July 1927, CP 212 (27) CAB 24/188, TNA.

14. Mackenzie King Diary, entries for 30 July 1927 and 4 August 1927, printed in Philip Williamson and Edward Baldwin, *Baldwin Papers: A Conservative Statesman, 1908–1947* (Cambridge, U.K.: Cambridge University Press, 2004), 198–200.

15. Martin Gilbert, ed., *Winston S. Churchill*, vol. 5, Companion Part 1 Documents, *The Exchequer Years, 1922–1929* (Boston: Houghton Mifflin, 1981), 1033.

16. Churchill memorandum, "Reduction and Limitation of Armaments: The Naval Conference," 29 June 1927, CP 189 (27), CAB 24/187, TNA.

17. Martin Gilbert, *Winston S. Churchill*, vol. 5, *The Prophet of Truth, 1922–1939* (Boston: Houghton Mifflin, 1977), 251.

18. B. J. C. McKercher, "'A Certain Irritation': The White House, the State Department, and the Desire for a Naval Settlement with Great Britain, 1927–1930," *Diplomatic History* 31, no. 5 (November 2007), 847–48.

19. Ibid., 857, note 115.

20. Churchill speech in Birmingham, "Liberal Party Economic Policy," 3 February 1928, in *Winston S. Churchill: His Complete Speeches*, ed. Robert Rhodes James (New York: Chelsea, 1974), 5:4346.

21. Enclosure P. J. Grigg to Hankey, Personal and Private, 10 February 1928, Hankey Papers, Churchill College.

22. Unsigned memorandum in Hoover's handwriting, n.d. [but Summer 1929], quoted in B. J. C. McKercher, *Transition of Power: Britain's Loss of Global Pre-eminence to the United States, 1930–1945* (Cambridge, U.K.: Cambridge University Press, 1999), 61, note 115.

23. Keith Middlemas, ed., *Thomas Jones: Whitehall Diary* (London: Oxford University Press, 1969), 2:165–66. Lord Grey turned down Baldwin's offer. It is not known whom Baldwin might have asked to serve as First Lord of the Admiralty. To make an agreement with the United States, Baldwin would have needed to put in place a First Lord who was willing to curtail the ship-building demands of the Royal Navy's uniformed chiefs.

24. Churchill's wife Clementine thought that her husband's "known hostility to America might stand in the way" of his heading the Foreign Office if the Tories had won the 1929 election and remained in office. Clementine Churchill to Winston Churchill, 14 November 1928, in *Speaking for Themselves: The Personal Letters of Winston and Clementine Churchill*, ed. Mary Soames (New York: Doubleday, 1998), 332.

25. A. P. Waterfield, "Naval Conference," 17 December 1929, T172/1693, cited in G. C. Peden, *The Treasury and British Public Policy, 1906–1959* (Oxford, U.K.: Oxford University Press, 2000), 216.

26. See B. J. C. McKercher, "From Enmity to Cooperation: The Second Baldwin Government and the Improvement of Anglo-American Relations, November 1928–June 1929," *Albion* 24 (1992), 65–88.

27. James B. Crowley, *Japan's Quest for Autonomy: National Security and Foreign Policy, 1930–1938* (Princeton, N.J.: Princeton University Press, 1966), 31–32.

28. Winston S. Churchill, *The Second World War*, vol. 3, *The Grand Alliance* (Boston: Houghton Mifflin, 1950), 603.

29. Haruo Tohmatsu and H. P. Willmott, *A Gathering Darkness: The Coming of War to the Far East and the Pacific, 1921–1942* (Lanham, Md.: SR Books, 2004), 11. Another provocative study drawing parallels between Japan's confrontation with the West and that of Muslim extremists is offered by Ian Buruma and Avishai Margalit, *Occidentalism: The West in the Eyes of Its Enemies* (New York: Penguin, 2004).

30. Herbert P. Bix, *Hirohito and the Making of Modern Japan* (New York: HarperCollins, 2000), 208, 226.

31. David C. Evans and Mark R. Peattie, *Kaigun: Strategy, Tactics, and Technology in the Imperial Japanese Navy, 1887–1941* (Annapolis, Md.: Naval

Institute Press, 1997), 238–39, 249. On the development of Japanese naval aviation, see Mark R. Peattie, *Sunburst: The Rise of Japanese Naval Air Power, 1909–1941* (Annapolis, Md.: Naval Institute Press, 2001).

32. Keyes to Churchill, 24 March 1925, in *The Keyes Papers*, vol. 2, *1919–1938*, ed. Paul G. Halpern (London: Naval Records Society, 1980), 112.

33. Samuel P. Huntington, *The Clash of Civilizations and the Remaking of World Order* (New York: Simon and Schuster, 1996), 209.

34. See Arthur J. Marder, *Old Friends, New Enemies: The Royal Navy and the Imperial Japanese Navy—Strategic Illusions, 1936–1941* (Oxford, U.K.: Clarendon, 1981), 365–521; and Arthur J. Marder, Mark Jacobsen, and John Horsfield, *Old Friends, New Enemies: The Royal Navy and the Imperial Japanese Navy*, vol. 2, *The Pacific War, 1942–1945* (Oxford, U.K.: Clarendon, 1990), 81–151.

35. Crowley, *Japan's Quest for Autonomy*, 66. A sympathetic portrait of Kato Kanji is offered by Ian Gow, *Military Intervention in Pre-war Japanese Politics: Admiral Katō Kanji and the "Washington System"* (London: Routledge, Curzon, 2004). A more balanced assessment is presented by Sadao Asada, *From Mahan to Pearl Harbor: The Imperial Japanese Navy and the United States* (Annapolis, Md.: Naval Institute Press, 2006).

36. Hiroyuki Agawa, *The Reluctant Admiral: Yamamoto and the Imperial Navy* (Tokyo: Kodansha, 1979), 37–38.

37. On the strategy of Tirpitz and imperial Germany's grand strategy, see Holger H. Herwig, "Imperial Germany: Continental Titan, Global Aspirant," in *China Goes to Sea: Maritime Transformation in Comparative Historical Perspective,* ed. Andrew S. Erickson, Lyle J. Goldstein, and Carnes Lord (Annapolis, Md.: Naval Institute Press, 2009), 171–98. On the unwillingness of Tirpitz to reach a negotiated settlement of the arms competition with Britain, see John H. Maurer, "Arms Control and the Anglo-German Naval Race before World War I: Lessons for Today?," *Political Science Quarterly* 112, no. 2 (Summer 1997), 285–306.

38. For a lucid appraisal of the Japanese strategic calculations for prevailing in a naval arms race, see Evans and Peattie, *Kaigun*, 293–98.

39. Stephen E. Pelz, *Race to Pearl Harbor: The Failure of the Second London Naval Conference and the Onset of World War II* (Cambridge, U.K.: Harvard University Press, 1974), 212–26.

CONTRIBUTORS

SADAO ASADA is professor emeritus at Doshisha University in Kyoto, Japan. A graduate of Carleton College, he holds a PhD from Yale University in American history. His publications include the award-winning *Japanese-American Relations between the Wars: Naval Policy and the Decision Making Process* (in Japanese), *From Mahan to Pearl Harbor: The Imperial Japanese Navy and the United States* (Naval Institute Press, 2006), and *Culture Shock and Japanese-American Relations: Historical Essays* (University of Missouri Press, 2007).

CHRISTOPHER M. BELL is professor of history at Dalhousie University. He is the author of *Churchill and Sea Power* (Oxford University Press, 2012) and *The Royal Navy, Seapower and Strategy between the Wars* (Stanford University Press, 2000), and coeditor of *Naval Mutinies of the Twentieth Century: An International Perspective* (Frank Cass, 2003).

JOHN R. FERRIS is professor of history at the University of Calgary, honorary professor at the Department of International Politics, the University of Wales, Aberystwyth, and adjunct professor at the Department of War Studies, Royal Military College of Canada. He was Cryptologic Scholar in Residence at the National Security Agency in 2008–2009. He has published widely in strategic, international, and intelligence history.

NORMAN FRIEDMAN is a strategist and historian concerned throughout his career with the way in which policy and technology intersect, in fields as disparate as national missile defense, nuclear strategy, and mobilization policy. He spent more than a decade at a major U.S. think tank, and another decade as consultant to the secretary of the Navy. He has consulted for many major defense corporations. Dr. Friedman's more than thirty-five published books include *U.S. Cruisers: An Illustrated Design History*, histories of U.S. and British destroyers (which were much affected by interwar treaties), and *British Cruisers: Two World Wars and After* (the first of a projected two volumes on British cruisers). Future projects include an account of First World War naval weapons, stressing their relation to the tactics of the time. Dr. Friedman has also published *Network Centric Warfare: How Navies Learned to Fight Smarter in Three World Wars*, which includes a detailed discussion of the way in which a revolution in command and control affected British cruiser policy, particularly as it was intended for trade protection. In 2001, Dr. Friedman won the Westminster Medal of the Royal United Services Institute (for the best military history of 2000) for his Cold War history, *The Fifty-Year War: Conflict and Strategy in the Cold War*, and he won the Alfred Thayer Mahan award of the Naval Order of the United States for his *Seapower as Strategy*. Dr. Friedman lectures widely on defense issues in forums such as the National Defence University, the Naval War College, and the Royal United Services Institute. He contributes a monthly column on world naval developments to the U.S. Naval Institute's *Proceeding* magazine and writes articles for journals worldwide. Dr. Friedman holds a PhD in theoretical physics from Columbia University.

PAUL G. HALPERN is an emeritus professor at Florida State University. He has written *The Mediterranean Naval Situation, 1908–1914; The Naval War in the Mediterranean, 1914–1918; A Naval History of World War I*; and *The Battle of the Otranto Straits*. His biography of Admiral Anton Haus, an Austrian naval commander, was published in Austria. He has also edited three volumes of *The Keyes Papers* for the Navy Records Society and is currently working on two volumes for the society dealing with the Royal Navy's Mediterranean Fleet in the 1920s and 1930s.

JOHN T. KUEHN is a former U.S. naval aviator who has completed cruises on board four different aircraft carriers. He flew reconnaissance missions during the last decade of the Cold War, in the First Gulf War (Desert Storm), and in the Balkans (Deliberate Force over Bosnia). Commander Kuehn has served on the faculty of the U.S. Army Command and General Staff College at Fort Leavenworth, Kansas, since July 2000, retiring from the naval service in 2004. He earned a PhD in history from Kansas State University in 2007. He is the author of *Agents of Innovation* and *Eyewitness Pacific Theater*, with Dennis Giangreco.

JOHN H. MAURER is the Alfred Thayer Mahan Professor of Sea Power at the Naval War College in Newport, Rhode Island, where he has served as the chair of the Strategy and Policy Department. He is a graduate of Yale University and holds an MALD and PhD in international relations from the Fletcher School of Law and Diplomacy, Tufts University. Before joining the faculty of the Naval War College, he served as executive editor of *Orbis: A Journal of World Affairs* and held the position of senior research fellow at the Foreign Policy Research Institute. He served on the secretary of the Navy's advisory committee on naval history. In addition, he is the author or editor of books examining the outbreak of the First World War, military interventions in the developing world, naval arms control between the two world wars, and Winston Churchill's views on British foreign policy and strategy. His current research includes work on the politics, economics, and strategies of great-power arms competitions during the past hundred years, and a study about Winston Churchill and Great Britain's decline as a world power. He has received the U.S. Navy's Meritorious and Superior Civilian Service Award.

INDEX